# The Not So Famous Battersea Boy

## Brian Gaskin

This book
is dedicated to

Mark, Andrew and Charlotte

# Acknowledgements

With grateful thanks to Kim Kimber
www.kimkimber.co.uk
for editing this book.


My thanks also to James Fanthorpe
www.xlbookcoverdesign.co.uk
for the cover design.

# Preface

Unlike Sir George Shearing, Roger Moore, Timothy Spall, Buster Merryfield, or the So Solid Crew to name but a few, this Battersea Boy is not so famous.

It was 6°C, windy and raining in London on 7th March, 1956, the day I was born into a poor working-class family from Battersea at 7.50 am, to Mum Elsie, wife of Stanley James Gaskin and parents to Paul James. I was born in St Thomas' Hospital London, on the south side of the River Thames facing the Houses of Parliament next to Westminster Bridge, so although not a true cockney I am proud to call myself a true Londoner.

When it was time for mum and baby to leave hospital and go home to our little terrace house in Battersea, South London, the weather was a barometer – no pun intended – of how my life was to unfold. Little did I know then what a great but heartbreaking, wonderful, amazing story I would begin to live and, later, tell to all.

# Chapter One

Having spent my first few days in hospital Mum and Dad brought me home to the tiny house in which I was to spend the first eleven years of my life. I weighed in at a respectable 7Ib 4oz, nothing unusual for a healthy boy at that time, and no doubt many others were similar in size.

Our house in Wickersley Road, Battersea, London SW11, was an old Victorian terrace house, typical of a working-class area in industrial London. There was no garden, although we did have two of London's most famous green spaces within walking distance; Clapham Common and Battersea Park. Both were to play a prominent part in my life.

The terraced house was just one of many drab and dirty dwellings in Battersea at that time. For years, dirt and grime had come belching out of the chimneys of the industrial factories along the south side of the River Thames. From the mid-1930s, Battersea Power Station itself had blasted out all kinds of nasty pollutants over the poor working class of South London.

*Fact: if the wind was blowing hard enough for the pollutants to blow towards Buckingham Palace the power station did not generate.*

Our little home was around eighty years old in 1956 and was showing signs of severe wear and tear. As Dad was a Wandsworth Council tenant, he was not prepared to pay out any of his hard-earned wages to improve it, no matter what.

We had the downstairs part of the house while another council tenant, Mrs Kennett, lived upstairs. Mrs Kennett was, by all accounts, the archetypal little old lady living on her own. The council offered to sell the whole house to Mum and Dad for £500, to be paid back by the weekly £1.00 rent, until the amount was paid off. Mrs Kennett told Dad that her 10/- shillings (equivalent to 50p today) a week rent would help to pay off the debt, but Dad was not interested, citing that the upkeep of the house would be too expensive. In fact, later on, the council offered Mum and Dad an even bigger house on the corner of Clapham Common Southside and Cedars Road for £1,000. Now, if Dad wasn't prepared to pay £500 he was hardly likely to pay £1000. Shame really, as in September 2017 the house was being offered for sale with a guide price of a staggering £7.2m!

At the front of our house was a small wall that originally had iron railings fitted, but these were removed by the local council workmen and sent off with all sorts of other metal objects that the household could give up, such as old pots and pans, and bikes, in fact, anything that was made of metal or iron, to become part of the war effort for World War ll. There was a bay window with just the right sized windowsill that seemed to have been especially made for a small child's bottom to sit perched upon until such time as Dad could be seen coming home from work on his beloved motorbike and sidecar. The first one that I remember was a 1000cc Ariel Square four, so named as the engine had two cylinders in the front and a further two behind, before moving on to a BSA 650cc Thunderbolt, or was it a Norton Dominator?

Dad replaced his motorbike with a car when Paul and I were too big to fit comfortably with Mum into the sidecar. The first of these was a Standard Vanguard which had the engine blown up by my older half-brother, Christopher Stanley, on the A5 driving back to Battersea from Aylesbury. Next was a green Austin A35 that Mum hated, followed by a magnificent maroon Ford Zephyr Mark Two. Paul told me why Dad had bought it. It appears that Dad's half-brother, George, had a Mark One and Dad, having seen the Mark Two for sale in Naylor & Root car salesroom in Wandsworth, decided to buy it. A bit of sibling rivalry going on there I think.

I have decided not to include my half-brother too much in this book as he is fifteen years older than me and hasn't featured greatly in my life. The period when Dad was married to

Christopher's mother is not for me to comment on.

When Dad came home from work, all the kids who had been hanging around the front of the house with Paul and I would magically disappear for fear of a clip around the ear if caught lingering there. It's funny, but as there were so few cars around when I was small if one came trundling down the street a group of us kids would congregate behind it and start cheering and shouting. God knows why!

Entry to the house was through a small, but heavy, front door with a boot scraper to the right-hand side, a relic from the past when mud and all sorts of unmentionables would be scraped off boots or shoes so as not to be taken inside. A short, high-ceilinged passageway revealed a room to the right, the front room, that doubled as a parlour, a room reserved for those occasions that warranted entry; Sunday high tea, visits from family and, of course, Christmas and New Year.

Just by the stairs leading to where Mrs Kennet lived was room number two, Mum and Dad's bedroom, where initially yours truly had a cot by the window. Funny, I can remember standing in my cot peering over the top of the wooden railing into Mum and Dad's bedroom, silent and dark but for the glow of moonlight, but not much else from my early childhood. I don't know if it's my imagination or not but it seemed as though I used to stare out for ages, not at all frightened, transfixed by all the shapes and shadows of the room.

I can also remember, later on, sharing a put-up bed with Paul in the front room that, by day, was out of bounds but at night was transformed into our bedroom. It was cold in the wintertime as, for some reason, the top sash window always seemed to be open an inch or two. We had a thick eiderdown and flannelette sheets, and every now and again Mum would find a big blanket or two for us so we kept really warm.

However, the real heart of our little home was the sitting/dining/family room, all grand titles for one room where we ate, watched telly and, later on in time, Paul and I would do our homework, play board games or cards and watch some of

TV's greatest moments. Amongst these were The Beatles first remarkable appearance on Sunday, 13th October, 1963, on ATV's *Sunday Night at the London Palladium* hosted by the late Sir Bruce Forsyth, plain old Bruce then, or the latest news reports of John F. Kennedy, the 35th president of the United States, who was assassinated on Friday, 22nd November, 1963 at 12.30 pm Central Standard Time in Dallas, Texas, while riding in a motorcade through Dealey Plaza.

We boys also watched many heavyweight boxing bouts by Muhammad Ali 'The Greatest' and, of course, the greatest sporting achievement by any professional England team; the 1966 FIFA World Cup. It seems almost like yesterday that on that sunniest of days, Saturday, 30th July, the eighth staging of the World Cup, England beat West Germany 4–2 in the final, winning the Jules Rimet Trophy.

With this victory, England won their first (and only to date) FIFA World Cup. I remember when BBC commentator Kenneth Wolstenholme made his now famous comment just before Sir Geoff Hurst scored England's third goal in the dying seconds, "Some people are on the pitch...they think it's all over...it is now." Paul burst into tears. I suspect we all had moist eyes.

It fills me with immense pride and usually brings a lump in my throat, even today, that back then when England was the best place in the world to live, that we had beaten the best and were rightly crowned World Cup winners. Another of Kenneth Wolstenholme's comments which really makes my chest swell is, "It's twelve inches tall, it's made of solid gold and it means that England are the world champions." Sweet words indeed. That's enough now as I might shed a tear or two at the memory.

Finally, there was the 'scullery', the tiniest of rooms where dear old Mum did all the cooking, washing and every other chore imaginable and where we all had to get washed in the only family sink. Very Dickensian, but I didn't know any better at the time and just accepted that this was normal.

Towards the back of the house, down three steps and past a

couple of under stairs cupboards, one being where the coal was kept, was the side-back door which lead to the narrow walkway that passed for the garden area.

Outside was where the real horror lurked; the family's toilet. Mum kept it spotless and smelling fresh, of course, but the unseen terrors that lurked inside were terrifying to a small boy even when old enough and able enough to use it unaided. Hiding inside were the biggest, baddest spiders imaginable and when the door was opened they would stay still and stare at their next victim, ME! How I hated that loo and never want to experience anything like it again.

In the so-called backyard, Dad kept an aviary full of budgerigars and canaries that he showed from time to time at Battersea Town Hall on Lavender Hill. I was too young, at the time, to know how well he did but there always seemed to be different brightly-coloured rosettes lying around.

So there you have it, a home that was old and shabby but filled with love and kindness, until I was about five that is, and starting primary school, then Dad's belt started to come off, but more of that later.

About this time, Mrs Kennett passed away and an Irish family moved in upstairs. For some reason or another, my parents didn't take too kindly to them. I think the feeling was mutual and so began a number of years of tension between the two families.

This was finally resolved when the house, along with all the others in Wickersley Road, was designated by the council to be pulled down in a programme that become known as slum clearance.

Mum was born on 11th September, 1921, the sixth child of Sidney and Adelaide Hogg of Twilly Street, Wandsworth, in South London. Mum was one of five girls and two boys. Granddad was a waterman/lighterman on the River Thames, in keeping with the family tradition, as his father and grandfather had been before him. As for Nanny, I don't know much about her side of the family, only that she was the sweetest, dearest little old granny anyone could have. Her house in Twilly Street was always a favourite place to visit, we didn't go that many times but it was always great to see Nanny Hogg. I remember, in pride of place in the front room, she had a very classy wood and glass display cabinet filled with china and glass, amassed over her lifetime. Her kitchen was always filled with the smells of home cooking and to the side of it was a little room with a green baize table where Nanny taught me how to play patience, accompanied by a slice of cake or a biscuit or two and a glass of milk, of course. At the end of her small back garden ran the River Wandle where, according to folklore, Granddad caught fish. I'm not sure if I believe that or not as whenever I saw the river, it had old bits of bike, shopping trollies and all sorts of general rubbish dumped in it, in common with many other streams in London at that time.

When Mum was 14 years old she went to work in a big house somewhere in Wimbledon as a cook's maid. She would later do an apprenticeship to become a head cook – that's where she learned to cook so well but, just before her 18th birthday, World War II was declared after Germany invaded Poland. Along with many other women, Mum went to work in a munitions factory, making not only the uniforms, but all manner of equipment for the military. She would travel by underground train from Tooting Broadway on the Northern Line to Bank Station where she would change trains and catch the District Line to Bromley by Bow, then onwards by bus to the factory in Plaistow where, for the next six years, six days a week, of her young adult life she did her bit for the war effort.

Always a keen cyclist, I remember Mum saying that she and her cousin Connie rode their bicycles down to Devon when they had their annual summer holidays. Mum often spoke about it being a wonderful time in a beautiful setting and such a long way from dirty, war-ravaged London.

Dad, on the other hand, came from a very poor working-class family who first lived in Queenstown Road, Battersea, where he was born on 14th September, 1921, before the family moved to Wycliffe Road. Dad had one older and one younger brother, Edward and Albert, and an older sister Dorothy. Granddad Edward Jeremiah was a farrier who worked for a company called Thomas Tilling that supplied horses to the working tradesmen of London; the milkman, the coalman, the binman, and also to the London Fire Brigade. Sometimes Granddad would take Dad to work with him on a Saturday morning so Dad could earn a penny or two. I believe it was during this time in his life that Dad begun his lifelong love of horses, and whenever we went out to the countryside he would always stop to feed and stroke them.

From the stories Dad told me, he had a hard childhood. For example, Granddad got paid on a Saturday afternoon and, when he got home, he would give Nan her housekeeping money for the week. After dinner, he would have a hot bath before going to the local pub, The Hanbury Arms, which was literally just across the road from home. But before he got all dressed up to go out Dad would have to take the couple of bob (two shillings, or 10p) that Nanny Gaskin gave him and run as fast as he could to the local pawn shop to get Granddad's best suit out of hock, then run back again and have it hanging in Granddad's wardrobe before he noticed it was missing.

Every Saturday night, once Granddad had gone over to the pub, Nan gave Dad another shilling – saying that she expected a penny or two change – to get the Sunday joint from the local butcher. As they didn't have cold storage in those days the butcher would sell off the meat cheaper the later in the evening it got towards closing time and, if Dad timed it right, he could get a good joint of beef with change left over. Well, one night he got the beef but no change, and when he got home Nan beat him so hard with her stick that he was black and blue for a week, AND he had to take the beef back to get a smaller piece and get that change!

When he returned to the butchers, and told the story through sobbing eyes, not only did the kindly butcher tell Dad that he could keep the beef, but he forgot to tell Dad that the joint he bought was, for that week only, to include two big pork sausages and to have a penny change. Nan was delighted with the extras but, alas, didn't shower Dad with much praise.

Dad didn't seem to have much luck where food was concerned. When Dad's older sister, Dorothy, was 'walking out' with her young man, Nan invited him for Sunday afternoon tea. It was Dad's job, again, to rush up to the bakers shop on Saturday night and buy seven stale cakes for a tanner (6d, or 2½ new pence) for Sunday tea.

All the kids had a good old scrub up, including back of the neck and behind the ears. Dad and the rest of the family sat around the dinner table, which was elegantly laid out with a sparkling white tablecloth *AND* best tableware, to await Dorothy's beau, Chummy. Upon arrival, and having been introduced to Nan and Granddad, Chummy sat next to Nan, and Dorothy next to Granddad with Dad, Edward and Albert seated towards the end of the table. Chummy was offered the plate of cakes, but he insisted that Nan go first. What a creep!

He then insisted that Dorothy and Granddad choose before him, and the three boys could take their pick of the four cakes that were left, but Nan ordered them in a stern voice, "Leave the last cream cake alone." Dad had had his eye on that cake all the while it had been sitting there on the plate, and once tea had been drunk and cakes eaten, Dad was primed like a cat and ready to pounce when the adults got down from the table. *That cake was his*!

But to his horror he heard those most dreaded of words from his dear mother's mouth, "Would you like the last cream cake, Chummy?"

*Argh no*, thought Dad, and he was relieved to hear the words, "Oh no, thank you, Mrs Gaskin." Phew! That was a close one.

But then Nan came back with, "I'm sure a big strong lad like you could find room for it, we don't want it going to waste, do we?" *No, we don't,* thought Dad, *because I'm having it!*

Chummy said, "Oh, all right, if you insist." He took the

prized last cake and proceeded to devour it. Dad never did like Chummy after that.

Dad had lots of stories. Another he told me was about the time Granddad took a new team of four replacement horses to Battersea Fire Station for the changeover, and he had to take the returning horses back to Tilling's so that they could go for their three monthly rest. Having been hooked up to a small dolly cart, the horses proved to be quite a handful for Granddad to control. Nonetheless, he stopped off at home to take Nan, in her best hat, Dad aged about six and his younger brother, Albert, who was a baby at the time, to see Nan's mum at Elephant and Castle, not far from Tilling's yard. Nan and Granddad sat on the tiny bench seat at the front of the cart with Albert wrapped up in a shawl and Dad in the back of the cart by the tailboard. As they were travelling along the Wandsworth Road, a loud bell, like the ones fire stations used back then as a call out, rang out and the four horse team bolted like they were going to a fire.

Working at the fire station, they were as strong and muscular as any horse could be and Granddad, not being the biggest of men, had a real struggle to control the wild snorting beasts, using the flimsy reigns and whip that went with the cart to steady them. According to Dad, Nan and baby Albert nearly went overboard a couple of times while Dad desperately clung on to whatever he could get his hands on. They got to Vauxhall Cross, where the train lines crisscrossed each other in the road, and Granddad feared for all their lives. If a wheel or two had caught in the train lines the little cart would have been flung high in the air, occupants and all. With one mighty effort, Granddad managed to get the horses under control. Nan, Dad and Albert made the rest of the journey by tram. Poor Granddad was in the doghouse for a while.

Sometime around 1952, Mum caught the eye of Dad as they both worked in the local laundry at the corner of Twilly Street and Garrett Lane in Wandsworth. The romance blossomed and they got married in Wandsworth Town hall in the summer of 1953. In June 1954 Paul James Gaskin, my older brother was born, and I appeared two years later in March 1956. Dad once told me this story about life at the laundry and what they got up to. As he was the senior man to a young, unintelligent colleague he would kid him into believing that high up inside the water storage tank, some 25ft above the ground and only reached by an extendable ladder, was an abundance of goldfish.

Being keen to see them the young man was sworn to secrecy and at knocking off time (probably 6.00 pm) one Friday night Dad propped the ladder up alongside the water tank so the man could take a peek inside. Once he was up the ladder, Dad took it away and, feeling rather pleased with himself, went home.

Come Saturday morning it was a different story. It appears that, after a while perched so high up, the young man became agitated and frightened and proceeded to yell at the top of his voice for somebody to get him down. I think Dad categorically denied any involvement in the incident despite the continued accusations of the victim. I suspect Dad's boss knew what had happened but let it pass as no real harm was done.

Dad was a hardworking man who, by the time I could understand such things, was working for a company called Morgan Crucible Ltd, a large factory located on the edge of the River Thames alongside Battersea Bridge. He worked hard in a dirty, dangerous environment and, at times, he would come home in a bad mood and, unfortunately, take it out on Paul or me. Later in life, when Paul and I spoke about this, we never really blamed Dad for that because he believed this was the right way to bring up his children. We suspect his father would have done similar to him and his brothers, and I am not going to dwell on that side of Dad, but it was all too easy for him to remove his belt and let me feel the leather of it on my backside. Sometimes I would get a clip round the ear or a hard smack. In the early part of my life I think I was afraid of him more than I was afraid of anything else. In fact, I had a bad stutter that lasted into my early twenties, and I believe this was down to Dad's physical treatment of me.

One Christmas, when I was about three years old, Paul and I

each received a little pedal tricycle with a small storage bin on the back fitted between the rear wheels. One tricycle was red and the other blue but which one belonged to who has been lost in the fuzziness of time, I'm afraid. Anyhow, we were both very excited and we raced up the street as fast as our little legs would take us, each trying to be in front of the other. Paul was first, as was usually the case in most things that we did.

At the end of the road we turned a sharp right and…wallop! I ran into a lady doing her shopping, who was not best pleased that I had laddered one of her stockings in the collision. Once she had got out of Paul where we lived she frogmarched us back home to confront Mum for the 1/6 (8p) that it would cost to buy new stockings. Mum paid up, of course, but I was in her bad books for a while.

It must have been about this time that an incident took place that had been talked about, on and off, with Mum, Dad and Paul over the years, that had become known in the family as 'the Devil made me do it'.

This is where Battersea Park comes into my life, with me being just about three years old. The story goes like this…I had not been seen all day and although Mum was not initially unduly worried as kids in those days were usually with older brothers or sisters or with friends and their brothers and sisters no one could remember seeing me for a while, so a search party was sent out to find me. They looked up and down the adjoining streets, in and around the block of flats that were no more than 50 yards away, down through the courts as far as the main road, but all to no avail. When Dad and a few of the others dads started getting home from work they too joined in and many a tea was put on the back ring that night.

All the searching hadn't produced a result so the local police were called in to help. By this time, Mum and Dad and, no doubt, Paul were extremely concerned as I had been missing for so long. Search parties were being organised to go further afield, but wait who's this little figure coming out of the darkness and into the glow of the street light in the courts pedalling away like mad on his little three wheel trike with a big grin on his face, pleased to see everybody? Yes, it was I, wondering what all these people were doing outside our house and why were the police there?

When Mum saw me she ran over and picked me up crying and holding me tightly to her. "Where have you been?" Dad asked.

To which I replied, "To Battersea Park." I don't think the people gathered around believed what they had heard. The park was about a mile away and to reach it a couple of main roads with heavy traffic would have to be crossed there and back, a major feat for a three year old on a trike. Whether I did or not, I don't know, but when Dad asked why I had gone to the park my reply was, "The Devil made me do it."

Many visits to Battersea Park followed, over the years, to play in the adventure park or on the swings or play football and cricket with a crowd of mates or even just to wander around. One favourite was to play at being explorers around the large boulders  situated by the boating lake. It was always a dare to see who could lean out the furthest without falling in. I never did but I suspect one or two of the others succumbed to Newton's law on gravity.

Many a time either going to or coming back from the park we would find a bomb site and devise a game where a dead rat would be placed atop a pile of bricks and the first one to knock said rat off would be declared the unofficial World Champion rat knocker off.

Once we had had our fun we would go to the little sweet shop, called Fox's, next to John Burns School in Hanbury Road and buy a small bag of assorted sweets; black jacks, fruit salads, jelly babies, flying saucers, and liquorice whirls and all for tuppence, 2d (1p). Scoffing them down it never occurred to us that, perhaps, after handling the odd rat or two we should have washed our hands first. We never gave it a thought as all we were interested in was our sweets ha-ha. My favourite treat from Fox's, or any other sweet shop for that matter, was the

Orange Jubbly. The appeal of a Jubbly was not the drink so much, although the orange flavoured juice inside was delicious, but the packaging – it was a four-sided tetrahedron – and looked a bit like a pyramid. I must admit I didn't realise they were supposed to be drinks, as I only had them as ice lollies. You cut off one end of the package and ate the ice lolly by gradually pushing it out of the packaging, which was made from a sort of heavy waxed cardboard, pure heaven.

The above-mentioned bomb sites were a result of German Luftwaffe bombs that fell upon Battersea during the start of the Blitz in from 7 September 1940, when the Germans changed tactics and started to bomb the civilian population of London in an effort to make the people call for an end to the war. Those brave souls endured during a period of intense bombing of London and other cities that continued until the following May 1941.

For the next consecutive 57 days, London was bombed either during the day or night. This period in the history of England will go down, as Sir Winston Churchill put it, as 'our finest hour'. Okay, so he was talking about the brave few of the RAF who turned back the mighty German war machine but I think the people of London and England as a whole deserve the accolade just as much.

During the great freezing winter of 1963, I remember Christopher and Paul taking me to Clapham Common to build a snowman. However, as the snow was so deep I could barely follow them on to the common, I had to jump into the footsteps Chris and Paul had made as the snow was so deep.

We always had a proper traditional Christmas. Arding & Hobbs department store in Clapham Junction had the best Santa's Grotto and I can remember Mum taking Paul and me there on many occasions. There was always a queue of boys and girls dressed in their Sunday best. Well, we were going to see Father Christmas after all.

At Christmas the ceiling and walls at home were adorned with decorations. We had a real tree that Dad somehow managed to keep upright in a box or a bucket filled with whatever it was that would keep it okay for a couple of weeks. Cards from family and friends stood on any available space on the sideboard and other bits of furniture in the front room, and if there were too many a piece of string would be stretched between two static objects and the cards hung from it.

Nuts, sweets, chocolates and dates were placed in glass dishes, bowls and trays that Mum would lay out, along with the cards, as best as she could, on the tables. Dad not being a big drinker of alcohol would have a few bottles of beer put aside along with a couple of little bottles of Babycham for Mum. A bottle of Advocaat would take pride of place in the middle, in case visitors might like a 'snowball'. No one ever did, of course, because other than our special Auntie Ivy, Mum's sister, people just didn't visit us.

Under the tree, presents were wrapped up in brightly-coloured paper, depicting characters such as Father Christmas, reindeer or snowmen, covering every inch of whatever Santa had brought for us. What these presents were is unknown to me now. I guess they were appropriate and popular for the time. The ever so neatly wrapped presents didn't look like that for long. Both Mum and Dad tried to hold Paul and I back from them, for a little while at least, but alas to no avail. The paper was ripped to bits in a frenzy of who would be first to open all their presents. We played with the toys or looked at the comic annuals that had been given to us for a while until Dad told us it was time to get washed and dressed and ready for Christmas dinner, now we're talking. Christmas dinner will always be special for me and the ones I had as a kid were the best ever and never to be beaten as my *mum* cooked them.

As I mentioned before, Mum was an exceptional cook and the highlight of my year was the delicious assortment of foods that adorned our table at Christmas. Shop bought crackers were laid on the table and pulled with enthusiasm. A loud bang came from the cracker as it was opened, pouring out its contents of: 1) A corny joke. 2) A colourful paper hat. 3) A cheap and nasty toy. Paul and I would eagerly wait and see what special trinket lay inside; a whistle, a sewing set – who wants that? A small penknife or a tiny pair of scissors.

Then Mum would come in with Dad's dinner, followed by ours, Mum bringing up the rear. There were no starters just straight in to the most mouth-watering chicken – no turkey, beef of pork for us – stuffed with Paxo Sage & Onion stuffing. There were also Brussels sprouts, peas, carrots, roast parsnips, boiled and roast potatoes all piled up as high as the plate could take. Christmas night tea was anything that had been left over made into sandwiches; cheese, picked onions, Branston pickle and crisps. This would be followed by the last of the Christmas pudding and mince pies, a few nuts, sweets and, perhaps, a small tangerine to round it all off. I would then climb into bed, with a new favourite toy, secure in the knowledge that all was okay with my world and this would be repeated in exactly one year's time. I will always fondly remember the wonderful Christmases that Mum and Dad laid on for us.

Thanks, Mum and Dad xxx

# Chapter Two

Jumping forward to the first week of September 1961, when I was five, I had to attend the local school a few hundred yards from home. It was called John Burns Primary School, after the Member of Parliament John Elliot Burns (20th October, 1858–24th January, 1943) who was an English trade unionist and politician, particularly associated with London politics, who had lived at number 56 Wickersley Road.

Burns was a socialist and then a Liberal Member of Parliament and Minister; he was anti-alcohol and a keen sportsman. After retiring from politics, he became an expert in London history and coined the phrase 'The Thames is liquid history'. When the Liberal cabinet made a decision for war on 2 August 1914, he resigned and played no further role in politics.

Mum, like all mums before and since, took me by the hand, together with my brother Paul, and walked me to my first day of school. There were separate entrances for infants and juniors, boys and girls. When we reached the outside, I remember going in through the 'Infants-Boys' entrance for the primary school as Paul went into the 'Junior Boys' entrance. Being twenty-two months older than I, Paul was, in my eyes, an old hand at this school business.

Not much of what happened has been retained by the old grey matter but I do have an inkling that we all sat on the floor in the main hall and were spoken to by the headmistress, Mrs Hughes. She was the most wonderful, elderly grandmother figure, big bosomed in a green twill suit, who became an icon of love and respect to all the assembled children on that first day.

I, like many a child who went to John Burns at this time, still speak of the great fondness, love, and respect we had for the school and its teachers that we held dear some fifty-five years later. In no particular order, I will try and paint a picture of those wonderful school years.

Originally called Basnett Road School, it was built in 1900, and renamed John Burns School in the early 1960s. It was a grand and imposing building to a little five year old who wondered what lay inside. I had never seen a building like it before and tried to imagine what terrors or delights it had in store for me. I needn't have worried because, from my first day until the last at John Burns, I can honestly say they were the happiest of school days. Mrs Hughes was an absolute wonder and my main teacher Mr Airey, a New Zealander from Napier near Lake Taupo on the North Island, was one of the best. I still believe he's the best teacher I ever had.

He would show us photo slides of his homeland and the rivers, valleys, and mountains all looked so absolutely wonderful. When he showed us the location on a map, it might just as well have been on the moon it was so, far away.

I remember one time he taught the class how to play with traditional Maori sticks and sing a Maori song that I remembered for a long time but, alas, many years have now passed and now I cannot recall how the song went.

Christmas at John Burns was always a fun time. I remember we would make paper chains from brightly-coloured sticky paper and hang them from the high ceiling in our classroom. We would draw and paint many Christmas scenes and they too would be hung up on the walls of the classroom. We also had a little Christmas party – you don't get that these days it's all about having a disco – when we were allowed to bring in little bits of food that mums had made to be shared around. We would dance to 45 rpm records played on a Dansette record player, brought in by one of the teachers. I remember taking in a couple of records with my name marked on them so we knew whose was whose. Weren't we all so grown-up dancing and singing along to the songs!

When I was approximately seven years of age, Paul and I went to Silverthorne Road Junior School which, to the naked eye, looked just like John Burns School, a couple of nights a week to attend Silverthorne Road Boys Club. It was here that Paul and I helped to create the club badge. We would play table tennis and board games. The older boys, perhaps, played snooker, amongst other things. Paul went along for the football. He was a good footballer and would eventually play for Silverthorne Road Boys Club first eleven who would go on to have many a success in the junior boys competitions held in the Wandsworth and Battersea area. One of his teammates, a boy called Trevor Lee, went on to play professional Football for Millwall, Colchester United, Gillingham, Leyton Orient, Bournemouth, Cardiff City, Northampton Town, and Fulham.

Another boy, Alan Alden, had one professional game for Chelsea Football Club, and one or two other boys made the professional ranks but, unfortunately, neither Paul nor I can remember their names.

On our way home we would usually have enough money to buy a bag of chips and crackling, drenched in salt and vinegar which, if you were lucky, would have bits of fish in it, mmm…lovely. Or, if we were nearly skint, we would just get a bag of crackling for tuppence from the chippy at the Queenstown Road end of Robertson Street. We would slowly eat these on our way home.

Around this time, Dad's older half-brother, George, was starting to appear at our house on a regular basis to have a chat with him. Of course, being too young to know what was going on I was completely in the dark as to why he visited us so often. As I said before, we rarely had visitors. It was only much, much later in life, when I was in my twenties, that all become clear and Dad told me why this uncle came to visit. You see, this man was not particularly law abiding and through some dodgy deals found himself with large bundles of cash, and I do mean large, so large in fact that he had to get rid of most of it before the taxman came snooping around. He couldn't just hide it under the bed or buy a new car every couple of months, although he did try part exchanging his Mark Ten Jaguar for a Rolls-Royce once, but my Auntie Kath soon sent him back with a flea in his ear when this happened. He had to get his Jag back because, as my aunt told him, "The neighbours will never talk to us again!" After all, they only lived in Sutton, Surrey, hardly the stockbroker belt. Anyhow, Uncle George persuaded Dad with a bung or two, no doubt, that they should go to Paris – highly unlikely as Dad never had a passport in his life – check into a hotel for a couple of nights and spend as much cash as they could get through.

Part of the story goes like this, upon arriving in Paris they checked into a suave hotel then went to the restaurant for dinner just like any other guests. Only this pair couldn't speak or read any French and, upon being given the menu, they couldn't make head or tail of it. By a stroke of good fortune, the 'French' waiter who was serving them actually came from Tooting in South West London and, on the sly, asked if they would like double egg and chips washed down with a beer from the bar. What a lifesaver he turned out to be and deserved the big tip Uncle George gave him at the end of their stay. A likely tale, I know, but it sounded half believable when Dad told it.

Apparently, this was one of many such trips they took together, that included continental touring holidays one of which resulted in his Ford Executive car being written off in Greece, so he went along to the Ford dealer in Athens and bought another one for cash. Uncle George also bought a large boat which never left the dock at Penton Hook Marina, which is situated between Staines and Chertsey, on the western bank of the river, close to Thorpe Park in Surrey.

Another relation, Cousin Derek, that's my Aunt Vera's – Mum's younger sister – eldest son, would often turn up unexpectedly, usually in the early evening and offer to take me and Paul to the funfair that was in Battersea Park at the time. Whether he did or not I can't remember, but Derek was always a favourite of mine when I was a kid. He looked like a Teddy Boy but certainly wasn't one. He knew how to handle himself though, as he had been a very good amateur boxer.

When my Aunt Vera died suddenly in 1986, when I was 30

years old, I went to Dunphail, Morayshire, in Scotland, for her funeral representing my Mum who was then too frail to attend. Vera had been working as a housemaid in a country estate owned by one of Scotland's wealthiest landowners/ businessmen, Sir Hector Laing. I travelled on the overnight coach from Victoria Coach Station one cold November morning, travelling firstly up the M1 to Birmingham, then overnight on the M6 to Carlisle then on the A(M)74 to Cumbernauld in Glasgow where I changed coaches to Aviemore via the M80/A9. This part of the journey took all day and we didn't stop for refreshments or the lavatory, this was catered for on board, so I just got my head down and went to sleep. In the early breaking light I was suddenly awakened by the unmistakable sound of a fast moving RAF Harrier Jump Jet flying low through a glen. I missed him but saw the second one come screaming after his mate.

As I had my hair cut short in those days and was carrying a kind of kit bag, a fellow passenger, who was about the same age, thought that, like him, I was travelling to either RAF Kinloss or RAF Lossimouth, both situated in Morayshire on the Moray Firth. No! I explained that I was a civilian going to my aunt's funeral.

It was late afternoon when we arrived in Aviemore and flecks of snow had begun to fall, as I waited for my cousin John, Derek's younger brother to come and pick me up. As the squaddie was waiting for Military Transport to take him to his base we decided to have a couple of drams in a local bar and see whoever came for us first. That was John, so, with a brisk handshake and a cheerio, we parted company and I went to Dunphail to meet up with Derek and co.

That night I stayed in the local hotel/pub/restaurant/Post Office, common in remote parts of Scotland. Bright and early the next morning, after a much looked forward to cooked breakfast, I got dressed in my best, and only, suit, and waited for Derek or John to come and take me to the local church in Edinkillie, situated on the banks of the River Divie about nine miles south of Forres. It is a beautiful location and in summer is very pretty with the wild flowers and towering trees that surround it, but not on this day. Although bright and crisp, the temperature was hovering around freezing as we waited for the hearse to arrive.

Shortly after we arrived at the church, Derek beckoned me forward to be a pallbearer, an honour that I cherish to this day. After a short but moving service Auntie Vera was taken the short distance to the little cemetery near the church.

After seeing his mother lowered into her final resting place Derek somehow had arranged for his mother's companion 'Tina', a bright-eyed and lively spaniel, together with a new unopened bottle of Scotch Whisky to be present and told me that we were both going to go on Tina's favourite walk down to the river. Not much was said as the dog lead the way and not much was said on the way back, but between us we had emptied the bottle and forever a special bond was made.

I attended the wake at the cottage that Vera had shared with her partner Jim but, after a short while, I made my excuses, and went back to the hotel to get changed and pack my bag. I then waited for John who was to drive me to Aviemore to catch the late afternoon coach back to London.

The temperature had dropped to below freezing, and it was beginning to snow, as John dropped me outside the same bar where we had met the day before. With a wave goodbye to John, I went into the bar and quickly ordered a double scotch, my favourite, The Famous Grouse, and asked the barman how they ever survived such cold weather. He replied, "This is na cold, wait until we get to the New Year, then you can call it cold." I was only too happy to get on the warm coach when it arrived and settle down for the long journey home.

Let's go back to the summer of 1967. I remember walking with Mum, who had my little suitcase in hand, to John Burns School to meet the coach that was to take me and my classmates to Clapham Junction railway station, at that time one of the busiest in the world. From there we would catch the train to

Portsmouth, Hampshire, on the south coast of England, and catch the ferry to Ryde to begin our school holiday on the Isle of Wight. The whole class, together with Mrs Hughes, Mr Airey, and other teachers stayed at a holiday camp site at Whitecliff Bay. What a great time I had on my first real holiday.

I admit to feeling a little homesick during the week as I had never been away from home before. I did have a small connection to home, though, as Mum sent me my weekly comic, *The Topper,* which I think arrived on Thursday. My homesickness soon passed as I got stuck into my comic. Thanks Mum!

It was a lovely holiday camp that I believe is still operating to this day, situated on the cliffs above the beach. It is a couple of minutes' walk down a sloping pathway to the beach where we could play ball games or swim in the sea. I remember one particular time when one of the teachers decided we should go for a walk along the beach, not having taken into account the tide and what time it came in. Inevitably, we got stuck on the rocks and as the water came in, and got higher and higher, we had to climb higher and higher also. Eventually, we became stuck halfway up the cliff waiting for the water to recede. It was getting dark, and only now did the teacher realise that we were in great danger but somebody, somewhere, had obviously raised the alarm because a Mountain Rescue team appeared above us and one of them started to climb down. Attaching ropes to us one at time he guided us back up the cliff towards his colleagues and, in due course, we were all rescued.

I shudder to think of the dressing down the poor teacher involved received from Mrs Hughes when we got back to the holiday camp. She was a formidable disciplinarian when necessary. Needless to say, we were treated like gods amongst our peers and many a tale, most probably exaggerated by all those involved, was told to the open ears of our eagerly awaiting classmates.

I think me and a good few others spent a lot of our holiday money on the holiday camp's juke box. It always seemed to be playing the song 'A Whiter Shade of Pale' by Procol Harum. I think a few of us boys had eyes for some of the girls, and this seemed to be the appropriate song to play to the one we liked anonymously and from afar. Happy days.

After one week of the most marvellous holiday, it was time to pack up and travel back to John Burns School. On Saturday afternoon, the mums came to collect their kids who were, no doubt, happy to see them and tell them all about the great time they had had. And just in time for Saturday afternoon tea.

The only other standout moment from primary school that I remember is taking part in a school play called *The Mikado,* by Gilbert & Sullivan. I was one of the three chorus girls.

All too soon it was time for me to leave my beloved John Burns Junior School and all that it had meant to me for six wonderful years from September 1961– July 1967. Oh how I was going to miss Mrs Hughes and Mr Airey, and all my classmates who were not going to Spencer Park Comprehensive School in September but were instead going to Battersea County School. On my final day, Mrs Hughes gave all the leavers a copy of the Bible, and I cried as she gave me mine as I knew that was probably the last time I would see all of them.

The family moved from Wickersley Road in July of 1967 to a house no more than a quarter of a mile away on the other side of Lavender Hill. It was a modern three bedroom house with a proper bathroom and gardens in Nansen Road. This was to be home until I left altogether in 1975, aged nineteen. But there is a lot more to tell before then.

Not long after moving into Nansen Road I managed to get myself not one but two paper rounds; one in the morning every day before school and again at weekends, and one when I came home from school every evening, Monday to Friday. Mum got me up at about 5.30 am so I could be at the shop by 6.00 am to start on the round. The satchel that held all the morning newspapers was slung over the neck and one shoulder to take the weight. I can tell you those bags, when full, weighed a ton! I didn't mind, though, because I soon worked out that if I changed the route slightly I would get round quickly and finish in the adjacent road to home, where one of the houses had a weekly *Titbits* (Google it!) delivered and it meant that I could have a good look before popping it through the letterbox.

Sundays were a nightmare though, as the Sunday papers all had large thick supplements inside and it meant doing half the round then going back to the shop to collect the second half. The bag was far too heavy to do it all in one go. In addition to the evening paper round I worked in a fish and chip shop at the bottom of Stormont Road. As soon as I finished the evening paper round and had taken the bag back to the newsagent's shop I would go next door and let myself into the backyard of the fish and chip shop. Then I would set about making the chips, firstly putting a big galvanised bucket full of potatoes through a peeling machine, getting the right quantity peeled. I would then put them through the chip cutting machine where it would spit them out into a big bath. I did this from about 5.00–6.30 pm Tuesday to Friday evening – they were closed on a Monday – then from about 10.00 –12.00 am on Saturday morning.

On Saturday, the chippy would give me a large plate of rock/cod and chips, in addition to my wages, which was most welcome especially on the days I went on to watch Chelsea Football Club play at Stamford Bridge. I forget how much I got paid for the two jobs combined but I know it was a pretty penny.

Speaking of Chelsea Football Club, I went to my first match at the old Stamford Bridge ground in Fulham Road, SW6, with Dad and Paul on 30th August, 1961 when Chelsea beat Manchester United 2-0. The goalscorers were Barry Bridges and Bobby Tambling, and we were three of 42,248 supporters that day. I was just five years old. It's amazing to note that, unlike today, all the players of both teams comprised on home-grown talent rather than internationals bought in for extortionate fees. Chelsea fielded eleven Englishmen, Manchester United eight Englishmen, one Scot and two Irishmen. Oh, how things have changed.

Stamford Bridge opened as a sporting arena on 28 April 1877, and for the first twenty-seven years of its existence the London Athletic Club used it almost exclusively for the traditionally popular Victorian pursuit of athletics meetings, during the construction of the stadium thousands of tons of material excavated from the building of the Piccadilly Underground line was used to shape the high terracing for standing spectators. Capacity was originally planned to be 100,000, the second largest in the country behind a decaying Crystal Palace Stadium in South London and, at the time, the FA Cup Final venue.

In 1904, the ownership of the modest ground changed hands when Henry Augustus (Gus) Mears and his brother, Joseph Mears, obtained the deeds, having previously acquired additional land (formerly a large market garden) with the aim of hosting a new sport they had fallen in love with – football. The game had swept the north of England and the Midlands and interest was growing rapidly in the capital city.

Initially the stadium was offered to nearby Fulham FC, but they turned down the chance and so instead a new team, Chelsea Football Club, was born in March 1905. Chelsea FC moved into the new Stamford Bridge stadium for the start of the season a few months later. It was quickly a success with a 60,000 capacity crowd in the first year, promotion to Football League Division One after three FA Cup finals were held there between 1920 and 1922.

Dad took me to as many games as he could paying 1/6- (one old shilling and six pence, 7½p in today's money) for him, and six old pence for me. When I was a bit older I would go on my own, walking from Nansen Road to the ground, a journey of about three miles taking about ninety minutes to walk. If I had enough pocket money I would catch the number 137 bus from Cedars Road to Sloane Square and, again, if I had enough for the bus fare I would take a number 11 that stopped by the Kings Road Bridge. From there it was a two minute cut through the flats to the ground. One particular house on route would store your pushbike outside by its railings. The owners looked after many supporters' bikes, each paying three old pence for the privilege.

It was such a thrill in those days to go to 'the Bridge' to watch my beloved Blues, even if it wasn't always the result I wanted. Chelsea were relegated from the old First Division of English football and yo-yoed backwards and forwards between leagues one and two from 1975 until 1989 when they won the old division two championship and were promoted to England's top flight where they have remained ever since.

I attended many memorable games during the years I saw them play, and went to several FA Cup Finals at the Old Wembley Stadium. I even visited Stockholm in 1998 for the UEFA Cup Winners' Cup Final on 13th May, 1998 to determine the winner of the 1997–98 UEFA Cup Winners' Cup. It was contested by Chelsea of England and Stuttgart of Germany, Chelsea winning 1-0 with a 71st minute goal by Gianfranco Zola.

During the 2003-2004 season I was made redundant from Aon Ltd where I was working as a chauffeur, reluctantly I decided that I could not afford to renew the season ticket that I had held with them for many years, so after watching them for nigh on forty years one indifferent season after another, it was only when I stopped going that they have gone on to be one of the most successful teams in the land.

Back to September 1967 when I was about to become one of Spencer Park Comprehensive School's new boys, studying in a building with a long and interesting history.

The Royal Victoria Patriotic Building in Wandsworth, London, this Gothic style, Victorian building was built in 1859 to house girls orphaned during the Crimean War and known as the Royal Victoria Patriotic School.

The building was refurbished during World War I, including the installation of a new heating system, and used as the third London General Hospital. Many thousands of soldiers were treated at the hospital during the War and the rear was packed with marquees housing those wounded at the front. After the War, the building reverted to its earlier use as the Royal Victoria Patriotic School for girls, until the children were evacuated to Wales in 1939.

During World War II, over 30,000 immigrants to the UK were interrogated by MI5 in the building, at the 'London Reception Centre', and Dutch 'spy catcher' Colonel Oreste Pinto operated out of here at this time.

After World War II, the building was initially used as a teacher training college but was purchased by London County Council in 1952. From 1957 it housed Honeywell Secondary Mixed School, followed by Spencer Park Comprehensive School for Boys. The building eventually became structurally unsafe and the school moved to a new building in 1974, after which time The Royal Victoria Patriotic Building fell into disrepair, under threat of demolition. The building was saved by the Victorian Society and the Wandsworth Society, who campaigned for its preservation, and it then became a Grade II listed building.

In 1980, the Greater London Council (GLC), London County Council's successor, granted a lease with the option to buy the building for £1 to developer, Tuberg Property Company. The restoration took six years, but just before the official GLC handover the main hall was destroyed by arson. The hall was restored from a photographic survey, made just two weeks earlier. The Civic Trust awarded a commendation in 1985 for the hall ceiling, and another in 1987 for the restoration of the building as a whole. The restoration also won the Europa Nostra Order of Merit in 1987.

Underneath the headmaster's study was rumoured to be an escape tunnel leading down to the railway line that connected London via Clapham Junction railway station to the south and southwest of England. Fact or fiction, who knows?

I don't remember much about my first day but I know, like Paul, I was in the green house called Kelvin Wilberforce. Our housemaster was a tall, blond-haired man called Mr Humber who was not the kind of man to be taken lightly. He took my science lessons and he stood no nonsense from any of us new boys. Quite often he would throw the blackboard rubber at a boy he suspected of talking, giggling or simply not paying attention.

In the morning we had to assemble in class order, military fashion, by 8.45 am. We would have to stand perfectly still and in complete silence, not saying a word to anybody about anything, otherwise you would be called out to face your housemaster or, even worse, the headmaster if warranted. Then we would march into school to our respective classrooms where we were expected to stand behind our desk to wait for the teacher to arrive before we were allowed to sit down. The class register was then taken prior to the beginning of our lessons.

Being an old Victorian building the classrooms were quite wide and long with high ceilings. I think there were about thirty children to a class in each house, and there were four classes. I think I was in green number three, Kelvin Wilberforce.

Secondary school was certainly a lot different from primary school as we had to wear school uniform; a black blazer with the school badge, white shirt, red and black diagonal stripe tie, grey trousers and black shoes.

The school had its own chapel and we had to attend once a week from 9.00–9.30 am. Each boy was expected to go, no excuses were accepted. Then it was off to class. Again, I cannot remember my school teachers' names other than Mr Humber except for one; a Welshman who took engineering classes whose name was Mr Evans. He was an elderly man who always wore a khaki suit, not military style just khaki in colour. He had a saying which always made us laugh, not in front of him, of course, but if any boy did anything wrong he would say in his thick welsh accent, "That boy yer. Come yer." So, naturally, we would march around in the playground saying, "Come day, come week, come month, come YER."

We had a PE teacher who thought that we were recruits for the Royal Marine Commandos disguised as children by the way he tried to make us do a USMC/Navy Seal test every time he took PE.

He would have us trying to do all manner of squats, chin pull-ups, and climbing up the ceiling rope and abseiling down – upside down. We also had to run on the spot, for God knows how long, but I didn't care, as I was the fat boy who sat in the corner, ha-ha. He did get his comeuppance though, as I shall reveal a little later.

Unfortunately, he also took us for swimming lessons which, to be honest, for me wasn't too bad as I was quite a good swimmer at eleven years of age. Dad had taught me how to swim by the age of about five at Latchmere Road Swimming Baths, so called because a laundry and bath house was in the same building. Bizarrely, so was the morgue. Anyhow, one of the good things about the baths was if you forgot your swimming costume you had the choice of going into the 1d – one old penny – bare bums for boys or girls, separately of course. Outrageous, I hear you cry but don't forget that this was in a far more innocent and simpler time. I never went in the bare bums as Mum always made sure I had my swimming trunks and enough money.

I used to go to the baths practically every day during the school holidays and at least once a week in term time and, naturally, I became a strong swimmer and not such a bad board diver either. Well, at least I thought so.

Spencer Park had its own outdoor swimming pool that every class, in every year, had to have in its syllabus every school week throughout the year, no matter how cold it was in the water or out of it – I suppose to justify having it. As it wasn't heated, we knew how awful it was going to be in the winter time.

Mr PE man would have us all line up on the side of the pool and, on his command, we all had to jump in. Anyone who didn't would feel his boot encouraging entry. After thirty minutes it was over and we all hurried back to the changing rooms for a hot shower.

It was in this swimming pool that I am proud to say that I took my ASA Life Saving Bronze, Silver and Gold badges on consecutive days, all thanks to Dad getting me into swimming at an early age. Actually, as I have two left feet and have never been any good at football, I would spend every spare moment in the swimming pool when finances allowed. It's something that I really miss now as I am not physically able to do it.

In my second year the school must have been desperate for teachers because, during a science lesson by Mr Humber, the headmaster came into the room followed by loveliness herself, a stunning blonde woman aged about twenty-two, straight out of teacher training college. Can you imagine the impact on thirty testosterone-fuelled twelve to thirteen year old boys?

After the introduction, it was announced that she was to take over Mr Humber's class the following week. *Great!* we all thought but it got even better as she was to take maths as well, which meant she would be using the up and roll over blackboards, we couldn't wait.

Sure enough, it happened as we all hoped it would and there was uproar. There were a few red faces and a few stern ones too. You see, when any teacher used the roll over blackboards they had to bend down to move the next section up and over to reveal a clean section, but sometimes the top section of the blackboard had to be pushed to the top so it could roll over. As this could be quite high, it normally required standing on tiptoes if you weren't quite tall enough. Definitely not advisable if you're doing it in a mini skirt in front of about thirty eager boys who knew exactly what was going to happen. Worse was to come as in Mr Humber's science class that she had taken over the inevitable happened.

The Department of Education had insisted that sex education was to be taught in all secondary schools from that year. Let's just say that some of the front row boys were well beyond the birds and bees stage when putting questions to little Miss Blondie, who ran out of the room in tears. Later the whole front row got the cane for that.

And so what became of Mr PE man I hear you cry. Well, in true 'couldn't make it up' style he and aforesaid Miss Blondie were caught having the three letter word in the showers late one night after school by one of the cleaners who obviously informed the headmaster. The following morning, low and behold, he was gone – hooray, shame about her though.

The best school day of the week for me was sports day because, come lunchtime on the day, we would be bussed from Spencer Park to Priest Hill at Ewell, near Epsom, to play football or rugby. As I said, I had two left feet when it came to playing football, but I excelled at rugby. This was okay until I received a bad injury to my back which caused me problems until I was about fifty-five years of age and needed to have surgery on a badly formed disc in my lower back.

The playing fields were commanded by Mr Wallace, the head of sports at Spencer Park. He had a really loud, cutting voice and if he saw something he didn't like going on out on the playing fields he would shout, "That boy there," and every boy on every football and rugby pitch in earshot would stop dead in their tracks for fear of being the one who was singled out.

As I said earlier, I have been a lifelong fan of Chelsea Football Club and, in 1970, when Chelsea won the FA Cup, Mr Wallace asked the manager Dave Sexton to bring the FA Cup to school so that we could see it. He also asked one or two of the professional players at Chelsea and Fulham Football Clubs to train the boys at Priest Hill. For those who played rugby, every fourth week we were made to play football and, on this particular week, the FA Cup winning captain of Chelsea, Ron Harris was to be referee of the game I was participating in. He didn't just referee he played sometimes as well. My claim to fame is that I was tackled by Ron Harris. Being a winner, he tackled me like I was a fellow professional and I must have gone five feet up in the air and landed on my backside to which the only words from Ron Harris were, "Come on, get up, that was only a tap." Not from my end it wasn't, Ron, it felt like I had just been hit by an Exocet missile.

# Chapter Three

In July 1971, aged fifteen, I left Spencer Park School and made my way into the big wide world of work. I didn't want to, as in my final year of school I had decided to try for the Royal Navy Officer training school. My teachers thought that my grades would be good enough but there was an educational stumbling block in my way, Physics. You see, on the curriculum at the time I could not study Physics so my dream of a career in the Royal Navy fell apart. I was too pig-headed to enlist as a rating at the time as my head was filled with much grander things, good job really, in a way, as my life might have taken a very different path.

In 1982 the Argentinean government led by General Galtieri, the president, was under enormous pressure to reform the political landscape of Argentina and decided that an invasion of the Malvinas Islands would deflect from the problems that he was facing and unite the country. So, on 2$^{nd}$ April, 1982, Argentine forces launched the invasion of the Falkland Islands, beginning the Falklands War.

The Argentines mounted amphibious landings, and the invasion ended with the final surrender of Government House. The British Prime Minister, Margaret Thatcher, and her government quickly ordered Her Majesty's Combined Forces of the Royal Navy, Army and Royal Air Force to put together a task force to sail to the South Atlantic to regain the Falkland Islands as it was a British Sovereign Territory.

Dad didn't believe that strongly in education and convinced me that, "Education was not for us, go out and get a job, that's the best thing for you." In those days you didn't normally argue with what your dad told you to do, so reluctantly I left school age fifteen.

On that first Monday morning after leaving school and

having no job to go to Dad was not best pleased. He proceeded to literally turf me out of bed at 6.00 am and I was told in a stern voice, "Go and get a job." Well, after looking around and not being inspired to work in a shop or factory or everybody's favourite the Post Office, I was a bit stumped. Then Mum suggested that, perhaps, she would ask if they had any vacancies suitable for me at the small commercial printers where she worked.

The Fraser Print & Label Co had premises on Lavender Hill and a small printing works, the old Queens Theatre, 1A Prairie Street, off Queenstown Road, the company also had a large Victorian house in Queenstown Road, next to the Victoria pub, at the junction of Silverthorne Road. The manager told Mum to bring me along the next day and, "We'll take a look at him." Early the next morning Mum and I walked to the printworks, a journey which took about twenty minutes, firstly walking to Lavender Hill where shops such as the newsagents and William's the greengrocers were beginning to open, past the Home and Colonial store, the bakers and butchers and then turning into Queenstown Road.

Mum and I would walk as far as the zebra crossing at the junction of the courts that Paul and I had used many a time to go to the Silverthorne Boys Club. Opposite was the 'The Oil Shop', a long gone relic of many decades of supplying the local populous with all sort of essentials from a yard broom to a rubber plug for the sink, a paste brush to a few screws or nails for those necessary DIY jobs that occasionally needed doing around the house.

Passing the petrol station on our left and crossing over Stanley Grove we were now on the home stretch, passing a number of tall Victorian houses on our left we eventually came to what was to be our regular morning stop for a newspaper and twenty Guards Cigarettes for me and a packet of Weights Cigarettes for Mum. In those days the majority of the population smoked, Paul was about the only person I knew who didn't.

We arrived early on that first day and I didn't really know what to expect. I was greeted by Mr Baker the works manager, a rather tall and imposing figure who I think had served in the army and lost a leg so was invalided out. Now here he was managing this small, friendly company on behalf of Mr Fraser the owner. There wasn't really an interview; Mum was so well liked that it was a formality me getting a job there. I was set to work straight away, firstly having to make the early morning tea. I was taken through to the small rest/tea room that was right next to Mr Baker's office, where he could keep an eye on us no doubt. I thought, *Oh no, that's not for me!*

After being shown what to do by the tea lady, 'Eli', I politely gave out the cups of tea and coffee as required and didn't make a fuss, but when the lunch time tea had to be made I saw my chance to get out of tea making altogether. You see I doubled the amount of tea leaves – there were no tea bags in those days – and poured lukewarm water into the large, almost industrial sized, teapot, stirred it all up and proceeded to pour out the contents into the individuals' personal tea cups/mugs without using the strainer to catch the tea leaves. The resulting mess that was served up caused Eli to redo it, and do it for evermore, thus no more tea making for me. I remember doing a lot of lifting and carrying after that.

The first week went by quickly and, to be honest, I didn't think that I wanted to stay there for that long. The following week was pretty much the same as the first, and on the Friday I got my first pay packet. It came in a small, brown envelope with a clear window on the front where the change could be seen, and a turned over top left hand corner where the corners of any notes could be counted as, once opened, any mistakes couldn't be rectified. I remember that my first week's take home pay was exactly £7.00. When I got home later that day Dad said that I could keep the full amount as it was my first week's pay. After that, I was to give Mum £5.00 housekeeping money a week. It was only fair, I suppose, as being a big lad I probably ate that amount every week, ha-ha.

It was around this time that Paul remarked to me, "If you don't stop eating so much you will be dead from a heart attack by the time you're seventeen." Thanks, bruv, I love you too.

After a few weeks of doing all sorts of manual jobs, I started learning how to count out the correct number of printed sheets required by the customer, pack and stack boxes for dispatch, affix address labels, lick the envelopes down and affix the stamps to them – yuk! Mum later told me there was a moist pad to dab the envelopes and stamps on to avoid getting the disgusting fishy taste from licking the said stamps and envelopes. And still no sign of doing any proper print work!

After a couple of weeks or so, I started getting to know some of the people who worked there. For example, Harry, the ninety-year-old ex-business man who travelled from Brixton on the 137 bus every day to do a morning's work sweeping up because he liked to keep busy. In fact, Harry was old school, often doffing his hat to the ladies upon arrival and giving up his seat in the staff room if a lady needed it. I learned a lot about doing the right thing from Harry.

Then there was Tom, the lithograph machine operator, who thought he could sing like Elvis Presley but sounded pretty awful. When at full voice many a missile would be sent his way, mainly by Mr Baker, I should add.

Numerous other men and women around Mum's age, whose names I have forgotten, made up the workforce. One girl, Gillian, was about my age and worked alongside Mum in the packing department. She was a freckled, bespectacled redhead who had aroused my interest, and we hit it off straight away, much to Mum's annoyance as she never really liked Jill. I think Mum felt that there were better fish in the sea, as the saying goes, but I liked her and that's all there was to it.

I was then put to work removing the large printed sheet of paper from the silkscreen printer's table so the printer could position another in exactly the right spot to continue printing. If I was too slow, the wooden frame containing the silk screen pattern would be pulled back down clipping my hand or finger, a reminder that I should be quicker next time.

There were three or four young men working in this section of the factory, all nice guys, but I became friends with two in particular, one Irish lad and one Polish. All the old girls fancied the Irish lad and flirted and teased him all the time. Some of the language quite shocked me coming from one or two women I knew to be the mums of my old classmates from John Burns Primary School. The Polish lad was very interesting as he was an art student working to pay his way while travelling around the world, something I have never really contemplated doing.

As the weeks went by, I became used to the routine of getting up and setting off to work with Mum. I was offered overtime for both morning and evening and so, with nothing better to do, I eagerly accepted. It wasn't that hard to stay on for an hour or two longer than my normal end time of 5.00 pm, especially if I was working in Queenstown Road where they did mainly silk screen printing.

As I was now part of the gang, on Fridays after work I was invited to go to the pub next door, The Victoria. Although I was underage I was big for my age and got away with it mainly, I think, because I never went near the bar to buy a drink. A pint of beer in those days cost 1/6 (7½ pence). I started drinking light and bitter as you got slightly more beer in the glass and when the light ale was poured in it came to more than a pint.

Around about this time, in 1973, I started to bump into the same three or four teenagers that were about my age and I started to go out with them a couple of times a week after work. Usually, we would go to one another's houses and play records in our bedrooms. It was here that I first heard and began to like, amongst others, Led Zeppelin, Deep Purple, Eric Clapton and Cream. One of the group loved Rod Stewart another Afrobeat band, Osibisa, and someone else liked a weird-sounding singer called Richie Havens.

We were just like most other teenagers of our age sneaking into pubs, playing football and going to the Devas Boys Club at the Lavender Hill end of Stormont Road, our usual meeting place. Mostly we went to The Crown pub, on Lavender Hill, for a pint or two before we decided on what the evening's entertainment would be. One of the lads, Phil, was a bit of a joker. He always doing daft things like smoking a fag through his nose, pulling a face, or farting at the most inappropriate of times, thus immediately causing the rest of us to fall about in fits of teenage laughter. Oh yeah, another trait of Phil's was that it was easier to get blood out of a stone than get him to buy a round or buy a packet of cigarettes. Still he was our mate so we didn't mind too much.

He lived almost opposite the pub and sometimes we would go to his house, a big, old Victorian building that had a glass-fronted car salesroom on the ground floor. There were always a couple of cars both inside, and out on the pavement, for sale but whether his dad ran the car salesroom or not I never really knew. It was here that Phil introduced us to Psychedelic Rock. Phil's older brother played guitar in a band and obviously followed the genre and this had rubbed off on Phil. We would end up hearing all strange and weird musical sounds heighted by lava lamps and joss sticks in his bedroom.

I loved Phil. I think it was through Phil that we started going to the Chelsea Drugstore on the King's Road, not far from Sloane Square. It had been a club that rock and film stars had frequented in the sixties and so became one of the 'in' places to go and be seen. In fact, there is a line about it in the Rolling Stones song 'You Can't Always Get What You Want' and, having seen those heady days gone by, it was now a great venue to hear rock music.

We would go on a Saturday night having first popped into The Crown for a couple of beers. We caught the number 137 bus at the top of Queenstown Road which travelled down Battersea Park Road, past Battersea Park, over Chelsea Bridge past the grounds of The Royal Hospital Chelsea, before we jumped off just short of Sloane Square. It was then a few minutes' walk along the King's Road to the pub.

After going for a number of weeks we started to get to know

the resident DJ Mark, a really nice guy aged about twenty-five. He told us that when he was a child, living with his parents, Paul McCartney of The Beatles had been his next door neighbour. We all scoffed at this but we had to eat our words when he showed us family snaps of all members of The Beatles at various picnics or BBQs in their respective back gardens.

Mark always had a couple of large, wide, briefcase-type bags loaded with albums that he would bring with him to every gig. He would try and get people to dance, but that was almost impossible as the pub would be absolutely packed. One favourite track he would mix up would be the opening minute or two of Silver Machine by Hawkwind with the opening sounds of the *Dr Who* theme from the BBC show, a masterpiece which got everybody cheering and raising their drinks to him. As it was always so busy, we usually bought two rounds at once because the queue to get served was so long.

Mark the DJ was of Asian descent and lived in a small flat in Tooting with his wife. We were by now good friends with him and he would invite us back to his flat for a beer and something to eat. His wife would usually have made food and left it out before going to bed, as it was usually well past midnight when Mark arrived home. The food was my introduction to South Asian cuisine and I found it absolutely fabulous; meat, rice, spices, peppers and vegetables. Many a night we would stay until the early hours of the morning talking about every subject imaginable. I really enjoyed those nights and they were very much a part of my growing up and understanding how other people lived their lives and the things that they believed in.

After a couple years, Mark and his wife moved to a flat in Highbury, North London, so we didn't go back so often as it was quite a journey back to Battersea, especially late at night. One day he told us, with the biggest smile imaginable, that he had got a job with one of the new independent radio stations in the Newcastle area, Metro Radio. He moved away and, sadly, that was the last we heard of him as there were no mobile phones, email, or social media in those days.

Later on, we all started to get girlfriends which meant that our usual Friday and Saturday nights were curtailed, so we decided to have a few beers on a Monday evening before going to an Indian restaurant for a curry. Not very original but it was what people started to do in those days. I always had a lamb vindaloo, as there was not so much variety as there is now, but one or two of the others would insist on having a chicken or lamb madras. Phil always studied the menu for far longer than was necessary and after mumbling about trying this or that for a change, he always ordered the same bloody thing, a Spanish omelette!

One night we had been out for a few beers and ended up in a not so good Indian restaurant on Battersea Park Road. Having been seated at a table, we were each given a menu and, as soon as the food and lagers had been ordered, the usual chat, boasting and leg pulling started. When the food arrived, it was dive in and devour. Those that had been brave or daft enough to order the madras soon regretted it as the sweat began to pour from their brows.

On this particular night, though, the occupants on the next table caught our attention. They were overheard saying things like, "The food's not up to much, Charles, is it?" And "Neither is the wine, darling." Yes, you've guessed it; the 'Hooray Henrys' from across the water had started to invade Battersea. You see, we all lived in the area and were proud of being Battersea boys and, at the time, we didn't appreciate them moving over the river, buying our houses for next to nothing, doing them up and selling them on for a tidy profit, thank you very much! We told the other diners as much, coming close to fisticuffs, and demanded that they leave or we would not be returning there for our curry supper. We told the owner it was them or us, but I don't actually remember going back there again.

The group started to drift apart and not see as much of each other. Most of us had girlfriends and that meant the inevitable was going to happen, we were only going to see each other once a week on a Monday night. We decided to change things around a bit and go on a massive pub crawl and far and away the best beer was that brewed by the Young's Ram Brewery in Wandsworth High Street which we took great pride in drinking. In those days, the brewery had 135 tied pubs in and around London and they had a scheme called the '135 Club'. To become a full member each one of their pubs had to be visited and at least a half pint consumed. The Guvnor would then sign beside the name of his pub on a printed list of the 135 pubs as proof that you had drunk there. Once all 135 pubs had been visited, the printed list would be sent to the brewery and those who had been successful in completing it would get a special blue tie with 135 embroidered in roman numerals above the brewery mascot, a Ram; a tour of the brewery and a firkin of bitter, seventy-two pints. Plus the signed sheet back.

At the beginning of this epic journey we decided to go to the furthest pubs first and work our way in towards the brewery, calculating that, at most, we could do five or six each week on a Monday night. It would, therefore, take us about seven months to complete our task. Handy really, as one of the group said if we could do it before his birthday we could have a massive party at his house as his mum and dad would be on holiday at the time. So there it was, we had a target to aim for.

Around this time I got fed up with the print game and having recently passed my driving test, I was determined to chuck it in and get a job driving for a living. And what a great job it turned out to be. I worked as a delivery driver for the Victoria Wine Company that had shops all over London. I worked in one of their West End shops, the one in St James's, London SW1. The manager was a middle-aged Irishman who had been in the game for years. There was also a woman who did the admin and served in the shop, an educated upper class lad who turned out to be a great laugh and yours truly, the van driver. That job was the first one that I really liked going to every day.

One day, after I had made a few deliveries, the manager took me to one side and, giving me the key that operated a small, private lift, told me to deliver a box of spirits and soft drinks mixers to an address around the corner. I was to put the box into the small lift and use the key to send it to the top flat in the building and come straight back to the shop. Under no circumstances was I to go up in the lift. Well, that had 'you gotta do it' written all over it. So, I got in the lift and travelled the few floors up to the private flat on the top floor. When it reached the flat, the door opened to reveal a stark naked young woman in her early twenties who had the most gorgeous figure. I stood frozen to the spot having got the shock of my life, but she didn't bat an eyelid. She looked at me in a way that meant I had to scarper pretty damn quick. Then, I heard a male voice shout, "Get rid of him and come back here." As she turned around I could see him in a state of full frontal excitedness; her punter for the afternoon.

Hurriedly returning to the shop I kept my mouth shut and hoped nothing would be said. Well, it never was, so all okay there. Another time, I was looking for somewhere to park in Jermyn Street, just around the corner from the shop. Having spotted an empty parking space I made straight for it only to beaten by a yellow Lamborghini Miura that had shot out of Bury Street right in front of my nose and nicked my parking space. Right, I thought to myself, I am having you mate. As I drew up almost alongside the Lambo the passenger got out, Ronnie Wood, lead guitarist of the Faces, later become a full member of the Rolling Stones said, "Has he taken your spot?" referring to the driver. Of course, I replied, "Yes, he bloody well has."

Ronnie Wood told me to tell the driver to "F***ing well move it," as it was my space.

Too right, but as the driver got out and asked if it was all right to park I meekly replied, "Yeah, that's okay," to which Ronnie Wood called me the biggest…well you know what… under the sun. What else could I do, the driver was Rod Stewart after all!

I do have to mention an elderly Lord and Lady who lived in an apartment in the Ritz Hotel, Piccadilly. I was instructed to make all deliveries personally to the apartment and, upon ringing the front door bell, the family butler would open it and beckon me in. When Her Ladyship saw me she would invite me into the kitchen for a cup of tea, toast and a chat on how the world was treating me.

One particular day, she told me that His Lordship was having trouble with the "Old Bentley" and asked me if I could visit the underground car park/garage to see if I could help him to get it going. When he saw me approaching, he said, "Brian, be a good man and take a look at it for me would you," and promptly disappeared!

I knew nothing about old cars, and not much about newer cars either come to that. Rather than muck about I had a look inside the glove box and found that he was a member of the Bentley Owners Club, Royal Automobile Club, and the Automobile Association – of course he was – so I went upstairs and asked the concierge in the hotel if I could use the phone to call the RAC. I did so and waited for the man to arrive. Well, His Lordship must have been somebody important because the mechanic arrived within about ten minutes and duly got the car started and was soon on his way.

I went up to His Lordship's flat to give him the good news and he was overjoyed. Her Ladyship then invited me to sit down at the kitchen table for more tea. Then she told me something that I have never forgotten, and rings true even today. She said that all their lives she and His Lordship had treated the people who worked for them with great respect and dignity, and paid them a fair wage. "Now, here's the truth of it," she said. "If you kind people didn't help us we would not be able to have lived the life we have done." Now that is old school gentry, pure class. Today's get rich quick 'sod you, Jack, I'm all right' brigade could learn a valuable lesson or two from Her Ladyship.

After a while, I realised that the pay at Victoria Wine was not as good as I could earn elsewhere so I decided that it was time for a change and started working for a local Battersea company delivering electrical goods around London. As I had use of the company van, I would do the driving for the '135 Club', and watch my mates getting pissed.

I had good reason to be careful when it came to drinking and driving as I had a great let off on one occasion. We had been to the White Hart in Richmond upon Thames one night in summer, a lovely pub close to Richmond Bridge. We had stayed there all evening with me drinking pints of bitter shandy while all the others were on the very strong Ram Special Bitter until chucking out time; 10.30 pm in those days. I drove home with two of the lads on the passenger bench seat beside me and the other two in the back, one of whom was Phil. As we drove through Sheen I was overtaken by a posh boy in his E-Type Jaguar, with his equally posh girl by his side, and was instantly egged on by the boys to give him a race. This I did, and we were both doing a ridiculous speed along Sheen High Street.

As we approached a set of traffic lights at speed, not giving a thought to anybody else, the traffic lights suddenly turned red. Matey Boy in the E-Type shot straight through the red light. Fortunately, I had the good sense not to as, unbeknown to Matey Boy or me, a police car that had been waiting at the opposite light and suddenly gave chase. Mr E-Type Jag, to our great delight, and with a lot of cheering from inside the van was nicked by the police for going through the red light and maybe for speeding too, result. We all laughed until Phil pleaded to be let out from the back as he was about to be sick. We just about made it to the side of the road as he threw up into the gutter. The rest of us lit up a fag and had a jolly good laugh about it.

This incident made me realise how easy it would have been for me to be nicked. I would probably end up losing my job as well, so it was a wise decision by me not to drink and drive, to get behind the steering wheel of a car is one of the most reckless, thoughtless things one can do.

# **Chapter Four**

I asked the girl at work out. Gillian, you remember her? And after a couple of dates her mum invited me round for Sunday tea, as was usual in those days. The following Sunday I went round to her house in Pitcairn Street, off the Wandsworth Road. I knocked on the front door of a house very like the one that I had been brought up in at Wickersley Road, except that this house had a basement flat and was three storeys high. I was met be a small, late middle-aged woman called Vera, Gillian's mother.

Vera was the wife of William (Bill) Bryant who was, at that time, suffering from and having treatment for lung cancer at the Royal Brompton Hospital, Chelsea, a place that many years later I became only too familiar with myself.

Sunday tea passed quickly as the family were going to the hospital to visit Bill. They were being taken there by Vera's brother-in-law, Bert, a nice old gentleman married to, Vera's sister, Joan, who lived in a flat in a tower block behind South Wimbledon Tube Station, towards the southern end of the Northern Line.

During the next six months I became a regular visitor with Gillian and her family to see her dad in hospital, usually on a Sunday. Bill had become extremely frail and weighed a little over six stones. He looked extremely ill the last time that I saw him. I have forgotten exactly when Bill died but it all seemed to have happened very quickly. The next thing I knew, Christmas was fast approaching and I wondered how the family would cope but Christmas and New Year 1974 came and went and, although things were not normal, we all seemed to survive it well enough.

Meanwhile, it was becoming increasingly obvious to Mum that it was getting serious between Gillian and I. We were always chatting in work whenever we could get away with it. Gillian was beginning to get hassle from her mum and was not at all happy at home. Then her mother met a fella; a fortyish, trainspotter who lived with his elderly mum and worked on the buses. Says it all, doesn't it! Anyone who knows me well will know exactly what I thought of him.

This was the final straw for Jill and, as we were getting serious, we decided to find a place of our own together. We were both about nineteen at the time, young I know but we felt old enough to break away from our families and go it alone. We approached Lambeth Borough Council to see if they could help, and they offered us a tiny flat in a terraced house at number 93b Lollard Street, in Lambeth. The flat was close to Lambeth Walk made famous by a World War II song called 'Doing the Lambeth Walk', that accompanied film footage in cinemas of the German Army goose stepping in time to the beat.

We occupied the upstairs. The flat had an outside toilet at the back of the house, right outside the tiny kitchen which itself was just about big enough to fit a cooker and washing machine in. Next to that was the dining room (ha, well we called it that) where we had a kitchen table, and a couple of small bits of furniture, a cupboard and sideboard I think. Then came the bedroom that had a large fitted wardrobe for the both of us and, finally, at the front of the house was the front/living room which was quite large so we were able to squeeze our second-hand three piece suite, telly and a couple of other second-hand bits of furniture into it. So we started on a chapter of my life that may bring a tear or two to your eyes, but more of that later.

By now I had put the driving job behind me and was working for the Home Office Reprographic Department, situated just over Lambeth Bridge, as the stationery storekeeper. It was my job to keep the Home Office Reprographic Department supplied with all the necessary items to keep it running.

I didn't really like the position, but it was a job after all and it became a stepping stone for something else in the future. I couldn't see myself working for long in the Civil Service as, unless you have experienced it, it is difficult to describe the mentality of the people who work there. To my mind, it is full of people who are not capable of working anywhere else as they can only do things by the book and would not last five minutes in the private sector.

Gillian had managed to get herself a job at ICI Headquarters on Milbank, located on the north side of Lambeth Bridge, where she worked in the Directors' Dining Room as a waitress. The pay wasn't good but, at the end of her shift, the cooks would share out the leftover cooked food to the staff who were finishing their shift after the last director had gone back to work. On many occasions we ate the finest steak, beef, pork chops, lamb and chicken cuts for free at tea time. Lovely Jubbly!

Every Friday, when we got home from work, we would open up our pay packets and count out our wages into one pile, then put the rent into one white envelope, the motorbike tax and insurance into another (I owned a lovely Suzuki Re5), housekeeping in another and so on and so forth until all the bills were covered. What little was left over was ours for the week, and although it didn't amount to much, we were happy enough because we never had much money when we were growing up and couldn't afford to go out very often. We found other ways to enjoy ourselves which meant maybe going for a walk to St. James Park on a summer evening, but usually we would spend our evenings in front of the telly like most people did. Occasionally, we would go to our nearest pub, The George in Lambeth Walk, although in those days we had a choice of seven pubs all within a five to ten minute walk. If we had time we would go out on the motorbike, a 1976 Rotary engine Suzuki RE5 – a rare and, nowadays,  valuable, bike. It was my pride and joy and gave me one of the most satisfying moments ever riding a big motorbike but, alas, it also had a sting in the tail.

We had been out for a Sunday afternoon ride to Richmond upon Thames and, on the way back, I decided to go via the A40 which meant that we would travel along the elevated section into London. I was using the outside lane following a queue of cars doing about 60 mph and keeping up with the traffic when, out of nowhere, an unmarked police car put on his blues and twos and indicated for me to stop on the hard shoulder. I pulled over, as instructed, and awaited my fate. Now, the engine on that particular motorcycle generates a tremendous amount of heat and, consequently, the exhaust pipes get extremely hot. They have a thick, black-coated metal guard on top of them just in case one's foot or leg should touch them. The officer told me that it was tough luck that I was at the end of the queue of traffic that had been speeding in a 50 mph zone and I was going to get a ticket which meant three points on my licence and a £30 fine and that I should be more aware of what was going on around me in future. I know he had not seen an RE5 before and was keen to inspect it. The bike was scrutinised by him; he checked the tyres, he checked the lights and indicators, all correct so far. Now he was going to check the chain for the correct tension but, as the bike was on its side stand the exhaust pipe was very low to the ground. The police officer put his hand under the exhaust pipe to check the chain, letting out an all mighty cry of pain as his wrist touched the underneath of the exhaust pipe causing a terrific burn.

I have never seen anybody move so fast to get to a first aid kit as he did. I felt a sense of moral justice and mentioned to the police officer that maybe 'he should be more aware of what he was doing in future'. I chuckled as they let me go on my way. In my mirrors, I could see one officer furiously starting to bandage the wrist of the other unfortunate one who had a grimace on his face as he was being attended to. I could do nothing else but smile as I rode off, with Jill clinging on riding pillion as usual.

I had decided that if Jill and I were going to have a future I would have to leave the Civil Service, primarily as the pay was low and would not allow us to move on, buy our own house and start a family. I decided to go on a government-funded course to qualify as a universal toolroom grinder and, for six weeks, I rode on the RE5 to the Training Skills Agency in Plaistow, East London, to do my training. Once completed, I was offered a job at Kemworthy Tools, in South Wimbledon, who were to be my employer for the next seven years. To be honest, I was useless at the job but the foreman must have seen some good in me for me to have stayed so long.

As I said before, the Suzuki RE5 really was my pride and joy. It never gave me any problems and was a sheer joy to ride. During the summer of 1976, I rode from Lambeth to South Wimbledon every day.

How glad was I that I had retrained? The money I was earning, especially the bonus, which some months was more than my monthly pay, was more than I had ever earned in my life.

The man I worked next to was a highly-skilled engineer, a likeable chap who had done a lot of amateur go-karting in his day and kept up with the sport by refurbishing engines for racers that he knew. He had given up the sport after an accident. While racing a mate at the old Crystal Palace motor racing circuit, they both crashed and his friend suffered irreparable brain trauma. In those days the circuit used, would you believe, railway sleepers as safety barriers. My colleague was well known on the racing circuit and many a driver from the era would pop in to see him.

One of my work colleagues, who was a bit younger than me, had a Suzuki GS 850cc shaft driven motorbike. I think he was a little envious of my bike because when it was parked next to mine our work colleagues used to look at mine first.

One winter morning, on my way to work, I was riding on an icy road and, as I approached a set of traffic lights, I assumed the car in front was going to continue through the amber light and let me follow. However, he changed his mind and started to brake right in front of me. I was left with nowhere to go and, thinking quickly, I carefully put my left leg down on to the icy road, pressing down with my right foot on to the foot rest and breaking lightly, I managed to manoeuvre the bike gently into the nearside kerb.

I got away with that one but realised that it wouldn't be long before I could expect something more serious to happen. I knew I had to sell the bike as I couldn't expect Jill to keep going on the pillion in all weathers as she had been doing for a while now.

It was around this time that Jill started to have, for no apparent reason, little falls every so often which was completely out of character for her. As there seemed no obvious reason for the falls, and her family couldn't shed any light on the matter, we carried on as normal. What a devastating error it turned out to be for her not to see the GP but, for now, everything seemed to going well enough.

Jill had lost her job at the directors' restaurant at ICI when it closed in the summer of 1976, leaving out of work. As I was, by then, earning good money at the engineering factory, we decided that, perhaps, with all the stress of losing her father and the split from her mother that she should spend some time away from work and concentrate on making a good home for us both.

One day, around September time, she mentioned to me that we should, perhaps, add a little one to our family. No, not that, a puppy! So, one Saturday morning, we went to Battersea Dogs Home, which was no more than a couple of miles away from where we lived, to look for a suitable dog and we found the perfect one. After looking into a large, open spaced kennel that held a black Labrador mum with about ten little black puppies, all barking and trying to stand up as high as they could to get our attention, one in particular stood out to both of us and we decided to see if the pup was available. After going through the paperwork we were told to come back in a couple of weeks' time when she would be ready, she being named 'Susie'.

The following Saturday morning we took a bus to the dogs' home and collected Susie who was still so small that I put her into the big inside pocket of my coat to keep her warm.

We had bought a dog basket and laid a nice soft blanket

inside with a couple of new toys and, when we put Susie inside, she snuggled down. A good sign, so we thought, but how wrong we were. Come bedtime, having put an old clock under her blanket, supposedly to mimic her mum's heartbeat, we placed her basket into the alcove behind the stairs and, leaving a dimmed light on, we went to bed ourselves. Well, when I say went to bed what really happened was as soon as I disappeared out of view she cried her way into the bedroom and shot to the darkest place possible, under the bed.

Having not even got into bed I had to fish her out. Jill thought my coaxing techniques, which mainly consisted of, "Susie, come on, look, I've got a teddy for you to play with, come on then," highly hilarious. This pup was not coming out for a stupid teddy.

So yours truly now had to lift the bed up and hope Jill could catch Susie, only to see her wagging her little tail and going to 'mummy' as if butter wouldn't melt.

We now faced a dilemma; did we try all over again to get her out on to the landing and into her basket, let her sleep in her basket in our bedroom or should muggins sit up with pup until pup goes to sleep? You guessed it, the muggins option won. So that's me then, for God knows how long, sitting in the front room with a table lamp on trying to dim the room and entice sleep into her, fending off a playful pup at an unholy hour of the night.

Eventually, both of us fell asleep and, every now and again, I would awake to see a little black bundle of fur curled up on my lap fast asleep. I think it was that night the little darling stole my heart. I loved that dog as much as any human could an animal until the day we parted.

As Susie grew, we started taking her out to places such as Richmond Park or Battersea Park for long walks, which usually meant that we ended up in one pub or another. Battersea Park, by the way, had a nice bar on the river pathway situated between Battersea and Albert Bridges. It had an open front that enabled visitors to sit out and admire the River Thames flowing by, but Richmond Park turned out to be our favourite. Being a Labrador, from an early age, Susie started to venture into one of the big ponds in the park and would become ever more daring, swimming out further and further. Being so young, probably six months old by now, I would be quite anxious the further she went but I needn't have worried. She was a superb swimmer and brought many joyous times with her antics, even to the extent that when the pond was frozen she would frantically stamp on the ice by the shoreline in an attempt to break through for her swim.

Jill began to gradually get more and more unsteady on her feet and many times when I got home from work she would bemoan another fall while out shopping or taking Susie for a walk. We both ignorantly joked about her needing to water down her favourite drink, Port and Lemon, although she didn't really drink alcohol, being almost teetotal, it was strange. I also thought I noticed a difference in her reasoning and understanding of simple matters in everyday conversation but brushed it to one side.

That first year of 1976, in our own little flat, was coming to an end and our thoughts turned to Christmas. Like everybody else we started to buy the odd few things, mainly baubles and decorations for the tree and, sneakily, the odd present, which in a small flat hiding them was no small feat I can tell you.

One thing I do remember is how cold it was in the flat. It had old-fashioned sash windows that let in a terrible draught so I had to get quite ingenious and wondered if cling film, fixed around certain parts of the wooden frame, would keep the draught out? Well, yes it did but only to a point, it was still really cold. The back door had a gap underneath that any self-respecting limbo dancer could manage to get under with ease, and the whole place just never got warm.

We decided that there was only one thing for it; we would have to change the front room and bedroom around. The front room had a built-in gas fire and we supplemented this with a paraffin heater on the other side of the room, a thick knitted 'worm' draught excluder in front of the door and as many blankets and coats on the bed as we could assemble. Oh, and Susie would also creep up on to the bed during the night too.

Actually, we used the room by the small kitchen, our so-called dining room, to spend our nights in as that also had a built-in gas fire, whereas the bedroom did not. I moved the telly into one corner of the room and it really was quite comfortable. At Christmastime, we put the tree up in this room and everything in our world seemed to be in order.

The New Year came and went and we were really enjoying our lives, so much, in fact, that I asked Jill to marry me. Happily, she said yes and we fixed a date in our minds to get married on 7th July, 1977: 7/7/77. All the sevens; luck must surely be on our side with those numbers.

Neither of us wanted, or could afford, a big church wedding which didn't go down with future mum-in-law Vera one bit. In fact, it led to a lot of arguing and rows and battles. Nevertheless, Jill and I insisted it was what we wanted and we were going to do it our way.

We went to Lambeth Registry Office, a horrible, grey, drab old council building in Brixton Road, Lambeth, about half a mile from the Town Hall, where we saw a clerk, filled out a form and paid the fee. The date was to be confirmed later, and that was it, thank you very much and goodbye.

That damn building was one that I was to return to three times over the next few years for other reasons, but for now all was done and it was a case of planning the wedding, buying clothes, inviting a few family and friends, and asking Mum if we could have a small reception at the family home in Nansen Road. To which Mum and Dad said yes, of course.

The time flew that year as we eagerly anticipated the coming wedding day. Jill's falls had diminished quite a bit, although she had not returned to work, mainly because I was now earning such a good wage. Somehow, we just carried on in the routine of living like a married couple; me working and Jill looking after the flat and caring for Susie.

Susie was turning out to be a fine, loving dog; full of life, obedient, loyal and easy to keep under control. Over the years, she was to become our solid companion when things turned out badly for us.

The wedding day came around quickly and, as tradition has it, I had a stag night albeit a few nights before the actual day. I spent the night of the eve of the wedding in my old bed in Nansen Road. I have to be honest, my recollection of the day has been clouded over time as things didn't go to plan over the next few years for Jill and me. I think future events filled my mind more with how to cope with, as yet unknown events, than with the joy of getting married.

Dad was working for a small, private bank in the City of London as their external messenger, a job which was totally different from any of the factory based work that he had done for most of his adult working life. Here was a nice clean office based job that paid a good wage and meant that Dad could more or less be his own boss. All he had to do was to make sure that the mail was collected early from the Post Office sorting office near The Central Criminal Court, commonly referred to as the Old Bailey from the street on which it stands, and deliver it back to the bank's mailroom at its offices in St Andrews Street in EC4 ready for the clerks to deal with and sort before the office officially opened at 9.00 am. He also had to collect financial mail from various banks in the city during the day up till 3.00 pm, after which time he could call it a day and go home.

One day Dad asked me, "Are you free to do some work at the bank at the weekend?" They wanted a bit of easy decorating doing in one or two of the offices; just emulsion the walls and paint the skirting boards to brighten the place up a bit.

I said, "Yes, of course I'll help you."

Jill and I could use the extra money and from where we lived in Lambeth, it was literally fifteen minutes or less by car. Dad asked Paul as well and the three of us arranged to meet early on the Saturday morning at the bank. Dad opened up and, of course, the first thing we did was make our way down to the staff room for a cup of tea.

When Dad thought that the time was right we went to his car, well, the bank's car actually to unload the materials, paint, brushes, buckets, dust sheets, steps, etc, in preparation for the work to be done. As there was three of us, it took no time at all to clear the office of furniture and get stuck into the job. We would quickly finish one office and move on to the next, then the next and so on. Not too many mind, as we didn't want to kill the golden goose at the first attempt. Dad said he would tell his boss it took ten hours on both Saturday and Sunday although, in reality, we only did about six on each day. Dad said if his boss was happy with the job it could lead to a lot more work. The best thing about it was that the bank was paying us £7.00 an hour, cash in hand, which for 1977 was extremely good money.

Sure enough, Dad's boss was pleased with the job and the following weekend we were all back again for another 'ten' hours on the Saturday and Sunday. Only this time there was a twist. Paul had a part-time job as a night cleaner at the *Daily Mirror* where the newspaper was printed and after the night's run Paul, with others, would go in and clean the machines and floors down. Dad knew this, of course, and persuaded his boss that the microfiche (the technology that was around before the workstation became common place on every desk in every office) department needed the wooden floors polished, a job that was just right for Paul.

So armed with mops, buckets, cleaning fluids, stain and polish off Paul would go for a couple of hours while Dad and me, well, mostly me, would get on with all sorts of other jobs; repairing desks, relaying carpet tiles, replacing electrical sockets or moving furniture from one office to another, all sorts really, and all for £7.00 an hour.

On one occasion, Dad's boss asked if we would be kind enough to get rid of some old desk name plates that were clogging up the safe room in the basement. When I next popped in to see him and Mum – there were no mobile phones in those days – on my way home from work, as I did once or twice a week, he told me all about it.

"Desk name plates," I said.

"Yes!"

"Aluminium," I said.

"Yes!

"And the boss wants *us* to get rid of them?"

"Yes!" he said.

"Dad," I said, "aluminium prices have gone through the roof just now."

"Have they now?" he replied, with a big, knowing grin on his face. My grin was just as wide.

So the following Saturday Dad, Paul and I went down to the bank's large, walk-in safe room and, joy upon joy, there in the corner was our very own pile of treasure. We quickly we loaded up the firm's car, a Vauxhall Chevette estate, if I remember correctly, with about a half a ton (500kg) of aluminium. Paul and I set off for the local scrap metal merchant located somewhere on the south side of Blackfriars Bridge. I am sure the car must have been overloaded, as it was very heavy to drive, anyway we made it there in one piece, pulled into the scrap yard and on to the weigh bridge where Paul and I got out of the car so it could be weighed. Then we offloaded the alli' into a cage which was then weighed and, with a suppressed grin on our faces, waited for the Guvnor to bring us our money, all £1200 of it. Yes, £1200! In cash, there were no cheques or credit cards in that line of work. Feeling really chuffed with ourselves Paul and I made our way back to the bank to give Dad the good news. Like us, he couldn't believe how much we had made, plus we were still earning £7.00 an hour don't forget, ha-ha.

We went into that bank most weekends for the next five or six years until one fateful day when it all came crashing to an end, but more of that later.

As we were doing so well, Jill and I decided that we would

have a week's holiday somewhere along the south coast. We hadn't had a traditional honeymoon back in July 1977 and this would be our first time away together, with Susie in tow, of course.

I looked through the small ads in one of the papers and found a self-catering holiday camp on Portland Bill in Dorset that was dog friendly. I booked a week for us in early June 1980, just after Jill's 25th birthday. On the Saturday morning, we packed the car up, dog and all, and started on our first holiday. Firstly, we drove through South London; Battersea and Wandsworth, then through the northern side of Wimbledon Common and, no, we didn't see any Wombles!

We got on to the A3 at the Kingston bypass and followed it all the way down towards Claygate, in Surrey, where we worked our way around towards Hampton Court, eventually picking up the M3 in the Sunbury-on-Thames area for the journey down to Dorset.

It was a pleasant, warm, sunny day and, after a stop on the way for a cuppa and to let Susie have a run, we finally pulled into the holiday camp mid-afternoon. After booking in, we were taken to our chalet room in a modern, single storey building overlooking a wild and overgrown field with a manmade pathway leading down to a small, sandy beach by the sea. It was a lovely, quiet place whose name eludes me.

After a couple of days had passed, we sat outside the chalet having a drink. I was sitting in a wooden deckchair, Susie was laying down puffing away in the warm sun and Jill was lying on a wooden sun lounger. I looked over towards Jill, who was in a bikini, and remarked, "Maybe you should cut out the cream buns, darling," looking at her tubby belly.

"Well, I wasn't going to tell you just yet," she said. "I think I might be pregnant?" I nearly dropped my beer. I just sat there speechless for a second or two before rushing over to hug the mother of my child-to-be.

The rest of that week was taken up with all kinds of plans for the future, how and when we were going to tell Mum, Dad, and Mum-in-law, how we were going to rearrange the flat to suit the furniture we would have to buy. But then we thought, *No, hang on a minute, let's not go rushing into things. Let's take one step at a time, as it was early days yet.*

By this time, Paul had been married for a couple of years to a girl he met at work, Lyn, and she too was pregnant with their first child. She was expecting in July of 1980, when, sure enough, little James was born and happy days had arrived for all of us.

When Jill and I returned home she went to the GP surgery and was referred to the anti-natal clinic at St Thomas' Hospital – where yours truly had been born twenty-four years earlier – once the pregnancy had been confirmed.

Jill took it all in her stride but, worryingly, the falls had come back and were increasing in their frequency. The doctors at St Thomas's didn't seem unduly worried and the regular visits continued for some time until the doctors decided that, to be on the safe side, Jill should go into hospital for the last few weeks of her pregnancy.

During the weeks and months leading up to the big day the guys at work would occasionally ask me how it was going, pulling my leg with age old wisecracks, such as, "If it looks like you, I pity the poor little blighter," but it was all said with the best intentions.

One chap, upon hearing the news, told me that he made wooden cots and would happily make one for us if we would like him too. When he showed us photos of his handy work Jill and I were only too keen for him to get started. What he came up with was beautifully made. It had an insert on the inside of the headboard of a stork in flight with a baby being carried in a blanket in its mouth to the new mother-to-be. It was a beautiful piece of work that must have taken him hours to complete, a work of art.

The due date was getting closer, the baby being expected in late November. *What a wonderful early Christmas present*, I thought as I made my way to the hospital to see Jill. Every night, after work, I would take Susie out for her walkies then walk through Lambeth Palace Gardens, using it as a short cut to the hospital. I couldn't have been happier; it was one of the best times of my life.

On one of these nightly visits Jill told me that the doctors had decided, in the interest of mother and baby, to schedule a caesarean section on the evening of Thursday, 27th November, 1980. In just a few days we were going to be a family. Our very own little bundle of joy was going to enter the world to the most loving parents.

# Chapter Five

After work, and with the best wishes of the guys, various aunts and uncles and my mother-in-law, I went to Mum and Dad's house to have dinner before making my way to St Thomas' Hospital ready for the big event. I quickly made my way to the maternity unit where Jill was waiting for me. She was nervous, excited, and apprehensive, all rolled into one, but happy to be going down to the theatre to deliver our baby. These were the most joyous, happy moments together. In just a short while our lives would change forever.

When the time came a happy, smiling, young nurse, accompanied by a porter, came to collect Jill and take her in the bed to the delivery theatre. I followed on behind, trying to keep up with the brisk pace the porter was making and, soon enough, we reached the theatre's outer waiting area. I hugged my wife, wished her good luck and told her that I would be there when she awoke the next morning. Unlike today, where it is acceptable for the husband to be present during a caesarean section birth, back then it definitely was not.

They disappeared into the theatre and I found my way into the waiting room, just outside the now closed doors where it was all about to take place. I sat down on my own in a fairly large room that had obviously had had many fathers and relatives in it during the day all waiting for the happiest of news, just as I was preparing to do.

After about forty minutes, the same nurse that had accompanied Jill down to the delivery theatre, still dressed in her green theatre gown, came and found me to tell me the happy news that I had become the father of a baby boy.

I cannot adequately describe how I felt that moment when she told me that I had become a father. It's indescribable; one's outlook on life changes in an instant in the knowledge that you have been partly responsible for giving life to another human being and all the responsibility that goes with it. I was elated, happy and proud. The first people that I was going to tell were my mum and dad who were waiting at home in Nansen Road for my telephone call. I spoke to Mum and remember saying to her laughing with pride and excitement, "Now little Jamie (James) would have a playmate." We laughed together and I told her that as soon as I had seen Mark, for that was the name we had decided upon if the baby was a boy, I would visit them the following day.

Soon after I put the telephone down, a doctor appeared, accompanied by the same nurse, and asked if I was Mr Gaskin. "Yes," I said shaking his hand with a smile on my face assuming that he wanted to congratulate me on the birth of my son, but the horror of his next few words were to set me up for a lifetime of sadness and heartbreak. My son had lived for but a few brief moments before he had died.

After saying how sorry he was, the doctor left me in the hands of the nurse who tried her best to soothe my pain but I was absolutely devastated at the news. And I mean utterly devastated. I sat down and cried, totally heartbroken. I had never experienced such pain, sadness and heartache in my life. I was a broken human being. My only thought was how I was going to tell my wife, after all that she had been through, that the one precious thing the she so craved and desired had died. Our baby had been so cruelly taken away from her, such a loving and caring woman, and one who was blissfully unaware of the devastating news that she would wake up to.

The nurse told me that the hospital's chaplain had arrived and asked to see me to give me some words of comfort in my time of grief. I agreed and the nurse introduced me to a large, imposing figure who came into the room and said something to me that I neither heard nor took in, such was my state of distress. After while later, the nurse came in and had a quiet word with the chaplain who turned to me and asked in a soft voice if I would like to come down to the chapel with him to see

Mark.

He and I walked together through the hospital, he with my arm in his, to the hospital's chapel where my son was now laid out peacefully at rest. My whole world had crashed around me and I was in a state of shock, not really able to take in the full horror of the events that were unfolding before me. When we arrived at the chapel, the chaplain let me go in first and then followed closely behind me, saying a prayer. My little Mark was wrapped in a crisp, white shawl, lying atop the chapel's altar. The chaplain invited me to say the Lord's Prayer with him, but I could only manage a couple of words. I was physically incapable of speaking as I looked down on my lifeless son in the darkened room with the cross bearing the figure of Our Lord Jesus Christ high on the wall above us.

When I looked into Mark's tiny face I saw myself there as I had been as a boy. The chaplain left me alone with Mark for a minute or two before gently ushering me outside. I never did get to touch or hold my son and, to be honest, I am not sure even now if I would have been able to.

The rest is a blur up until the time I left the hospital and was driving home to Mum and Dad's house, crying all the way, tears flowing down my cheeks as though a tap had been turned on. There was a heaviness in my body that I had never known before. Mum was surprised, and then devastated, to see me on her doorstep. No words needed to be said and she knew in a heartbeat that something terribly wrong had happened. I sat down on one of the kitchen chairs and Mum hugged, held and cradled me as I sobbed my broken heart out to her, barely able to blurt out that my precious, darling, newborn son had died.

Dad was by now standing in the doorframe of the kitchen having heard the words that I had just spoken, with a look of complete heartache etched on his face and reddening eyes, a look that I had never witnessed in any man before. The pain and sorrow that he and Mum must have felt may have been as great as mine; I'm sure that it was. Susie and Mum and Dad's Labrador, Sally, both came and sat next to me and looked up at me with a knowing look of sadness in their eyes. Animals can sense our emotions, and they knew something wasn't right.

A few hours later, I made my way back to St Thomas' Hospital knowing that I had to tell Jill what had happened before she asked to see Mark because I didn't want anybody else to tell her. It was my job to break the news to her and I was going to do it. They had moved Jill into a side room and, thankfully, she had not woken up by the time I got there. She was sleeping peacefully and I willed her to stay asleep for as long as she could before hearing the dreadful news. I pulled a chair up to her bedside, sat down and gently put my hand around hers. I just sat looking at her. I asked the nurse who was nearby to leave us alone as it was our grief and I didn't want to share it with anybody else for now, it was too raw.

A little while later Jill started to stir. I dreaded every second until I gently told her, through my sobbing, that her little baby boy, Mark, had died. After a brief pause she pulled my head down towards her and said, "It's okay, there will be others." Then she started to gently weep until she fell back to sleep again, leaving me holding her hand, never wanting to let it go.

But it wasn't okay. Our son had been taken from us and we didn't know why. I hated God, Mother Earth or whoever was responsible. What had we done to deserve this? It was so cruel to have given him such a short breath of life and then take it back again.

Later in the day, as Jill and I sat heartbroken in the side room that we had been given, Paul appeared at the door looking as upset as we felt. I can't remember what was said or what happened, as it was such a long time ago, and I don't think my brain will allow me to recollect exactly what happened that day. I do know that from that day on Paul has been a true brother to me, always being there if ever I needed him and, boy, was I going to need him in the years to come.

The next few days were a blur. Relatives came and went, some more tearful than others. A few of the men tried to keep a stiff upper lip but we could see that it wasn't working. All of our visitors said and did the right thing, except for one who made me angry. Whenever anybody tells me their stories about such a person I know exactly what they are about to say. That person was the dreaded social worker.

They told Jill to be strong and if there was anything that she needed – "Ha, that's a good one!" – don't hesitate to get in touch and we will do all we can for you. Yeah, right!

As for me, I was given the worst advice possible. "You're okay, you're a man you can handle it." Well, no, actually. I bloody couldn't. It is still extremely hard for me to talk about today.

The chaplain came to see us and was kind, gentle and understanding as you would expect. He broached the subject of a funeral as delicately as he could and explained a number of options to us. We decided to have little Mark cremated and let the hospital take care of arrangements as I wasn't in a fit state to do it. It was bad enough having to register his death at that drab building, Lambeth Registry Office. On a date that I don't remember Mark was cremated at Honor Oak Crematorium in South East London and his ashes were scattered at the same place shortly afterwards. Neither Jill nor I attended the service she being unable to as she had not recovered from the surgery and me because I was too distressed to do so. I have often given myself a hard time for not attending as I know Mark didn't have anybody with him from the family at the time, but I am sure that wherever you are, son, you've forgiven us.

Daddy still thinks about you nearly every day and doing the things that other dads do with their little boys, watching you grow up from baby to toddler, your first steps, your first words, first day at school, first school nativity, teaching you to swim, play football, give and receive cuddles from you, secondary school, girlfriends, first job, wife, your own children…It never happened that way, it's like in my book of life your page and subsequent pages were ripped out so all the above could never happen.

After a few more days of rest and recovery, Jill was finally able to leave the hospital and, in doing so, had to cruelly walk past the other nursing mothers who were either feeding or holding their babies. But not poor Jill, she had to walk past them all with a look of total sadness etched on her face. Life can be really tough at times.

When Jill was discharged from St Thomas's we were spoken to by the obstetrician who had cared for her in the final weeks of her pregnancy. He told us that we were still young enough to try again for another baby as there was no evidence to the contrary. We were both fit and healthy and should just put it down to 'One of those things', a dropped stitch in the fabric of life as the saying goes. I suppose he was right and time would heal our broken hearts. We could try again when we were ready.

We arrived home at our tiny flat and Susie was there to greet us. It's funny, you know, but animals do have a strange sense about them. Somehow she knew we were hurting and would stay by us, Jill mostly, and lay at our feet or sit close by with her big, brown, sad, knowing eyes looking up at us trying to share our pain, but also to reassure us at the same time.

I had let work know about Mark's death and, to their credit, they told me to genuinely take as much time off as I needed, on full pay of course. I returned two weeks later, a very hard thing to do. All the men said how sorry they were and not much more. What do you say to somebody whose baby had died?

My work colleagues were very good to me at this time, but I knew that they were 'carrying' me. I think they felt my pain and gave me the space I needed. Most of them were fathers themselves and I guess that they must have had their own thoughts about the situation. I found it difficult to get to grips with work and would often go to the toilets and sit in one of the cubicles biting hard into my handkerchief in an attempt to suppress the sound of me crying.

It is difficult to remember the events of late 1980. Christmas was approaching but all thoughts of presents and yuletide happiness were the furthest things from my mind as the one present that I craved was not able to be with us. It was hard to see Paul and Lyn with Jamie at Mum and Dad's as they all enjoyed having him there, and why shouldn't they? After all that is what Christmas is about isn't it, being surrounded by your children and grandchildren.

As happy as I was for them, I couldn't enjoy the get together as my broken heart wouldn't allow me too, I remember glancing over to Jill as Lyn lifted the by now six month old Jamie to her and gave him a bottle of milk. The look of longing on Jill's face just tore me apart inside and is a look that I will never forget.

I think we bought a tree and decorations for the flat but, in all honesty, it was just tradition that made us do it. To be like everybody else, I suppose, but our hearts really weren't in it. I assume we must have bought gifts for one another to try and carry on as normal.

It was now that the loss of Mark really started to hit home. Every time I heard a baby crying on TV or in the street, supermarket or pub, I couldn't stand the noise as it brought home to me that I had never heard Mark cry. This was so hard to deal with and stayed with me for many years, likewise the Christmas carol 'Silent Night', a carol I loved as a child but no more. Its haunting sound and storyline was just too much for me to bear and, whenever I heard it, I had to get away. That feeling has lasted to this day.

We spent Christmas day at my mother-in-law's and she made it as good as she could for us. She prepared a traditional spread similar to the one described earlier and made sure that we had enough presents around the tree. I'm not sure if we stayed Christmas night or not but I do know that we also spent Boxing Day with her. Oh, and Susie was with us the whole time.

On our way home to the flat we both knew what the other was thinking. Neither of us was looking forward to going home but we had to, we couldn't stay away any longer. When we got back it was cold, dark and empty, not how we wanted it to be. We wanted it to be bright, warm and alive. We just got on with it, I don't know how but we did. As we had a few days to ourselves and didn't want to see anybody it suited us fine.

New Year came and went without celebration and, pretty soon, it was time for me to go back to work and try and put it behind me. This was easier said than done, as Jill was at home by herself and, although she was good at keeping herself busy, I couldn't help thinking about what might have been.

Mum and Dad were very kind to us at this time and, although not much was said about us losing Mark, their second grandchild, every now and again I could see that either Mum or Dad had 'something in their eye'. I think Dad felt it even more than Mum. I had seen him doting on Jamie, buying him clothes almost every week – I think, in a funny kind of way, this was how he always wanted to be with Paul and me but wasn't able when we were young – and knew he longed to have two grandsons. Mum didn't say much but when I had my moments she was there to comfort me.

My birthday came and went without much celebration. By now life had settled into a pattern of work and sadness. Our grief was made worse by having to see Mum and Dad, quite rightly, making a fuss of Jamie whenever Paul and Lyn were there. I have to say that we both loved Jamie but maybe I didn't show it that much then, although I was honoured to be an uncle to the youngest member of the Gaskin family.

I noticed that Jill had started to have more falls than ever before and, being quite concerned, I urged her to go to the doctor. However, she needn't have bothered as the old fossil that passed as a doctor told her not to be so clumsy and to pull herself together. Well, thank you very much.

We spent many Saturdays in the company of my in-laws and, quite often, went to a Private Members' Club in Wimbledon where my father-in-law had been a member for many years. This was basically a drinking club, situated above some lock up garages at the back of Wimbledon High Street and frequented, amongst others, by members of the local constabulary. The members obviously knew about us losing a baby but none of them, male or female, made an issue of it and just treated us as normal people.

I enjoyed going to the club to drown my sorrows. The beer was cheap and as the night went on Joyce, the barmaid, would pull almost full pints of bitter when ordering a light and bitter, so much so that I started to drink it again. It meant that you could get a pint and a half for the price of a pint, ha-ha.

Many a night I insisted on driving home having drunk far too much alcohol. Most times I don't remember how I got us home to Kennington safely, probably because I knew my way home like the back of my hand. I would drive the eight miles or so on roads that were very familiar to me. Anyway, most of the officers from Wimbledon police station drove home in a similar state and the middle ranking officers made sure that any problems just disappeared, if you know what I mean. Of course, this all took place during a time that was very different from today.

At Christmas the club would be turned into the most fabulous of places. A large Christmas tree – real, of course – was placed in the furthest corner away from the bar, for obvious reasons, and decorated with lights, tinsel and baubles. A multitude of different shaped and coloured decorations hung across the ceiling and adorned the walls. The tables, including the snooker table, would be covered up and on Boxing Day night would hold homemade sandwiches, sausage rolls, mince pies, cuts of meat, crisps, peanuts and all sorts of other delights, brought in by the customers.

One Christmas night, just before midnight, a group of Bobbies, maybe six or eight of them, came into the club for a drink before they made their way home at the end of their shift. A couple of them had remarked to one of the middle ranking officers who were at the club, that a police car from another district was waiting in the High Street ready to pounce on the first drunk driver they encountered. "Not on my watch," said the aforementioned officer and proceeded to bring the occupants of the police car into the club whereupon a free beer was administered, to the point where the officers could hardly nick anybody for being as drunk as they were getting that way themselves. Thankfully, I don't think this is likely to happen in the world we live in today.

I didn't really hit the booze as hard as it may seem but, on occasion, I would let my self-control down and just go for it. Daft really, as you will recall the episode near the end of Chapter Three.

Jill and I had some of the gloom hanging over us lifted by the news that in late November – ironically nearly a year to the day that we lost Mark – she was expecting again. Joyous as the news was, we were extremely nervous as the weeks rolled by towards a delivery date in late May 1982. Now it just so happened that Paul's wife, Lyn, had announced a few weeks earlier that she too was expecting again in April 1982.

Although delighted that Jill was pregnant, my thoughts had turned back to the events surrounding Mark's birth and death. It would be unbearable if the same thing happened again, wouldn't it? I kept telling myself, over and over again, not to be stupid. It was just bad luck with Mark, wasn't it? This time around nothing was going to go wrong. The obstetricians at St Thomas' Hospital were keeping a close eye on Jill and her weekly visits showed that everything was going as expected. Work were pleased for me and gave me as much time off as I needed to accompany Jill to the hospital, without stopping my wages or, indeed, the bonus that was due at the end of every month. I have to say that Kemworthy Tools was a very good employer.

With about two months to go before the baby was due, Lyn gave birth to a girl, Emma Louise, on 18th April, 1982. We were delighted for both Lyn and Paul and duly went to see the new baby. I had to put on the bravest face possible for the new parents, but when we made our way home I cried like a baby.

More tears were shed for Emma later but in entirely different circumstances.

As Jill's due date was fast approaching, the doctors decided to take her in early as they were concerned about the falls that she continued to have and didn't want to take a chance on the slightest thing happening that could jeopardise the baby. This period before the baby was born was very tiring, as I was having to get up early to take Susie out, feed her, go to work, dash home to take Susie out at lunchtime, go back to work, go home feed Susie take her out then go to St Thomas's to see Jill.

Something had to change. So, after about a fortnight of this, Mum and Dad had Susie every day so that I didn't have quite such an exhausting time. I was relieved not to be running about as much as I had been during the week. It was not so bad at the weekend as I could take Susie out for a long run in the morning and she would sleep for quite a time when we got back home at lunchtime, leaving me free to walk over to the hospital to visit Jill.

All was going well and, although she was bored, Jill looked the picture of health. Don't they say that most women bloom when they are pregnant? Jill certainly did and all the reports from the obstetricians attending to her were normal. Hopefully, this time there would be a happy outcome. At home I got all the things out that we had either bought or been given for Mark, ready for the new arrival. I especially made the handmade crib that we still had look just as it should have.

As Jill's birthday was on 29th May we began to speculate about when the baby might be born. It was due around that time and we thought how wonderful it would be if it was born on Jill's 27<sup>th</sup> birthday. Later, when I went to see Jill on Tuesday,

25<sup>th</sup> May she told me that she had been scheduled to have a caesarean section to deliver the baby on the morning of Thursday, 27<sup>th</sup> May and I should expect to hear about lunchtime. So it wasn't going to be on her birthday after all. I was extremely nervous, as I couldn't help thinking the unthinkable, but telling myself in the same instant to stop being so negative. Everything was going to be all right this time.

Having told Mum and Dad what was planned and taking Susie to them, once again, on the Wednesday night, I went home. I don't think I slept much that long night, as I was far too nervous, and hour after hour dragged by until, thank God, morning came. Now all I had to do was wait another six hours or so until it was time to make my way over to St Thomas's. I got there early so I could sit with Jill until it was time for her to go to the operating theatre for the caesarean section. At about 11.00 o'clock the nurses came to prepare her and I was duly kicked out of her room while they took care of her.

A little while later a nurse and a porter came to take her to the theatre where pretty soon, and with fingers crossed, she would have the baby. We didn't know if it was a boy or a girl as we wanted to be surprised, but had thought of naming the baby Charlotte Victoria if it was a girl and Andrew Simon if it was a boy. When we reached the outer room to the operating theatre I held Jill's hand tightly, bent over and said to her in a soft low voice, that was only for us, "Best of luck, this time everything will be all right, you'll see, I will be waiting for when you wake up." I kissed her on her forehead and let her go to have our baby.

I went to the waiting room and waited for the news that I hoped would make me the happiest father anywhere. I think that there was one other dad-to-be but we didn't engage in conversation, both too nervous I guess. We waited until it was our turn for the nurse to come and give us the good news. Sure enough, after about an hour, a nurse entered into the room and called out, "Mr Gaskin, please." *This is it*, I thought, and made myself known. "Come with me, please," she said, a bit too abruptly I thought. I followed her out and was led into a side room where a doctor was waiting for me.

"Mr Gaskin, I am terribly sorry to have to tell you this, but your baby died twenty minutes after delivery."

"NO! NO! NO!" I cried out in my pain as I collapsed in a heap in one of the empty chairs in the room. My already broken heart had been ripped apart for the second time. A feeling of total devastation consumed me as I sat there in disbelief at the most awful news. The doctor made a hasty exit, as I recall, leaving the poor nurse to deal with this quivering, sobbing wreck of a man.

Worse was to come as I realised that, once again, I would have to tell Jill that her baby had died. I made my way with the nurse to Jill's room getting there just as the porter was taking the bed into the room with Jill still fast asleep from the aesthetic, oblivious to the devastating news that I was to give to her.

The porter left and the nurse asked if I wanted the doctor to break the news to Jill. I declined her offer and said that I was going to be the one to do it and could she please leave us alone. A short time later, Jill awoke and I cowardly sobbed my heart out to her holding her close to me. I again heard her say, "It's all right, don't cry." Just then a doctor with the same nurse came in to see us. I never heard what he said as I was so deflated that I couldn't give a damn right there and then what anybody said.

What I went through on that day, ripped the soul out of my inner self. I cannot describe for the lack of words how I felt having gone through the loss of another baby, a beautiful little girl this time whom we named Charlotte Victoria Gaskin.

Once again, to my utter anger and frustration, after a few more days of rest and recovery Jill was finally able to leave the hospital and in doing so had to cruelly walk past the other nursing mothers who were either feeding or holding their babies. But not poor Jill she had to walk the gauntlet and go past them all with no beaming smile, just a look of total sadness etched on her face, enduring it not once but now twice. Life can be really cruel.

This time I made my own decision not to go and see Charlotte. I just couldn't gather up enough strength to do it and I am not even sure if Jill saw her. The appropriate arrangements were, again, taken care of by St Thomas' Hospital and, as with Mark, she was cremated and her ashes scattered in Honor Oak Cemetery. I now feel so guilty that she was all alone; please forgive me my little fallen angel. Your Daddy still loves you just as much today as always. Your page was ripped from our life book as well and, like Mark, all the things that we hoped to have done with you would also never happen.

But life goes on for the living. We had to get Jill well and home so that she could get on with her life. She was struggling physically to cope and we both noticed that the unsteady balance and walking problem was getting a little worse as the weeks and months went by. Nothing could seemingly be discovered by the experts at St Thomas' Hospital, as to why we had lost two babies. It was really disappointing but there you are that's how it was.

Attending outpatients clinic with Jill was a complete waste of time. The doctors showed a trace of concern about two lost babies but could not add anything to what they had said in the past, but now here came the rub, "You are both still young enough to try again and if you should decide we will have you in very early and keep a close eye on you for the last three months of any new pregnancy." Yeah, okay, but if you don't know what you're looking for that's one hell of a gamble, isn't it?

We got back into a pattern of daily life. I went back to work only to be met with an embarrassing silence and with just a curt smile or a nod between the other guys and me. Nothing had to be said, all knew it was all right not to mention the unmentionable, we all had to get on and do our work so it kind of kept the balance. It was about this time, I realise now, but not back then, that I was becoming more inward thinking and with my actions towards others. I didn't really want to talk about the events of the previous two years and I think other people, family as well as friends, let it go on that way as it meant that life was easier. I think that even Jill and I started to think that, unless absolutely necessary, it was easier not to mention our losses, but still every time I heard a baby cry or saw a new one in the street, I would become really emotional to the point where I just had to get away. I would go into another room at home or leave wherever we were. Mum always said that I had a soft heart and oh, how right she was. I never received any counselling to help me to come to terms with my loss and, in those days, it was very much a case of get over it and carry on.

It was doubly hard to go to my parents' house, usually on a Saturday, as now there were two young ones to face. Not that I didn't want everybody to revel in Paul and Lyn's new baby girl, Emma, but I so dearly longed not only for Mark to be playing with Jamie but to see and hear Charlotte cooing along with Emma. My heart broke a little bit more every time it happened. Funnily enough, I could see in Dad's eyes that he wanted to reach out to me but, however much he wanted to, he just couldn't.

Jill was much better at handling those kind of situations and, to be honest, I felt a little let down by her; why wasn't she feeling the same as me? Why was she just getting on with it? After all she carried them for nine months of her life both times and yet here she was seemingly unaffected by the loss of her two babies. Perhaps the female of the species really are the strongest?

Jill had not been back to work since we lost Mark, and she carried on being a housewife supporting me to cope with work. We did all the usual things that people do every day and even thought about going on holiday somewhere later in the year but never got around to it. We would drive out to a lot of different places, primarily just to be together and find nice areas for Susie to have a good run around.

Christmas came around again and very much followed the pattern of the previous couple that I have described above. We were still living in our little flat in Lollard Street and I was working with Dad and Paul most weekends. On the odd occasion, I would go to Stamford Bridge to watch Chelsea play and that gave me my own space and enabled me to get away from my demons for a few hours, having a beer or two if possible on the way home. I also enjoyed listening to the football results and related stories on the car radio on the way home.

I was now beginning to keep everything inside and bottle up my emotions, not talking to anybody about the way I felt, which I realised through another event some thirty-two years later, that we shall get that in due course, was doing me an immense amount of harm.

Jill and I were still attending the clinic at St Thomas' Hospital as they were trying to find out just what had gone wrong. It's hard to believe that in 1982/3 an answer to our most fundamental question, why? could still not be answered. One of the experts that we were introduced to was an eminent professor in all three of the disciplines connected to childbirth; gynaecology, obstetrics, and paediatrics. At least now some light might be shed on to our problems, or so we thought. Alas, still no progress, only the same dead end that we had encountered for such a long time.

We now gave serious thought as to whether we should put ourselves through the acute stress of trying for another baby. You cannot imagine the great emotional strain that getting the decision right had on us both, but at the end of the day the desire to create a new human life and nurture him or her to maturity was just too strong. We still didn't know of any real reason why we should not try and our thoughts were, "Surely, it cannot happen a third time?"

So, in September 1983, Jill announced to me that she was pregnant for the third time. This time, though, it was going to be a completely different pregnancy to the previous two. The professor at the hospital announced that Jill would be admitted immediately so that they could keep her under close observation and monitor her on a daily basis.

Logistically, this was going to be just as much of a slog as the undoubted emotional burden, not only would I have to go to work every day but now there was no way I could possibly get home for Susie on a daily basis so the poor thing would have to be by herself all day. It didn't seem to do her any long-term harm as I think that she just slept in her basket all day. I also think, as I have said before, that animals realise when things are tough for those around them and I believe that Susie knew what was required of her on this occasion.

Now, with more experience and foresight, I would have done things differently.

For me, however, it was a totally different story. I would get home and feed and exercise Susie before I grabbed a bite to eat and then shoot straight off to visit Jill in the hospital. Initially, this wasn't too bad but the prospect of six months of this routine was enough to test anybody's resolve and, sure enough, my stamina started to wane. It was extremely difficult to hold a conversation with Jill after the first few weeks as she had literally nothing to talk about once the settling in period had taken place and she had explained all about the routine monitoring of blood pressure checks, temperature checks, urine samples etc. She occasionally told me about different tests but I have forgotten exactly what these entailed.

Then, during one of my regular visits, she told me this story. A junior trainee doctor had come to see her as a matter of routine. The doctor asked the usual questions that Jill had answered a million times before, and then the doctor asked if she could examine Jill. She, of course, said yes and so a nurse pulled the screens around the bed and the examination started. Firstly, he used a stethoscope to check Jill's breathing, all okay there. Next up was a physical examination of the upper half of the body, again all okay there. Then he did a grip test of Jill's arms and hands, yes, no, wait a moment, something was not right. So the doctor repeated the grip test to Jill's hands and, again, said something wasn't quite right. The doctor told Jill to get dressed and said he would be back later.

*This was very strange,* Jill thought. She felt well, ate well and slept well and put it down to the junior doctor most probably putting two and two together and coming up with five! She thought no more about it until my next visit when she told me what had transpired. Barely had she finished telling me when the professor and another eminent looking gentlemen arrived. He introduced himself and, together with the professor, started to tell us that they thought Jill might have a condition called *Myotonica dystrophia.* They said that they would carry out more detailed tests but, at this stage, there was nothing to worry about. Jill and I shrugged our shoulders and continued chatting, before we mutually decided that there was nothing else to discuss about until next time. So with a kiss and a cheerio from me, I went back home to give Susie a bit of much-needed company.

The next night when I arrived at Jill's bedside it quickly became apparent that all was not well. I could see that Jill had been crying and the junior doctor who had examined her was by her bedside. When I approached, she extended her hand and said good evening, and asked me to wait while she fetched the professor to have a chat with us. As soon as she left, I asked Jill, "What's going on?"

"I'm not really sure," she said. She was worried about what she had been told earlier but didn't give me much time to ask further questions as the professor had arrived. He sat on the side of the bed and looked at us both with a serious expression on his face.

"Have either of you heard of *Myotonica dystrophia?*" he asked. We both said no and he began to explain what it was and what the consequences were for the sufferer, as follows:

*Myotonic dystrophy is the most common muscular dystrophy.*
*It occurs in every 5 per 100000 with onset between 15 and*

*40 years of age, The disease makes slow progress and is characterised by weakness, wasting and myotonia of involved muscles.*

*The condition reduces longevity.*

This was absolutely devastating news for Jill. An illness that had not come to light in the previous four years of visits to anti-natal clinics for both previous pregnancies, visits to see specialist mother and childcare doctors at St Thomas's, an eminent professor and his colleague, and not one of them had picked this up? It took a junior doctor to do so, how could this be? He apologised profusely and said that medicine was never an exact science until proven procedures had given definitive answers, and now here we were.

What he said next was the biggest, and I do mean the biggest, bombshell we had ever heard in our lives, the baby stood little to no chance of surviving once outside the womb due to a known effect of Myotonica dystrophiain pregnancy; a condition called *LungPulmonary hypoplasia,*

In layman's terms, it meant that the baby would die soon after birth and there was absolutely nothing that they could do, for as the professor put it, "The baby's lungs will not grow and what little lung baby does have would be like one of our adult lungs trying to keep an elephant alive!" That was the enormity of it.

Devastation, utter devastation hit us. Jill was past the point of a termination, already being past the twenty-four week limit. Yes, I am aware that in certain circumstances an abortion can be carried out, but it was not offered, and at the time we didn't know that one could be done. We were in a whole new world, not knowing what to do next or who to turn to for support. We felt isolated and alone.

# **Chapter Six**

Trying to digest the news was very difficult and many tears were shed together that night. I eventually made my way sorrowfully back home where, once inside the flat, I hugged Susie and sobbed. This was going to be a living nightmare. Jill had about ten to twelve weeks to go before the baby was due towards the end of February 198. We were in the run up to Christmas 1983. A bloody good Christmas and a happy New Year to look forward to then!

Every day would be a tortuous hell. How could this be so? What had gone wrong? If only the medical profession had picked up on this earlier it would have meant that some kind of understanding and closure could have been afforded to us and we most certainly would not have tried for a second or, indeed, third baby.

When I told Mum and Dad, later that evening, they were as devastated as we were. They didn't say much because, I guess, they didn't know what to say or how to say it.

When I went to see Jill, we were just going through the motions. What could either one of us say to each other under these circumstances? It was purgatory, every night was the same and, as the delivery date came closer, we tried to brace ourselves for the inevitable. Who am I trying to kid! No, we didn't, we just thought that we did. When the day came I sadly watched Jill go down to the delivery suite, both of us knowing the dreadful outcome that awaited us. I waited in Jill's room by myself, feeling hardly any emotion; that was to come later.

Jill came back to her room rather quickly and was asleep, of course. The two nurses made her comfortable, but hardly glanced at me. They were both aware of the situation and probably just didn't know what to say. They soon left and, in a short time, Jill had woken up, not yet tearful but terribly sad at the news to come. And come it did. The professor told us a boy had been delivered and that he had been put on to a respirator immediately after birth. All was normal except for the fact that the machine was the only thing keeping our son alive. We named our baby Andrew Simon Gaskin and he was born on Tuesday, 21st February, 1984.

The professor told us that he would monitor events and get back to us when he could. A terrible silence filled the room that afternoon. I had asked Jill how she felt after the operation, and she asked me how tired I was and that was all. Who had anything to say? About five hours later, the professor arrived with the inevitable news that Andrew was desperately ill and a decision had to be made about what to do next. He said, "In our considered opinion the only option that you have is to turn off the life support machine and let your son die, but we need your permission to do so."

Well, yes, we knew that and we had tried to prepare ourselves for this moment. Jill told him, "Turn the machine off and let our baby son die with as much dignity as he can."

It was time for us to shed more tears together, not only for what happened that day, but for the previous times when Mark and Charlotte didn't make it, now with the added realisation that that was the end of us being able to have children together.

Again we let the hospital take care of all the arrangements as we were so totally consumed by grief, pain and disappointment that neither of us could have attended a funeral. So again, and finally, I will say, I am sorry Andrew that you were all alone and had no family with you at the end, but Daddy has a special place in his heart for you just like I do for your brother Mark and your sister Charlotte, all three of you have a special place in my ripped apart heart that will always be ours and ours alone, sleep tight together my little lost angels until we are all together again.

After a few weeks things began to settle down. Jill was making a good physical recovery from the surgery but she still stumbled every so often. I was in a very emotional state, and although I had gone back to work my heart was not in it at all. I was constantly going through the all the emotions I had had for the last four years, and it was wearing me down. On the outside I was putting on a brave face but inside I was tearing myself to pieces.

Shortly after, Jill said that she didn't want to live in the flat any longer and suggested we move to be near her mother who had moved to the Rose Hill area of Carshalton in Surrey years earlier. I agreed and we arranged to see the social workers at St Thomas's to see if they could help. They greeted us cordially enough and after explaining the situation, which they already knew anyway, they said that they would speak to our local council, Lambeth Borough Council. They felt pretty sure that, under the circumstances, we would be helped to move fairly quickly. Sure enough, after a couple of weeks we had a firm offer to move into a small, two bedroom house at Newstead Walk in Carshalton, close to Rose Hill and about a ten minute walk to where Jill's mother lived.

On the Saturday after the offer was made we drove to the house and cast an eye over it from the outside. We liked what we saw and, on the following Monday morning, I telephoned the social workers when I got into work, having first asked the foreman if I could make a call during working hours – remember, there were no mobile phones in those days. By the end of the week I had collected the keys from the housing department at Sutton Borough Council who owned the property, and the following Saturday Jill and I went to look around the house.

It was a small, mid-terraced house with a tiny front and rear garden. Upon entering we walked straight into the front room, which was quite small, with a narrow passageway that led to a little kitchen. Further along there was a lavatory with a bathroom beyond. A door led out to the small back garden. Stairs from the passage way led to the two upstairs bedrooms, one at the front of the house, the master bedroom, the other one facing the rear. Although it was quite small, it was much better than the flat in Lollard Street so we decided to take it.

On Monday morning I asked work if I could disappear for a couple of hours and, with their blessing, I went to the council offices in Sutton to sign the paperwork and collect the rent book. The following weekend we packed all our belongings – that's a laugh, what belongings? – and moved in to our new home.

For the next couple of weeks I found myself putting a lick of paint here and there, putting up curtain poles and curtains in the living room and bedrooms, blinds in the kitchen and bathroom, installing the new cooker and washing machine in the kitchen and, most importantly, the television in the living room. It was soon looking like a proper home.

Jill had been to her mother's most days while I was back at work, mainly because we didn't know anybody and, I suppose, it was nice for her to be with her mother when she needed her most. I guess her mother was pleased to be looking after Jill again after all that she had been through during the past four years, but all was not as well as it seemed. In my opinion, Jill had been through more than was expected of a young woman. Yes, I know other people have been through worse and I can't imagine how they had coped, but Jill was not coping mentally and I could detect a difference in her thinking, and at times some of the things she said didn't make sense, her outlook was narrow.

Jill had started to make friends and was getting on with them well. The majority of her new friends had young children and I think this gave Jill a lot of comfort knowing that she was welcomed and thanked for the many times that she babysat. She relished doing it and was beginning to get back to her usual happy self. Jill was always very caring and kind and had the biggest heart of anybody that I have ever known. As for me, nothing could get me out of my lethargic mood, except for a glass or three of whisky. I was still going through the motions every day, my life was going nowhere. Well it was; downwards, not up as it should have been. I now hated work, hated visiting family and friends, hated just about everything. Then fate was to inflict another cruel twist on our already tortured lives.

You know sometimes in your life a kind of sixth sense takes over and you know what's going to happen before it does. That's exactly what happened early one Sunday morning in late April 1984. I received a telephone call and knew that it would be Mum telling me that Dad had been up all night complaining of pains in his chest and, sure as eggs is eggs, that's just what happened.

Mum was very tearful and said Dad would only go to hospital if I took him, so telling Jill the story we hurriedly got dressed and rushed home to Nansen Road where we found Mum and Dad quite distressed. I had never seen my dad looking in such a state before, and his eyes were bloodshot where he had obviously been crying from the pain in his chest. Mum had a look of anguish on her face that painted a sorry picture indeed. Leaving Jill to comfort Mum, who was very upset at seeing Dad in such a distressed condition and couldn't face going to the hospital with us, I helped Dad into the car and drove to St Thomas' Hospital – the last place that I wanted to be – as quickly and safely as I could.

Anyone who is familiar with St Thomas's will know that the front entrance on Lambeth Palace Road is elevated so ambulances have an easy access to deliver patients straight into the A&E department. In those days, private vehicles could do likewise, in an emergency, not so today though. Having parked in an appropriate place I helped Dad into A&E and called out, "HELP! I think my dad is having a heart attack!" Almost immediately a couple of nurses rushed over and, within seconds, had called for a 'crash trolley'. Dad was then whisked away into a cubicle and a blue curtain pulled around him for privacy. I found a seat nearby and a nurse came out and asked me for details. After telling her what had transpired and giving her names and addresses she told me not to worry and said that a doctor would be out to see me presently.

As I sat there waiting for news I could hear Dad saying, "I

don't mean to cause you any trouble." followed by, "I didn't want to bother you, it was my wife and son who insisted that I came." That's as maybe, I thought, but you're here now so let them do what they need to do.

A short while later, a doctor came out to see me and confirmed that Dad had suffered a heart attack. They were going to take him to a ward and keep him in so that they could carry out more tests and get a clearer picture as to what had actually occurred. They wheeled Dad out in a chair and beckoned me over to accompany him to a ward. He was wired up to a portable heart monitor and an oxygen mask was fitted over his nose and mouth. I could see that he was still red-eyed and looking worried, but he managed to give me a half smile as we made our way towards the ward.

St Thomas's was rebuilt in 1966 and is today a modern hospital with a new central square building, twelve stories high, that has all manner of departments and wards. So, I was very surprised when Dad was taken to one of the old Victorian wards that cared for the elderly, both male and female, that were often upsetting for the older generation. These wards were long and filled with up to twenty beds, ten on either side, each having a large, old-fashioned, metal framed bed with a hard mattress, thick cotton sheets and heavy woollen blanket and a small cupboard for personal belongings. The beds were set in front of a tall, multi-paned window, and only the top two rows opened in one piece so hardly any air came in, meaning that they were always hot and smelly places, not very nice at all.

Once Dad had been settled in his first words to me were, "I'm not bloody staying in here. Look at them they are all old and senile."

He did have a point but I told him that it wouldn't be for long and that I was sure that he would be moved to one of the wards in the new block as soon as a bed could be found. We were informed by a nurse that Dad was to have further tests that would probably take a while, so I decided to go back home to tell Mum what had happened, and return and see Dad a little later.

Mum was a lot calmer when I arrived at home. She told Jill and I that Dad had woken up during the early hours with a terrific grabbing pain across the top of his chest that had spread down his left arm. I guess he was fearful of what it might be and had told Mum that he would take a couple of Anadin tablets and see how he felt in the morning, when she called me at about 6.00 am to come and help.

I went back to see Dad a little later in the day. Mum had said that she was not ready to visit him just then, for whatever reason, and wanted to stay at home. Leaving Jill with her once again I set of for St Thomas's. It's only a few miles from Nansen Road and easily reached by driving along Wandsworth Road to Vauxhall Cross and then along the Albert Embankment, passing Lambeth Palace before reaching the hospital.

I remember when I was quite young, if Dad and Mum had taken us out somewhere for the day, maybe to Brands Hatch motor racing circuit in Kent, or to Littlehampton, Margate etc, Dad would often drive back through Lewisham and stop at a pub called the Old Father Thames on the Albert Embankment. He and Mum would go inside for a drink and Paul and I would have our soda pop and crisps in the car. I was now passing the very place that held such fond memories for me before going to a place that held such sorrowful ones.

Having parked the car in Royal Street, opposite the main entrance, I made my way into the hospital to the ward where Dad had been taken. When I arrived he told me that after they had carried out the tests on him, he had told the ward sister, the matron and the doctor treating him that if he wasn't found a bed in a better place 'away from all these dying people' he was going to discharge himself.

"No, you're bloody not," I told him. "Don't you realise that you have just had a heart attack?" It made no odds to him, he was adamant that he would much rather leave than stay in that ward. He told me how the tests had gone and once we had exhausted the small talk I reassured him that I would be up to see him again after work the next day. I left with those reassuring words that we all say at times like these, "Don't worry I'm sure all will be fine."

The next day after work I telephoned Mum from Kemworthy Tools to see how Dad was getting on. To my horror, she told me that Dad had discharged himself early on the Monday morning and was right now sitting on the settee in the front room having a cup of tea.

"What! He's doing what?" I told Mum that I was coming straight over to see what had happened. After letting Jill know that I wouldn't be home for dinner as I was going to see Mum and Dad, I jumped into the car and sped off. When I arrived, sure enough, Dad was sitting on the settee in the front room smoking one of the hand-rolled Old Holborn cigarettes that he had smoked since he was a kid.

"What are you doing here?" I asked.

"I couldn't stand it in that hospital," he replied. "I told them that I was going home." You can imagine how the conversation went after that can't you? Lots of toing and froing about the rights and wrongs of his actions, but the most telling remark from Dad was, "Look, Brian, I know that I am going to die soon, and I want it to be here, at home." What can you say to that?

Typical Dad, he then went on to tell Mum and me the story of how he came to leave the hospital. Apparently, he knew where his clothes and belongings were being kept, so early in the morning, when all was still quiet, he fetched his clothes, got dressed and casually told the nurse who had been on duty all night that he was leaving.

Naturally, she had tried to stop him but he was having none of it. Even the sister on duly couldn't prevent him from leaving and before anybody more senior came along, he had gone. I think that you will see the funny side of a serious situation when I explain how he got home. After walking out of the hospital's main entrance, he crossed to the other side of Lambeth Palace

Road and waited for a number 77 bus which would take him to the bus stop near to Stormont Road, from where he would make the ten minute walk home.

Now, unusually for Dad, he was not dressed in the best of clothes. He was very old school in this respect and would put on a collar and tie – if you don't know what this means ask your nan or granddad – to walk to the corner shop at the bottom of the road to buy his tobacco and cigarette papers. However, on this occasion, he hadn't had time to get dressed properly before I had taken him to the hospital and he was dressed in an old pair of dark grey trousers, a vest with no shirt and a dark tan, chunky cardigan with big brown buttons on the front. Oh and, to finish it off, a pair of carpet slippers.

When a bus eventually came along, Dad got on, paid the correct fare with the small amount of change that he had in his pocket and settled down for the short bus ride home. When they reached Vauxhall Cross the bus conductor called out to Dad that this was the stop he wanted as they were at 'Railton House'. For those who don't know what this means I will enlighten you.

Railton House was a hostel/shelter for homeless men, one of those places that no man would contemplate going into out of choice. The very thought that the bus conductor would think that this was where Dad lived sent him into a rage. He spat out to the poor man, "I don't f**king live there, you cheeky b**tard!!" With a quick ring of the bell the bus was quickly on its journey and, once at the correct bus stop, Dad alighted with a few more choice words under his breath no doubt.

After spending a couple of hours with Mum and Dad, I promised to call the next lunchtime and prompted Mum to call the local doctor's surgery first thing in the morning to let them know what had happened. Hopefully, a doctor would then call on Dad to see how he was doing and, sure enough. that's exactly what happened the next day. I was fairly happy with the situation when I next returned on the Wednesday evening of that week and found Dad looking better and in a good mood. Both Mum and Dad told me what the doctor had said. Firstly, he was not at all impressed that Dad had discharged himself from hospital, but nonetheless respected Dad's wishes that he wanted to be at home. Secondly, he had examined Dad and prescribed some tablets that would help to keep him calm and thirdly, NO MORE SMOKING!

So what was Dad doing having a fag? "Give up," he said. "How the hell does he expect me to give up? I have been smoking for the best part of fifty-five years, I am hardly likely to stop now am I?" Fair point, Dad, but at least you could try and cut down. Having spent a couple of hours with them I promised to return on the Saturday lunchtime.

On Saturday, 5th May 1984, the phone rang just as Jill and I were about to leave home in Carshalton to visit Mum and Dad. As it rang, I sensed it was not going to be good news, and it wasn't. It was Paul's wife, Lyn, telling us to get to Nansen Road as quickly as we could as things had taken a turn for the worse.

When we arrived Lyn met us and told me that Paul had gone to St James Hospital, in Tooting, with Dad. Mum was sitting at the table in the kitchen crying. I think it was Lyn who told me that Dad had died while sitting on the settee waiting for Mum to bring him another cup of tea and one of her homemade rock cakes which he loved so much. A doctor had been called to verify Dad's death, and a short time afterwards an ambulance had arrived to take Dad to the hospital.

I immediately set off on my own to St James's having left Jill with Mum and Lyn. I didn't want her going through the next couple of hours with me at the hospital after all she had suffered in the previous four years. When I got to the hospital I quickly found Paul who confirmed what had taken place. Dad had died from, what they knew to be, an unsurvivable heart attack. I can't remember if Christopher was there or not, or even the next series of events. All I can remember is asking to see Dad in the chapel of rest when.

At some stage that afternoon, I was taken to see my dad by the resident chaplain. Dad was dressed in a crisp white hospital gown that was pulled a little way down his chest. I sat next to him and said, "Oh Dad, Oh Dad," as the tears and memories began to flow. I held his hand and sat sadly and quietly with him for a while. Even then he made me smile as I noticed that his mouth was partially open, and I could see the gaps in his teeth that he referred to as his 'railings'. I kissed him on the forehead, said my loving goodbyes and left.

Time has not allowed me to remember much more of the rest of that day, or indeed the coming few days after those sad events, except that on the following Monday morning I went to the bank where Dad had worked to give them the bad news. The bank had changed its name after it had been acquired by the finance group Lloyds Banking and was now known as Lloyds Bowmaker. When I arrived I asked to see Dad's boss and was taken up to his office. After I had been introduced to him he sat behind his desk, eagerly awaiting the news I had about Dad. When I told him, he was genuinely stunned, as the reports that he had had from Dad over the telephone had obviously been quite positive. I think he thought that, after an appropriate amount of rest, Dad would be able to return to work and resume his duties.

I explained to him, in as much detail as I could, what had happened since Dad's first heart attack some eight days ago, culminating his death forty-eight hours earlier. The poor man was devastated and I felt pride in the fact that a highly successful man in the banking world was so affected by the news I had just given him. It told me just how much Dad must have been liked by his work colleagues. He gave me his condolences to pass on to Mum and the rest of the family and reassured me that the bank would expedite the necessary arrangements so Mum would suffer no financial hardship.

The passing of my father was naturally a sad event and one which must, and will, come to us all eventually, but there is one thing that, even today, thirty-five years later, still leaves me feeling angry. It is the fact that I was to play no part in any of the funeral arrangements. I assume it was handled entirely by

Chris and Paul as Mum would have left all the arrangements to them, but I was not asked for any input whatsoever. I was not asked if I wanted to have something included in the order of service, nor about an inscription on the headstone and so on. Maybe they thought I would prefer not to be involved having dealt with arrangements for my babies over the previous four years. However, it would have been nice to be asked and not just excluded with no mention of anything that I could have helped with. It wasn't to be the only occasion that this happened either.

From memory, I believe that the funeral took place about a week after Dad died and it was held at Putney Vale Cemetery, in Kingston Vale, on the main London Road the A3. This has always puzzled me as normally anyone from the part of Battersea where Nansen Road is situated would be buried in St. Mary's Cemetery in Wandsworth. Why Dad should have gone elsewhere is unclear to me; perhaps the cemetery couldn't accommodate him. Anyway, the service took place in the chapel and once the service was over Dad was laid to rest not too far from the main entrance into the cemetery.

I don't know how Mum, Chris or Paul felt about the way Dad passed away but for me, although it was a shock as it happened and all so quickly, I am comforted by the fact that he couldn't have suffered any of the pain, anguish, or terror many humans most probably endure when they are staring death in the face. It helped me to deal with the added grief I had to cope with so soon after my son Andrew's death.

Shortly after the funeral, we three brothers met at the White Hart public in Barnes, London, for a drink and a chat. During the evening, the question was asked by one of us, "I wonder if there is life after death?"

I think Paul gave the best answer, "Yes, I think so, because whenever we talk of Dad he will be alive in our hearts."

A few weeks after the funeral, things had started to become more normal. Whenever Jill and I could we went to see Mum for a chat and generally did the things that people do at these times. On one such visit, Mum told us that she and Paul had discussed the possibility of her moving into independent warden controlled accommodation in Ascot. She wouldn't be too far away from Paul and Lyn who, at the time were living in Bracknell, in Berkshire and it made sense because, if she needed anything, Paul and Lyn were nearby. Besides, Battersea was no longer the community filled place it once was and Mum would soon be isolated on a day to day basis.

During this time, I received a telephone call from Dad's former boss asking me to go and see him at the bank, if I could spare the time, as he had something to discuss with me. Intrigued, I agreed and we arranged a mutually convenient date. I was baffled as to why he wanted to see me and eagerly awaited the appointed day.

Dressed in *my* collar and tie I drove to the City of London, parked the car on a parking meter close to the bank and presented myself to the receptionist who took me to the meet the boss in his office. Having greeted me and gone through the usual niceties he asked me if I would like to take on the role that Dad had been doing during his time at the bank? Apparently they had tried out a number of temporary workers to fill the role but none of them had proved to be suitable. He thought that as I knew the building layout well, and had possibly learned what the role entailed from Dad, I would be a natural candidate to take over and would I give it consideration?

Well, actually, yes, I thought I would. I had not been happy at Kemworthy Tools for a while and this seemed like an ideal opportunity to get start afresh. I asked him to let me think about it for a day or two, and said I would give him my answer by the end of the week. My decision had already been made by the time I had shaken his hand and left his office. Of course I was going to say yes, who wouldn't? A nice clean, collar and tie job with better pay and conditions.

On the Friday of that week I telephoned him and accepted his offer. Delighted to hear the news, he said the bank would send a formal offer in the post and I should sign it and hand my notice in at Kemworthy Tools, after which time I was to call him with a start date.

Having done the above I presented myself, suited and booted, to Lloyds Bowmaker on a Monday morning, and was introduced to the team of mailroom staff that I would be working with. They were mostly women, mail sorters who worked part-time from early in the morning until lunchtime, and nearly all of them said that they were really sorry about Dad's passing and that he would be greatly missed.

I was shown around and told what my duties would be and given the keys to the car that was necessary to do the job. Mailbags containing correspondence for the bank had to be collected from the local Royal Mail sorting office in King William Street, London EC4, by 6.00 am, which, by the way, has long since closed and disappeared to make way for swanky new offices.

Jill was indifferent about me taking on this new role as she was continuing to lead her own life, and this resulted in us becoming ever more distant. If I am honest, it didn't make any difference to me as my feelings towards her were changing anyway. I was thinking more and more about leaving and starting again, but that was not going to happen anytime soon so the status quo was maintained for now at any rate.

One of my work colleagues was the chairman's chauffeur, a Scottish man funnily enough called 'Jock', ha-ha! He was approaching retirement and told me that he didn't want to be driving the Guvnor as much as he had been doing, and would I be interested in filling in for him on the odd occasion so that he could have a night off. This was an interesting development, especially as the car he drove was an S Class Mercedes Benz, albeit a funny mustard colour.

"Yeah, all right, Jock, you're on," I told him. And so, I started my foray into a world that I was to enjoy, well mostly, for the next thirty years, although I didn't know it at the time.

I had only been at Lloyds Bowmaker for about six months when the bank announced that it was relocating in the spring of

1985 to the financial district in Bournemouth, in Dorset. *Great*, I thought, *what a nice place to move too*. It was on the coast and one of England's best resorts, ideal for me and Jill, and Susie, of course. When I got home that evening I excitedly told Jill the news but was met with the reaction that I least expected. "Well, I'm not going," she said. "I am more than happy to stay here."

Deflated, I now realised that it was only a matter of time before we parted, how could she turn down a great opportunity like that? No matter how many times I tried to talk to her about it over the next couple of weeks she just wasn't interested, and so when the time came for work to know my intentions reluctantly I told them that I had decided not to go with them, partly telling them the reason why.

It was time to start looking around for something similar also located in the city. What caught my eye, however, was to send me in a different direction entirely. I spotted an advert in the *Evening Standard* which ran a lot of adverts for manual jobs, mainly on a Thursday each week, for mailroom staff, messengers, porters, security guards and, chauffeurs.

It was a chauffeur position that I quite liked the look of, the position of chairman's chauffeur at the government quango of the Manpower Services Commission (MSC), in High Holborn, not far from Lloyds Bowmaker. So I decided to apply, after all, what did I have to lose?

# Chapter Seven

Having made an application to the MSC at the advertised address I waited to see if I had been successful. After a couple of weeks, an official looking, brown envelope arrived. I eagerly opened it, and the letter inside said that they would like me to attend an interview at the MSC offices at Selkirk House, High Holborn. I attended the interview on the day advised in my best and only suit, a dark grey one hurriedly purchased from Marks & Spencer a couple of days earlier, white shirt and dark blue tie, and clean black shoes.

On arrival at the MSC offices I told the security guard on duty that I had an appointment at the chairman's office, and I was given a temporary pass allowing me 'escorted access only'. A telephone call was made and, after a few minutes, I was met at the front desk by a nice lady from the chairman's office (lead the way Ms Civil Service!). I followed her into the lift and upon reaching the executive floor I was led into a large office that had three secretaries, one female and two male one of whom had his own desk. The young man introduced himself and said that he would go and see if the chairman was free to interview me.

He reappeared a minute or two later and beckoned me into a large office where sitting in a leather armchair on one side of the room was the chairman, Bryan Nicholson. As soon as I entered he stood up and greeted me with a firm handshake and beaming smile. He then asked me a few questions about what work I had been doing over the last few years, although he already knew via my CV, he wanted to hear it in my own words, and he also wanted me to explain why I wanted to change jobs and become his chauffeur. I forget what I told him, but the interview was soon over and he called the young man back in. I later discovered this was his private secretary, as opposed to just being an office secretary, and it was his job to liaise with other senior members of the MSC and members of any government departments that the chairman was to hold meetings with.

The nice lady who had escorted me up to the chairman's office originally now escorted me back to the security desk in the main reception area, wished me good luck and said that they would be in touch fairly soon. I duly returned my temporary pass to the guard on duty and was escorted off the premises. When I got back home Jill asked me how I had got on. I told her all about it and said that I hoped to be called back for a second interview.

Daily life had become fairly routine for both of us. Jill was spending more and more time either at her mother's house or babysitting at her friends' houses and if it gave her some comfort then I was pleased for her. In between times she would take Susie out for a walk and, in most cases, take Susie with her to her mother's. I was still terribly sad, at times, over the loss of our babies. I have to admit that the realisation we would never have a child was weighting heavy on my heart and it began to have an impact on my relationship with Jill.

The letter that I had hoped for arrived in the post and I was excited to read that Mr Nicholson had invited me back for a second interview. The same process as before took place and, once I had arrived, I met the chairman for a second time. It was much quicker than the first interview. Once again, as I was being escorted from the building I was told that they would be in touch as soon as they could with an answer. So it was back to the daily grind of work, dog walking, shopping, etc. I really was pinning a lot on getting this job as I needed a new direction in my life.

After a few more days the brown envelope used by government departments in those days arrived. But this time it was an A4 sized window envelope and I knew straight away what that meant; that somehow with no chauffeur experience I had been offered the job. Sure enough, upon opening the envelope it was all there; confirmation of the appointment 'Chauffeur to the Chairman of the Manpower Services Agency', salary details, holiday entitlement and so on. There was also a paragraph that said something along the lines of: 'The vehicle will be administered by the Government Car Service, all fuel receipts etc should be forwarded to them at Marsham Street, the vehicle shall be kept clean and roadworthy at all times, no personal use of the car or telephone is allowed.' *That's fine by me*, I thought, *just let me get started*. On the date indicated, I telephoned the lady in the chairman's office, who I now knew was called Beryl, and told her that I would be accepting the offer.

One week later, I travelled by bus from Rose Hill to Morden Underground Station at the end of the Northern Line, and made my way to High Holborn Underground Station on the Central Line. As I was early, I stopped in a local café for a cup of tea and, at the appropriate time I presented myself to the security guard in the MSC reception armed with my letter of appointment. Beryl was notified that I had arrived and came to collect me. She then took me to have my photo taken for my full entry pass and when complete, with photo, name, and number, I went with Beryl to the chairman's office to be officially introduced to everyone. The chairman and his personal secretary were at the Sheffield office of the MSC for the day as this was where the daily workings of this government quango was done, not down in London as I had thought.

After the introductions and paperwork had been completed Beryl took me along the corridor to introduce me to the chief executive and his staff of two, a secretary and a chauffeur. I forget her name but I will never forget the chauffeur's, Bill Pritchard, the man who helped me enormously in passing on all the tricks of the trade that he had learned over the years. Then I was taken to see the car that had been delivered the previous Friday in readiness for Monday morning, a light green Vauxhall Carlton 2000cc CD Automatic with darkened windows. It actually didn't look too bad, especially when I saw what Bill was driving, a tan, wedge-shaped Austin Princess, Yuk! Sorry, Bill, but I know even you thought it was horrible.

As I was getting acquainted with the car, Bill appeared and suggested that we go for a cuppa and have a chat. I was all for that, so we went to the local café and Bill ordered the teas. Now I have to tell you that Bill had his tea a strange way, he only had a small teaspoon of milk with it and I always thought, but never said to him, what's the point of that, either have milk or don't.

Bill told me all the things to do and what not to do in the job, which I found to be a great help, as I was completely inexperienced back then.

When I returned to the office Beryl suggested that I acquaint myself with the main buildings that the chairman would be visiting in the course of his duties and, after I had done that, she suggested that I drive to the chairman's home and take note of exactly where he lived. Then I could go home and they would see me with the chairman the next morning. So I left with a list of places in central London to familiarise myself with, mainly in Westminster, as I needed to know the best places to park etc.

Because I signed the Official Secrets Act, which I still have to abide by to this day, I cannot be too specific as where those places were. However, I shall endeavour to do my best not to fall foul of the Act and tell some of the stories that happened over the next few years.

On that first morning, I drove the seven and a half miles from Carshalton to Mr Nicholson's Surrey home, a journey of about twenty minutes. Being in plenty of time I popped into the local newsagents to purchase a copy of the Financial Times for the chairman to read on the journey into the office. I waited a couple of minutes away for fear of being too early. The pickup time was 7.00 am, so at 6.55 I reversed the car up to the house and parked in a suitable position. At exactly seven o'clock Mr Nicholson left his house with his ministerial red box containing important government papers together with his own black briefcase. I held the rear nearside passenger door open for him and he greeted me with a cheery, "Good morning, Brian," as he got into the back of the car and picked up the *FT*. As we set off he asked if, in the mornings when he appeared from his house, I could take the red box from him and place in on the rear seat next to where he would sit, there was no need to open the door for him and could we have BBC Radio Four tuned into the radio and on at all times. He then asked which route I would be taking into town.

Before I could answer, he told me the way that he had been driving himself into the office and suggested I give it a try. This meant driving down through Mitcham, on to Amen Corner in Tooting, working our way through the back streets in Balham, running in line and past the London Underground stations on the Northern Line until we got to Stockwell, where we would then go along Kennington Lane, pass by the Imperial War Museum and work our way around to Waterloo Bridge, a journey that took just sixty minutes.

Anybody who knows that route, and I know a couple of people who do, will find that an unbelievably quick time – don't forget that, back then in the mid-1980s the traffic was nowhere near as bad as it is today. Once at the beginning of the bridge on the south side of the River Thames he would get out and walk the rest of the way to Selkirk House, weather permitting. This is what we did every working day for the next three years.

The first thing that I had to do when I got into the office was to take the red box to Beryl. She was always in the office by 7.30 am which gave her ample time to get the chairman's itinerary ready for the day ahead. As I gave her the red box she would give me a schedule of the chairman's movements for the day, having highlighted when I would be needed. She would give me a provisional itinerary every Monday morning for the week, sometimes for the next two weeks ahead, with a warning that these timings were likely to change. She also asked me to keep my pager on at all times, even at home, so messages could be sent directly to me if necessary – don't forget, there were no mobile phones in those days. She also asked me not to wander too far and stay in the chauffers' room so that I could be readily contacted by phone during the working day.

Bill had rigged out the large chauffeurs' room with a couple of comfy armchairs, television, video recorder, kettle and mugs etc. It was a regular home from home that Bill and I spent many hours in. Sometimes we would sit in the small garden at the side of Selkirk House with a cuppa and a bacon sandwich putting the world to rights.

Beryl was a great person to work with and she would always allow me to get away early from the office if the chairman was away or, indeed, not come in if the chairman was away himself either for personal or business reasons. I did need to go to the office to collect the red box the afternoon that he was due back, mostly from his visits to the office in Sheffield. He would take the train to St Pancras Station where I would meet him with the car positioned in the exact spot on the platform where his carriage would come to a stop. If anybody, mainly the police, asked me what I was doing I just showed them my government pass and they left me alone.

One of the best 'tricks' that Bill told me about was to purchase a Rupert Bear lapel badge, one where he was wearing a policeman's helmet, from one of the police officers stationed at the vehicle entrance for the House of Commons, situated under the clock tower that houses the famous bell Big Ben. We went there quite often as it was where the chairman would go to meet ministers. This badge was recognisable to all London police officers – Metropolitan, British Transport Police, and even the City of London Police – as it was a known that the wearer had contributed to the Metropolitan Police Widows and Orphans fund.

That little badge was a godsend, especially when I had to park the car in the street outside one of the offices that the chairman was visiting. Many times a traffic warden would approach the car and say in an officious voice, "You can't park there." Usually, when they saw the badge on my lapel, they would say, "Oh, you're okay mate, stay as long as you like," because they didn't know who I was in this unmarked car. They were not going to take the risk of asking for fear that I might be one of the Old Bill.

It worked a treat one day when I was parked outside the Waldorf Hotel on the Strand, opposite the BBC's Bush House, the building from where broadcasts to the Indian sub-continent were made. The diplomatic protection officer stationed outside the building was obviously bored, as little was going on, so he decided to brighten up his day by making every single car, van, taxi, motorbike, you name it, that was parked up from Drury Lane back down past the Waldorf to Catherine Street, to move. As he ordered them to drive off, one by one, he came up alongside the driver's door where I was sitting in the government car, saw the badge and said, "You're alright, son" and continued walking by.

Another time, while waiting in a restricted area at Heathrow where I was to meet the chairman from a flight from Germany, a police van pulled up alongside the car and an armed officer approached ready to tell me to leave. I wound the window down and turned slightly so he could see little Rupert badge resplendent in his policeman's helmet sitting on my lapel. He said, "Okay, mate," and went back to his colleagues in the police van and drove off. Many a time Rupert helped me out in this way.

The chairman had turned out to be an extremely nice person to work with. I never gave him cause to worry, or have any concerns about how I conducted myself, and I think he came to rely on my judgement as far as route planning and my driving abilities were concerned. I was lucky enough to be sent on two government driver training courses, the first to learn anti-hijacking and observation techniques and the second on how to control the car using evasive manoeuvres at eye-watering speeds.

The first course really opened my eyes as to how a car can be driven correctly utilising the observational and driving skill that all class one police drivers need to use when maintaining good driving within the legal limits of the road, learning how to safely be in pursuit of another vehicle and how to safely be part of a convoy of vehicles. We drove on public roads during the mornings which meant doing everything by the book while putting the previous afternoon's theory and instruction into practice.

The second course was mind blowing. Over two days, I was taught how to handle the car on a skid pan, skidding the car in a controlled way, both to the left and to the right, doing as many forward and reverse J turns it took until they became second nature, driving at high speed to get away from an attack car, and I do mean high speed! All in all I had a great time and thoroughly enjoyed myself at the taxpayers' expense, ha-ha!

Even though the hours were long I really enjoyed my new role, and I don't think Jill was too concerned that I was rarely at home in the evenings either. After I had been in the job for a number of months, I started to think about leaving home and divorcing Jill. I still desperately wanted to be a father, but how could I even think of doing such a thing after all that Jill had been through, what a lowlife I would be. Jill and I were becoming distant from each other and whether she recognised it or not I couldn't tell. I just got on with life as normal to maintain the status quo, but work was playing an ever more dominant role in my life. The hours I was putting in easily totalled twelve hours a day, at least three days a week, which I didn't mind, as it gave me something to focus on and I never worked at weekends.

From time to time, British Conservative politician Sir Peter Hugh Morrison (2nd June, 1944–13th July, 1995), Parliamentary Private Secretary (PPS) to Prime Minister Margaret Thatcher, would accompany the chairman to 10 Downing Street when Mrs Thatcher summoned him to a meeting. On one of these occasions I had to take the chairman to the Department of Employment building at Caxton House, in Caxton Street, SW1, where we would collect Sir Peter Morrison, before driving them both to 10 Downing Street to meet the Prime Minister. Easy, yes?

Well, as it turned out, it is an event that Sir Peter never let me forget! As we arrived at Caxton House the chairman leapt out of the car leaving the rear nearside passenger door open as he hurried to the front entrance where he met Sir Peter. They both hurried back to the car and, feeling people getting in the rear and hearing a voice shout "Let's go!" I pulled away, to hear further shouts of "Stop! Stop!" coming from the back.

I stopped and turned around in my seat to discover that Sir Peter hadn't quite got fully into the car and was only half in. What he said is unrepeatable here, and from then on whenever I drove him he always said, "Today's not the day you're going to kill me is it, Brian?"

One Friday lunchtime in summer, I took the chairman to his parents' home where he, by now Sir Bryan Nicholson and his wife Lady Mary Nicholson, had been invited to spend a weekend. Sir Peter's parents were Major John Granville Morrison, 1st Baron Margadale and Lady Margaret Smith and the family seat was The Fonthill Estate, near Salisbury, in Wiltshire. Once we arrived we passed through the main gates and continued on for a couple of minutes until we reached the main house set in about 9,000 acres of land.

We pulled up outside the house, a large, grey building that I think comprised of a ground floor and two upper floors, and Sir Bryan and Lady Mary walked up the wide, many stepped entrance to a wooden door to be greeted by a rather dowdy-looking old man. Muggings here was following behind with the luggage and when I got to the open front door I put the bags just inside. I couldn't see the Nicholsons so I closed the door and left. Once back inside the car I was just filling out paperwork before I left to make my way home when I noticed the old man again. He was now at the top of the staircase beckoning me over. *Oh blimey,* what does he want? I thought but nonetheless I went up to see him.

"Are you Brian?" he asked.

"Yes," I replied.

"Ah good," he said. "Sir Bryan tells me that you are driving all the way back to London, I would like to offer you some refreshments before you go. Walk down this corridor until you come to the kitchen where Mary will see to you." It then dawned on me that this scruffy old man was His Lordship! I thought he was the gardener!

"Thanks very much," I said as I began to make my way down the passageway to the kitchen. And what a passageway it was; old family paintings adorned the walls either side, coats of armour and actual suits of armour that formed a funny kind of guard of honour line for me as I continued on to meet Mary in the kitchen.

Before I got there I could hear what sounded like a pack of dogs inside the house and, sure enough, that's just what it was. In the far corner of the kitchen was a stable door, half open, and I could see a young woman feeding about a dozen or so dogs who were all positioning themselves in the best spot waiting to be fed. I asked the woman if she was Mary and she said, "Good God, no, sit down at the table and Mary will be along shortly."

After a minute of two in walked the most elegantly dressed lady I had ever seen in my life, very tall with immaculate hair and make-up, not too much but just enough to bring out the beauty of this middle-aged woman. She was wearing a summer dress which seemed to be quite fitting on this pleasant summer evening. She greeted me with a beaming smile and an outstretched had saying, "Hello, is it Brian? I'm very pleased to meet you. Papa tells me that you would like some refreshments before you travel back to London."

"Well, he offered," I replied stupidly. Cringe moment!

Having said no matter she went to the cupboard, and then the fridge, took out some food and put the kettle on, with a little bit of small talk in between. She prepared sandwiches, crustless naturally, small meat bites and a biscuit or two all served up on a silver tray with silver teapot, and a decorative Wedgewood cup and saucer. Pouring out the first cup she then wished me a safe journey home and bade me goodbye. She oozed class, sheer bloody class. When I asked the kennel maid, who had just finished feeding the dogs, if that had been Mary, smiling she said it was.

The Hon. Dame Mary Anne Morrison (born 17th May 1937) is a lady-in-waiting to Elizabeth II, and assumed the position in 1960. Ha-ha, how about that then, the hand that has waited on Her Majesty Queen Elizabeth II, had now served yours truly, not bad for a Battersea Boy after all.

Another time, I was driving Sir Bryan and his private secretary back to home from the Sheffield office via the A1, he asked if we could divert into Peterborough as he wanted to see an old colleague. Sir Bryan gave me the address and we headed towards Peterborough. His friend lived on the outskirts of a little village just south of the town, and we pulled up outside a large bungalow with a few acres of land. Sir Bryan's friend was waiting by the gate to greet us, and we were all invited inside and led to a splendid living room.

The private secretary and I were seated on one side of the room while Sir Bryan and his friend sat on the other by the French windows. The lady of the house served up light refreshments and after asked me if I would like to wash my hands as we still had quite a journey back to Sir Bryan's home in Surrey.

"No, thank you," I said followed by, "but could I use your lavatory, please?" The look of disbelief on their faces at what I had just said was priceless.

Once back in the car and on the road the private secretary relayed the story to Sir Bryan adding, "You can take the boy out of Battersea, but you can't take Battersea out of the boy." to which Sir Bryan just turned his head and glanced out of the car window. Top man, he didn't respond in a way that would embarrass me.

I continued to work at MSC, enjoying every single minute of my time there. With my level of security clearance I managed to go into many government buildings that ordinary members of the public would never have the privilege of seeing. Whenever I took Sir Bryan on a field trip he would usually be met by some of the most senior figures in private or business life, but he always asked if I was going to be looked after while he was being entertained. Quite often I would be treated to the same lunch or dinner that he had been served, albeit behind closed doors but I didn't worry too much about that.

All was going well until one evening, in the spring of 1987, while taking Sir Bryan home after work, he told me that he something confidential to tell me. He had been asked to be the new chairman of the Post Office and had decided that, when his tenure as chairman of the MSC came to an end, he was going to take up this new position. *Great*, I thought. *A new challenge for both of us*. Almost immediately, though, I was to become extremely disappointed. He told me that the Post Office already had a chairman's chauffeur and no matter how hard he tried to convince them that he wanted to take me along as part of his package, they informed him that their Trade Union would not allow it. So there it was, Sir Bryan was going to leave in a couple of months' time.

Beryl and others arranged for the office to go out for a lunch party to a local Indian restaurant in Bloomsbury, a few weeks later, close to the date when Sir Bryan was due to leave. He invited the same staff to a farewell dinner to be held one evening at an Italian restaurant in Covent Garden, next to the Royal Opera House. It was my first and last experience of nouvelle cuisine, and good job too. When the menu was presented to us I liked the look of the roast lamb thinking that it would be like a normal Sunday roast dinner. Oh how wrong I was, for when it was served up it had only two tiny, round, almost rare, pieces of meat with a couple of vegetables, and I do mean only a couple.

Well, the look on my face must have been a picture of bewilderment and was caught by Sir Bryan who took it all in but didn't say a word. The starter, and then pudding, which was two tiny melon balls had me baffled as to what this nouvelle cuisine was all about. It certainly didn't leave you feeling satisfied afterwards, that's for sure.

Once the evening was over and we departed in the car for Surrey, Sir Bryan got down to doing the day's work that was in the red box. He didn't make conversation until we approached the Mitcham area when he asked, "What did you think of the meal?" What did I think? I told him exactly what I thought about it and said that I was still hungry.

"Yes, me too," he replied. "If you see a fish and chip shop on the way home pull up outside and I will go in and get us cod and chips." And that is exactly what we did in a chippy near to where I lived at Rose Hill.

That summed the man up, yes he could wine and dine with the mightiest in the land, but was humble enough to stop and eat fish and chips with his driver as though it was the most natural thing in the world. Sir Bryan was the best boss that I ever had and there was never a cross word between us. Even today, I have nothing but the utmost respect for the man. He taught me a lot about how to present myself and how to do the right thing, not by telling me, all I did was observe him in action. It was an honour and a pleasure to have worked with him for three years, he and the job are sorely missed.

But life goes on and, to be honest, life at home wasn't that great. I guess both Jill and I had changed from the people we had been when we met as teenagers. I have no doubt that it was because our three little angels hadn't made us the family unit that we both longed for that we began to edge away from each other. Jill was enjoying her life with what she was doing. I was working long hours at MSC so I suppose it was inevitable that we would grow distant from one another.

Near the end of Sir Bryan's time at MSC, he told me about a conversation he had had with a colleague about a chauffeur position that had become available for a wealthy Arab businessman from Beirut, Lebanon, and his family, who were now living in London. He suggested that I might like to speak to his colleague about and that's what I did. To cut a long story short, I gave my notice at MSC and duly went to work for the Arab family, having said my goodbye to Sir Bryan and the office staff. It was with a heavy heart that I made my way home to Newstead Walk, but I was also a little excited about starting the new job the coming Monday morning.

# **Chapter Eight**

Early that Monday morning I set off by bus, tube and Shanks's Pony – Google it! – to the address that I was to report to in Sloane Street, London SW1, a small office located on the first floor above an estate agency where my new boss and his two colleagues had their offices. Upon arrival, I could not have been met with a warmer welcome by the two colleagues who gave me a quick tour around the offices. And boy, was it quick!

There was only one central office where they worked, a large office/sitting room for the boss, a small kitchen and a little store room/restroom for me. It was not a bad set-up as it had a lovely, comfy settee and a colour TV for the periods when I was not required.

The two guys were ex-city traders whose job it was to build up the boss's portfolio by trading daily stocks and shares on the London and International markets where appropriate. My first thought when told this was, *I bet you are both on a nice little earner!* But if that is what they did and they were good at it then why not. Actually, in due course, I was to see where they both lived; one in Marlow, and the other in Bourne End, Buckinghamshire, about three miles apart from each other. You should have seen their houses. Yes, they were definitely on a big wedge that's for sure.

The boss hadn't arrived at the office just yet as he usually didn't leave his home in Exhibition Road until about 9.30 am. Then he would walk the approximately one mile via Princes Gate and Knightsbridge to the office. I asked how often he did this, to which the reply came, "Oh most days."

At around 9.45 the boss, a Lebanese man of about fifty-five years old arrived and greeted me with a broad grin, firm handshake and a pleasant, "Good Morning, Brian" a greeting returned similarly, of course. He then told me that after he had drunk his first coffee of the morning he would take me to the underground car park of the Sloane Street Hotel where the car was kept during the day while not in use. The vehicle in question was a lime green Daimler XJ12 6.0 Double Six LWB with a dark tan interior. What a lovely looking car and not too shabby to drive either.

He explained that I would not be able to take the car home but recognised that I needed transport of some kind and so he had acquired a Renault 5 1.4 petrol automatic three-door hatchback for me to use, not to keep mind, just to use. *What a nice bloke,* I thought. *I think I might like this job!*

He went on to tell me that I would generally leave the office by 5 o'clock each day as he would make his own way home about then unless the weather was terrible and if it was I was to drive him instead. I didn't have to work weekends unless it was unavoidable, a couple of suits and shirts would be supplied for me and, last but not least, he said, "I hope you will be very happy with us."

So off we started, usually his secretary would tell me at the end of the day what would be required of me the following morning. I would either pick him up from his home or just come straight to the office whatever was necessary. At least twice a week I was to take his wife shopping to one of only three places; Harrods, the shop of choice for the rich and famous, located within walking distance of the office on the Brompton Road, but too far for the missus to walk from Exhibition Road, a small Arabic market shop in Moscow Road, London W2 and an Arabic confectionary shop in Upper Berkley Street, W2. I thought this was odd, it being right next door to the West London Synagogue, as Arab Muslims do not usually get along with Jews. Anyhow these were the only places that she ever shopped.

He was a successful businessman from Beirut who had fled with his immediate family before the civil war had started in 1974 with most, if not all, of his personal wealth. His wife would go to Harrods most weeks and buy household items ranging from the mundane, say tablecloths all the way up to large pieces of furniture, or electrical goods that were sent to Lebanon to family who hadn't been so fortunate in getting out as they had been.

Sometimes his wife asked me to escort her to Harrods Bank, located on the lower ground floor, as she would be withdrawing a large sum of money, usually £10,000 in cash. A lot of money today, a small fortune in 1987.

Wednesday, 3<sup>rd</sup> June, 1987 started fine, bright and warm, a good sign that the afternoon's 209<sup>th</sup> running of the world-famous horse race the Epsom Derby would be enjoyed by all that attended the most traditional of British days out. People would travel from all over the UK to be there, as well as large numbers from around the world. Top racehorse owners from the UK, America, the Middle and Far East would also attend, hoping that if they had entered a horse it would be theirs that would run out as the winner, and they would have the honour of having the winner's trophy presented to them by Her Majesty Queen Elizabeth II. I mention this, as little did I know when I arrived at the office that the day would be taken up with sitting with the boss trying to pick the winner from the day's race card. When I arrived at the office I assumed that it would be a day like any other, as I had only worked for the company for a few weeks I was still finding my feet, so to speak.

When the principal arrived he had his usual meeting with the two other guys over his traditional cup of Turkish coffee, Harrods No: 2 Blend, then asked for me to go and see him in his office. I naturally thought that it was to tell me I needed to collect his wife to take her to one of the three destinations already mentioned, and was surprised when he announced, "Brian, you and I are going to try and pick today's Derby winner."

"I don't really know that much about horse racing," I protested, but to no avail.

"We will sit at my desk and go through the day's race card and see what we think," he said. His secretary was instructed to hold all but the most essential calls as the other two guys left his office with a chuckle. I was asked to go to the local newsagents and get the morning papers, including *Sporting Life*, so that we could 'study the form' of the runners and riders of the day.

We went through the whole day's race card trying to sort out one or two runners in each race but, alas to no avail. We couldn't agree on anything, so the boss decided to put a £20 each way bet on every horse in every race. I don't know how much he laid out, a pretty penny I'm sure, but I do know that when I went back for the winnings, it was a lot more than he had paid out, where's the excitement in that though? Still, I wasn't complaining as, upon counting his winnings, he gave me ten crisp £20 notes as my reward for helping him.

As the summer rolled by I was enjoying the job as it was so much more relaxed than the hectic schedule that I had been used to at MSC. The pay was good, with the bonus of not having to pay for the running of a car, so we were doing quite well. In fact, so well that when the boss took his family on holiday for the whole month of August I suggested to Jill that we should go to Orlando, Florida, for the trip of a lifetime to see if things were going to get any better between us. Jill readily agreed to the idea and we both brought home a number of holiday brochures, and settled down to find a holiday that would suit. We came up with a two week stay in a hotel/motel with a rental car included, in the popular location of International Drive in the central area of Orlando, not too far from the city's main attraction, Walt Disney World.

When the time came, we put Susie into a local dog kennel for the duration of our holiday, and the following morning set of for Gatwick Airport. All went smoothly and quickly as we checked in, went through customs and boarded a McDonnell Douglas DC-10 aircraft to take us to Orlando. Upon arrival it took an age to clear customs but eventually we headed for the car rental desk where we collected our car and headed off to find our hotel.

We had an enjoyable two week holiday in the fun capital of

the world. We overate, like everybody does the first time that they go to Florida, and tried to pack in too much and came home having thoroughly enjoyed ourselves, or did we? We were even talking about returning, although deep down I knew this was not going to happen. Yes, we had or, at least, I had a great time but the holiday only confirmed that I really did need to get away.

Having returned to work it was very quiet until the family returned from their holiday and it was pretty much back into the routine as before. As it was turning into autumn the boss's wife wasn't keen on going out so often, and I was spending more and more days doing nothing. A great job, I hear you say. Yes, but not for a thirty-one year old, I wanted to be out there going places and discovering new places to build up my knowledge for the future and I wasn't going to do that by sitting in an office watching TV all day. In fact, it was getting so bad that I would find myself going for walks around the Sloane Street area. I would often walk to Harrods and browse the departments, in awe at the prices of some of the items on display. Or I would walk into Hyde Park to catch the Household Cavalry mounted soldiers exercising their horses or walk part way down the Kings Road window shopping before having a cup of coffee somewhere. No, this wasn't what I wanted at all, and I knew that I couldn't keep it up for much longer.

Soon Christmas was upon us and, once again, we spent it in precisely the same way as the previous couple of years, being bored at the in-laws. New Year came and went, and then it was back to work. I was going through the same old routine which was now beginning to bore me. Jill and I were not getting on and, all of a sudden, life wasn't good in any respect. The more time went on, I felt increasingly stifled at both home and work. My relationship with Jill wasn't improving, and I was really quite sorry that it had got as bad as it had. Work was no better. Yes, it's great for a while getting paid for sitting around doing nothing, but not every day. So I decided that, on the job front, it was time to make a change.

I thought about the best way to go about it and, having looked through the *Evening Standard* and various other publications to no avail, I dug a bit deeper and found that posted on the internet were job agencies that specialised in corporate and household vacancies for, amongst others, chauffeurs. So I began to scour the agencies, but registering my interest meant that I had to submit my Curriculum Vitae and any references that I had. I was then called into agencies eager to be interviewed by the consultant who handled the chauffeur vacancies on behalf of the particular agency in question. This was easier said than done. I had mentioned that I didn't do much every day, still, it was proving difficult to get away for up to ninety minutes at a time just for the registering process alone, let alone going for a job interview.

The CV that I had submitted was commented on favourably by most of the agencies. They were all impressed by the government position at MSC and the security driving courses that I had attended while employed there. The glowing reference from Sir Bryan Nicholson didn't do any harm either.

A few days after the registering process at the agencies, job offers started to be telephoned through to me, mostly for domestic chauffeurs to wealthy families that could afford one. I tended to stay clear of those as it was a corporate position that I was looking for. I assumed the pay and conditions would be better, ie paid overtime, holiday and sick pay, and not being at the beck and call of some obnoxious wealthy person. Being ordered about was not the road – no pun intended – that I wanted to go down.

One job that was I offered did catch my eye. It was to work for a Malaysian oil company based in New Zealand House on Pall Mall, near to Trafalgar Square not far from St James Park, an area that I knew well from my wine delivery job days a few years earlier. I attended the interview with the company's personnel officer who explained what they were looking for in the applicant for the position, salary and conditions. At the end of the interview I felt it had gone well, and it had as I was asked back for a second interview to be held at the same offices about a week later, only this time it was to be with the principal user of the chauffeur himself.

Having interviewed well a second time I felt that I was in with a good chance of being offered the position. A few days later the agency rang to say that the company were impressed by my CV, interviewing skills and personality and would like to offer me the job. Whoopee! I decided to accept, work out my one week's notice and join on the given date suggested. Now all I had to do was tell my current employer.

Leaving it until the end of the week, Friday, I went to the office as usual and waited for the boss to arrive. Having given him time to have his coffee and daily meetings with his two colleagues, I asked his secretary to find out if he could spare me a few minutes of his time. "Yes, of course," came the reply and I ventured into his office.

Having explained my reasons for handing in my notice, I thanked him for giving me a chance in the first place, being so kind and understanding during my time with him and his family. To my surprise, he said that he had wondered how long it would take me to come to this decision. You see, he told me that, although he would be sorry to see me go, he understood that the job with him would have suited a much older person, someone who was nearing retirement or had already retired. He said that he felt he had made a mistake in offering the job to a younger person in the first place. He went on to say that I didn't need to work out my notice and that he would pay me all that I was owed up to the leaving date and with a shake of hands that was it. I walked out of his office and headed for Knightsbridge Underground Station to catch a tube to Morden Station and begin my journey home.

On the Monday morning of my first day with the Malaysian oil company, I was met by the personnel manager and shown into the boss's office. Once the pleasantries where out the way he asked me to take the company car, an S Class Mercedes Benz, to his home in St John's Wood, just north of Regents

Park, where I was to collect his wife and take her to wherever she wanted to go.

Hang about, I thought this was a corporate job, not a personal one? But okay, it was my first day so let's see what happens. I located the car in the underground car park of New Zealand House, drove out on to Pall Mall and made my way to St John's Wood to collect his wife. I parked the car outside a large, white painted house in the style befitting the area, climbed the front steps, rang the bell and waited. Pretty quickly a small middle-aged lady appeared and, having recognised the car, greeted me with a grunt and a hand gesture that said, "Okay, I know who you are let's get going." As she obviously could not speak English, once in the car, she handed me a piece of paper with the address that she wanted taking to, a road just off Harley Street, W1. So off we went and, upon arriving near the address, I parked the car within five metres of the front door and pointed out where she should go. With a series of grunts, hand signals and the odd Malaysian word she told me to get the car closer to the front door, an impossible task as there were cars already parked on parking meters outside of the adders she wanted. When I tried to explain, she went into a flying rage, shouting and gesturing for me to move forward.

Not being used to this kind of behaviour, I got out of the car, walked around the back and opened the rear nearside passenger door and beckoned her out. She got out, still shouting and gesturing for as she made her way along the street to where she wanted to go.

*F**k this* I thought. I am not standing for that. So I left her there, drove back to New Zealand House, parked the car in the garage and went to see the boss. I told him what had happened, how I was not putting up with that kind of behaviour from anyone and, tossing him the car keys, I turned around and walked out never to see him or her again.

Once outside I found a phone box, called the agency and explained to them what had happened, after which time, I started to make my way home. When I got back, Jill was surprised to see me and, after relaying the story to her, I started to phone the other agencies to see if they had any suitable vacancies on their books. All said that they get in touch if anything suitable came up.

One called me straight back and said that a job was on their books for a corporate chauffeur at a Japanese Bank in the City of London if I was interested. Yes, of course I was. You see, back then if you worked for a bank in the City you knew it was going to be one of the better jobs around and especially a Japanese bank as the pay and working conditions were excellent. Having told the agency that I was keen to attend an interview they said they would send my CV.

It was about this time I decided that as Jill and I were really not that close any more it was about time I started to think about myself, so I decided to buy another motorcycle. This would be for me and just for me. Jill would never ride pillion again as her condition had got a lot worse and there was no way that she would be able to climb on board let alone be able to keep her balance.

One Saturday morning, I drove to the local motorcycle dealer in Carshalton and browsed the used stock. They had all manner of different motorcycles, from small commuter bikes right up to 1200cc monsters from BMW, Honda etc. I didn't want one as big as any of those, but I spotted a fairly new Honda VFR 750 RC sports tourer in the Honda sport racing colours of red, white, and blue, with low mileage. She looked absolutely gorgeous and was priced within my budget. *That's the one for me* I thought, as I left to go home and think it over. I had to find out how much the insurance, tax and servicing costs were going to be, but during the next few days all I could think about was that bike and how great it would be to get back riding again.

Having done my sums and got insurance quotes etc, I made up my mind to buy her if she was still available. The following weekend, I went to the bike shop on the bus knowing that if I liked what I saw I could take the bike straight home with me. I asked for a test ride, which was granted, and so with no further ado I set off through Carshalton to try her out. As soon as I pulled away and got my feet up on to the footrests I knew that I was going to buy her; what a well-balanced, powerful, easy to ride machine, probably the best in its class, and most certainly the best bike that I had ridden since the RE5. Once I returned to the bike shop we set about sealing the deal to buy her – as she had already been prepared to leave the shop it was just a formality of doing the paperwork, and then I was free to take her away.

Jill was totally belligerent about the whole affair, so I didn't go straight home, instead I took the bike for a ride to the top of Box Hill, in Tadworth, Surrey. Having got there I was feeling pretty chuffed with myself as I parked up and sat on a park bench at the side of the car park and admired the glorious machine that I had just purchased, in all her glory, on that beautiful sunny spring day. In March 2018 I spotted an identical one for sale at £59,999.

During this period, the job agency contacted me to say that the Japanese bank would like me to attend an interview as they liked my CV and thought that I would be just the kind of person that they were looking for. So I put on my suit and tie and made my way to the offices of Saito Bank, in Knightrider Street, London, EC4, a small block of offices located in between the Horn Public House and the Royal College of Arms. I was due to meet the personnel manager for my interview, a process that I always do well. I usually think that I am not likely to be successful and that helps me to be relaxed and be my natural self. Having signed in at the bank's security reception desk a telephone call was made to the personnel department and, shortly thereafter, I was met by the personnel manager herself. Little did I know at this time that she was, in fact, the only member of personnel staff employed by the bank. After the interview I made my way home and called the agency to let them know how it had gone.

A couple of days later I was called back for a second

interview at the bank to meet the person that I would be driving, if successful. It turned out to be an archetypal English City banker, a man of about fifty-five years old with wavy, grey hair who had obviously been in banking all his life and was now, at a guess, seeing out his final few years in the city in a lucrative position. I believed he was working with the Saito Bank to help them find their way into the London banking world as they were newly established as a wholly owned subsidiary of Saito Securities Europe PLC, located in much larger offices in Victoria Street, London SW1.

After the interview I was escorted off the premises by the personnel manager who didn't give anything away, it was very much a case of wait and see. As I walked outside the building a metallic brown Mercedes Benz S420 saloon car was parked directly by the main exit with the driver waiting beside it. The driver said that he was the bank's CEO's chauffeur and asked if I had been for the vacant chauffer position. "Yes," I said and we started a conversation about it. He told me how good the job was and how he hoped that I was successful with my application, why, I couldn't work out. He then went on to tell me how he had been asked to order a Mercedes Benz for the new director, but as he was not as senior as *his* boss the new man couldn't possibly be expected to have as good a car and a Mercedes Benz S300 had been ordered for him. What a stuck up snob I thought, it didn't matter to me what car I was going to drive the only thing that concerned me was getting the job in the first place.

As I was about to leave a Jaguar V12 pulled up behind the Mercedes and a slim, tall man, who was as it turns out was a lot younger than either the other man or me, alighted from the car. We shook hands and, after a brief conversation, I said my goodbyes and began the journey home. *How great it would be*, I thought, *if I got this job* – it was just what I was looking for.

Back at home the atmosphere was pleasant enough, but Jill wasn't really interested in hearing my thoughts. "As long as I had a job," she said, "that was the main thing." I called the agency to let them know how it had gone, and they said that as soon as they heard, either way, that they would let me know the bank's decision.

I spent the next couple of days taking Susie out for long walks and spending time getting to know the bike a bit better. Behind the house in Newstead Walk there was a small, council owned garage block where I kept my bike. The bank had insisted that, if successful with my application, I was to park the car overnight and at weekends in the garage and they would pay the weekly rent. But for now, it housed my bike.

On the Friday of that week I received a telephone call from the agency telling me that I had been successful in my application for the position of chauffeur with the Saito Bank and that I should receive an offer letter in the post that morning. I duly thanked them for their hard work and help in getting me the job, their 17½% commission of my basic annual salary probably made their day as much as getting the position made mine.

When the postman delivered the letters that morning a large, brown A4 sized envelope addressed to me, with the Saito Bank and its address franked in the top right-hand corner, was amongst the pile. As I sat down to open it and read the contents, feeling quite chuffed with myself, Jill said that she was taking Susie around to her mums and would be there for most of the day. Yet another disappointment that I had to put up with in my hour of triumph, a trait that I was to suffer a few more times in my life, but hey, who cares? I would enjoy the moment by myself if I had to. Sure enough, the letter inside the envelope made me an offer to join the bank in the position of chauffeur. If the terms and conditions were acceptable I was to call at my earliest convenience to arrange a start date, which I duly did.

I had about another week at home before I again made my way, suited and booted, by bus and tube to Blackfriars station and then on to the bank's offices where I signed in with security and was, once again, met by the personnel manager who arranged a photo pass for me that I was to show whenever asked. She then introduced me to the secretary who looked after the chairman and three other directors, a woman I was to work well with over the next ten years, and took me to meet with the director who I would be driving. After the pleasantries were dispensed with he told me that, in his opinion, due to my lack of experience (eh?), I was not his first choice, but he had been overruled by the banks company secretary, Mr Takahashi, who turned out to be a staunch ally for me in the future.

The principal that I was to drive, Mr Pickford, liked my CV and the fact that I lived a lot closer than another guy I was up against. He felt that this was important as I would not have so far to drive home. Furthermore, he told me that he was a terrible back-seat driver and would, when necessary, instruct me to go into whichever lane that he wanted to go in, what route to take etc. *Well, that's just great*, I thought, looking forward to working for another man like Sir Bryan. However, this man was the complete opposite.

I was then taken down to the chauffeur room to officially meet the other two guys. Nigel who, as it turns out, was so up himself it was hard to believe that he could be taken seriously by anybody (which he wasn't by the way), and Christopher Collet who, from that moment onwards, was to turn out to be one of my best friends to this day. We hit it off straight away, although we had one, and only one, slight disagreement that was over nothing, indeed we remain the firmest of friends.

I was taken to the NCP car park in Queen Victoria Street by Nigel and Chris, just a couple of minutes' walk from the office, where I was introduced to a brand new silver Mercedes Benz S300 saloon. We looked it over and each of us recorded the car telephone number, I was given all the relevant phone numbers necessary for the job and proceeded to store them on the phone. As the day went on I gradually met a few of the other people that I would be seeing on a daily basis from then on: David the post room messenger; Peter the maintenance man who was sent over from Saito Europe to look after the building, calling in specialists if he couldn't carry out particular repairs; the three chauffeurs from Saito Europe, Thomas, Nigel's older brother, Paul and Terry; various security personnel, and Miss Rawlings the directors' secretary.

Personal mobile phones were relatively new and, consequently, very expensive so the chauffeurs were issued with pagers to be kept with them and switched on at all times, so that we were contactable as and when needed. Miss Rawlings gave me a rough itinerary of the boss's movements for the following week every Friday afternoon and updated me on a daily basis every morning when we arrived at the office at about 9.00 am.

When it was time to take the boss home Miss Rawlings gave me ten minutes warning, so I had plenty of time to get the car and have it parked outside the office ready to go. Having done this I sat in the car and waited for the boss, and waited and waited and waited.

*What's going on here?* I thought. I called Miss Rawlings after ten minutes to find out what was happening. She couldn't update me much and was frustrated herself about having to wait until the boss made a move as she always liked to get away on time to catch her train home from Liverpool Street Station, a good fifteen minute walk away. Eventually, the boss came down and got in the car and we set off. He had given me his home address earlier in the day I looked it up in the *A-Z* street atlas of Greater London (there was no satnav in those days, everything was done by map ) and knew exactly where he lived. I had a picture in my mind of the best route to go by, but was I in for a shock. The actual route that we took was nowhere near the way that I had taken just a couple of years earlier with Sir Bryan who lived not that far from this new boss, the route should have been almost identical after about the first mile or so.

As we set off he was right about one thing, he was definitely a back-seat driver, calling out which roads to go down, where to turn off, double back if we hit traffic, etc. *Crikey!* I thought, *this is going to be a challenge if every journey is going to be like this*. Well, after a while, I started to pre-empt him, using my own initiative I would take slightly different roads to the ones he expected to take, this worked well until the inevitable happened and one of the streets I took was blocked for about ten minutes. He was not happy and kept throwing in remarks like, "Oh, that's done it, now I will be late for the squash club," or "I am going out with my wife for dinner tonight, you might have to take me straight to the restaurant now."

*F**k you*! I thought. We were never late home once in all the years that I drove him.

# Chapter Nine

A really funny event one morning put paid to his back-seat driving for good, thank goodness. We were headed towards Tolworth, in Surrey, just a few miles from the boss's home in Epsom, being on a particularly busy section of Kingston Road in the early morning rush hour and approaching the A3 into Wandsworth. The two lanes of traffic had slowed down to a snail's pace and, having glanced up from behind the newspaper that he was reading, he suddenly shouted out, "Quick, go into the left hand lane."

"What, are you sure?" I knew exactly where we would end up, and quite obviously he didn't, so dutifully I pulled into the left hand lane and promptly stopped...at a bus stop, much to the amusement of the queue of people standing in line waiting for their bus. Turning my head slightly towards him I politely enquired, "Are you making the rest of your journey by bus today sir?"

By now a bus was pulling into the bus stop and tooting his horn for us to move out of the way, and with the queue of people wondering what was going on, I glanced in the rear-view mirror and have never seen a man look so sheepish and embarrassed before. "No, no," he said. "I had better let you plan the route from now on." As I pulled back out into the mainstream traffic, he shrunk down in his seat and hid behind his newspaper. Sure enough, that was the last time he was to back-seat drive with me.

As the office was located on the edge of the Square Mile of the City of London, the boss hardly ever used me during the day as it was almost always easier and quicker for him to walk to external meetings or lunch engagements. That meant the prospect of kicking my heels every day, once again, but not so. Peter had rigged up a TV aerial on the roof of the building and fed a cable down to his room on the other side of the basement floor from the chauffeurs' room and could now watch TV. So we asked if he could install a cable splitter into his feed and run a cable across and on top of the suspended ceiling tiles to our room and he duly obliged. The chauffeurs' room now had a TV feed and we three chauffeurs clubbed together and bought a portable TV and video recorder.

At the start of my third week at Saito, a courier company started to drop off and collect documents and small parcels to the bank once in the morning and again in the early afternoon. They were delivered by my other best mate, Steve Ripley. He was about the same age as me and talked the same language, we hit it off immediately and, just like Chris, he has remained the closest and firmest of friends to this day.

After introducing himself to us, and with a mug of tea in his hand, we started to have a bit of a chinwag, during which Steve commented on a TV drama that had been on the night before about a roving gigolo who wormed his way into a middle-aged woman's affections as her husband seemed to be more interested going up and down the river in his motor cruiser than he did his wife. The more Steve told us about the story the more Chris and I laughed, not because of the TV show so much, but because, without knowing it, he was describing Nigel and his brother, Thomas, who had a boat between them. The description fitted them perfectly; a blazer and naval captain's hat was their clothing of choice when on the boat, and they were basically a couple of inverted snobs thinking they were something that they both were definitely not. Our laughter got even louder as Nigel realised what was going on and would comment dryly every now and again, "Oh very funny." At one point Chris and I stumbled out of the chauffeurs' room as we couldn't take it any more. Steve was baffled by all this until we told him later and he, like us, almost collapsed in fits of laughter. Nigel never lived it down although I must say I never suspected his wife of going off with a gigolo of any kind.

Our days were not particularly busy. After arriving at the

office with or without our respective bosses – they may have been on holiday, or at meetings elsewhere – a routine started to take shape. A cup of tea or coffee would be made and taken to a post room worktop, some 20 feet (7m) from the chauffeurs' room, where myself, Chris, Nigel, Peter and David, the post room man, would spend around an hour or so putting the world to rights – except for David who would continue to sort the morning's mail. These morning get-togethers were the highlight of the day as Peter was the joker in the pack. In another life he could have been an entertainer as he was always coming out with hilarious wisecracks and tall stories that had us in stitches.

The only thing that spoiled it was the a**hole of a premises manager, Derek Brown, a middle-aged failure of a man who thought that he something special. Well, I am here now, mister, to tell you how wrong you were. Derek was a pathetic excuse for a man who would bully David, who was not himself the brain of Britain but nonetheless it was not necessary for him to treat the man the way he did. In fact, a couple of years later Mr Brown brought in a new post room supervisor, William, over the head of David, needless to say the two never got on.

William was straight out of the same mould as Mr Brown, pleasant to your face but would stab you in the back given half a chance. He was extremely jealous of the chauffeurs, as was Mr Brown. All they saw us doing was sitting with our feet up in our room for most of the day but what they didn't realise, as I told Mr Brown one day, was that we worked in the evenings, until God only knows what time, waiting for our bosses who would attend a function most nights of the week. As I pointed out to Mr Brown he would be socialising with his family or friends after leaving the office at a reasonable 5 o'clock in the afternoon.

I felt sorry for Chris as he was the CEO's driver and, as Japanese custom dictated, when the boss went out for a meal or a karaoke night all the male Japanese staff junior to him would be expected to join him for the evening. What's wrong with that? I hear you thinking. Well, I will tell you…

Those evenings would go on until about midnight, usually three or four times a week. The CEO was in London on his own, his wife and children being back home in Japan as the kids were still in full-time education, and when it was time to leave he would offer his friend, and company secretary, Mr Takahashi a lift home. The same courtesy was then offered to the senior members of staff, right down to the most junior member of the team. They would all be offered a lift. If there were too many the rest would be allowed to get a black cab home. This meant, of course, that after dropping off the CEO who lived near to the Albert Hall in Kensington, Chris would then head towards West London to drop off Mr Takahashi, then go to God knows where to drop the others off in turn. This usually meant that poor Chris would often not get home until well after 1.00 am. Think about that Mr Brown, will ya!

Nigel and I had a much easier time of it as Nigel drove the elderly chairman who wasn't into that kind of thing, and I drove an upper-middle-class Englishman who definitely wasn't into that kind of thing. Chris suffered this until, some years later, his boss went back to Japan and he was transferred over to Saito Europe.

Steve christened the chauffeurs' room 'The Lodge' which amused us all greatly and the name stuck forevermore much to the dismay of Nigel who, we began to realise, had no sense of humour at all. Ah Nigel, what a snob he turned out to be. He lived with his wife and son in a pokey little terraced house in Mortlake, South West London but referred to it as a little 'bijou' cottage with a brook running at the end of the garden. When he mentioned this one day Steve said he knew exactly where he was talking about as one of Steve's more, how shall I put this, benefit scrounging, scumbag neighbours, had a daughter who, it turns out, took a dump one night on the bonnet of Nigel's Mercedes, charming! As for the brook, it turned out to be an overflow from the local industrial estate filled with all sorts of rubbish, supermarket trollies etc. Now here is a typical example of Peter's wit; upon hearing about when Nigel moved into his so-called bijou cottage with its waterway at the bottom of the garden he quipped, "What, did P&O move you in?" This remark, to this day, has Steve and I rolling about with laughter but I suspect you had to be there to appreciate the irony in it.

One day Nigel made the error of calling an estate agent from the post room telephone. During the conversation we overheard him say that he was looking for something new and it had to have a swimming pool and be under £125k. Big mistake, as a couple of hours later Peter took a telephone call on said post room phone for Nigel from the estate agent he had called earlier asking if he could call them back. Peter, playing dumb as to who they wanted to talk to as they referred to Nigel by his surname saying he had told them he was the bank's operations manager, said, "Oh, you mean Nige." Peter then told them that he was just a messenger and had been sent down to the local shops to buy 'bog rolls'. Funnily enough, Nigel never heard from that estate agent again!

As time went on, our mornings progressed into what we referred to as the 'Breakfast Club'. The chauffeurs, plus Peter, a young secretary nicknamed Foxy, and David clubbed together to buy hot dogs, rolls and onions so that we could all have breakfast. Chris, being an ex-chef, did the honours of preparing and cooking the dogs for us. On one memorable morning, William came in a bit earlier than normal right at the end of feeding time, enviously eyeing the last dog. Chris said, "One left, who wants it? Nobody, right I will have it then," and promptly threw it in the bin. That brought fits of laughter from us all gathered around as we could see that William was dying to have it.

We hadn't really thought the boiled onion bit through properly though as Chris had cooked them underneath the air conditioning unit which subsequently drew the smell up into the system. For a while, anywhere you went in the building the smell of onion could be detected, in itself quite amusing as it baffled staff looking around for the source of the smell, ha-ha.

Typically, William complained to Mr Brown who told us to stop having our homemade breakfast in the mail room – something shop bought was okay but cooking was not permitted. "Well, that's okay," we told him and promptly moved into Peter's maintenance room instead. Mr Brown had no authority over the maintenance room as that was Saito Europe territory and they allowed use of a microwave oven and a grill hob so the maintenance man could have hot food, as and when he wanted.

There were many more such stories from this time, but if I were to recollect them all to you my life story would go on and on. However, a couple more I just have to mention. Occasionally, a motorcycle courier would deliver urgent letters to the bank. Sometimes he would stay for a cuppa and we got to know him reasonably well. He was a typical biker and looked filthy dirty all the time. His hands were always stained with greasy residue and there was probably enough old engine oil under his fingernails to lubricate a lawn mower but, having said that, he was pleasant enough. We called him Moxie, not knowing if that was his real name or not, and he seemed to respond to it. On one occasion, the bank held its annual golf tournament at Liphook Golf Club, near Guildford, in Surrey. All the Japanese players had transport except for one, so Moxie volunteered to take this particular gentleman on the proviso that he could take part in the competition. The organiser, Thomas, agreed and that suited everybody nicely, except that Moxie couldn't play golf and his mode of transport was an old MK 3 Ford Escort that was as dirty and greasy as he was.

I didn't witness it but the story of the day went thus… Moxie, not being the best educated of men, had actually gone out the night before and had a skin full of beer, fallen asleep in the car and vomited over himself. He then woke up late and didn't have time to go home and change so turned up at the man's house looking like a bag of s**t. When Moxie picked up the Japanese man all was not well from the start as, before the passenger could get into the car, Moxie had to move various bits of bike or car engine off the front seat before it could be sat on. Worse was to follow for the poor Japanese passenger as halfway to the venue Moxie had to tap him up for £20 for petrol as the car was nearly out of fuel and Moxie was skint.

Once everybody had arrived and met in the clubhouse with the Japanese resplendent in outfits that would not have looked out of place at any professional tournament, lots were drawn to see who would partner who and rules agreed on such things as the longest drive, nearest the pin etc. Thomas had been tasked with arranging the various trophies for the day and, as he was pretty good at the longest drive, the cup he bought for that, in the hope that he would win, was more significant than the Champions League Winners trophy. The winner's trophy, however, was so small that it would fit into a trouser pocket.

And so the day's play began. The course was in pristine condition, the fairways and greens having been lovingly prepared by the green keepers. All was going well until it was time for Moxie to tee off. He could barely recognise one end of the club from another let alone know which one to use. With a bit of help from his partner, he pushed his tee firmly into the ground, placed his ball on top and took an almighty swing with a driver. Amazingly, it connected with the ball and drove it straight into the woods at the side of the first fairway. Oh dear, oh dear, oh dear! After the others had teed off Moxie went in pursuit of his ball that was somewhere in the woods. Rumour has it that all that could be heard from the woods was a club being used like a chainsaw with enough expletives to do Roy 'Chubby' Brown proud. After a little while, a ball came flying through the air out of the woods to land in the middle of the fairway with Moxie declaring that he had only made three strokes to get out, yeah right!

Thomas was playing reasonably well, but one of the other players in his group noticed that he had started with one ball, ie a Dunlop, but was now playing with a Slazenger.

This was entirely against all the rules and etiquette of golf. To cover up his obvious embarrassment at being caught cheating he claimed to have a headache and was confused. He said that he would retire from the day's play and went to the clubhouse, ashamed and defeated, ha-ha. Even worse was to come, however, and inevitably it involved our man Moxie. You see, as he was no golfer, he had proceeded to tear lumps out of the greens as he was attempting to put the ball into the hole to finish. This didn't go unnoticed by the powers that be and the club secretary came out to have a word with the players and Moxie in particular. Well, the inevitable happened and a big argument ensued, resulting in the participants being ordered to stop playing and abandon the day's play. The whole tournament was cancelled and Moxie legged it quicker than a rat up a drainpipe. The consequences for Thomas's involvement were to continue for some time to come, and I don't believe he was to organise a day's golf for Saito ever again.

By now, my home life had deteriorated to the point where I was seriously considering moving out of the matrimonial home, a decision that I had put off long enough out of loyalty to what Jill had gone through in the past, but it was now quite clear to us both that the end of our marriage was close. We had drifted apart and the gulf between us was immense. I was more than happy to be spending my time at work and didn't mind getting home late in the evening a few nights a week. Jill had usually gone to bed by the time I got in and the first thing I did was to take Susie out for her late night walk. After fifteen minutes or so we would return to home and Susie would get into her basket. I would make a cup of tea and watch a bit of telly before retiring to the bed in the spare room. This had been the norm for a long time, primarily because I was up early and didn't want to disturb Jill, and, besides, it didn't feel right to be sharing the same bed under the circumstances.

Jill was spending most of her time either at her mother's or with her friends and wasn't at all content to spend her time with me anymore. Weekends were worse and I found myself going out with Susie for ever-longer walks, going further and further away to avoid being at home alone or in an uncomfortable atmosphere.

To be honest, I wanted to be a father more than anything else. We had discussed with various health professionals the possibility of adoption, but because of Jill's medical condition we were advised against pursuing it. In my mind, the only way that was going to happen was if I split with Jill. If I was lucky enough to meet somebody else then maybe, just maybe, my dream of becoming a father would happen. So, in the late spring of 1990, I packed up my belongings and told Jill that I was leaving. Although I think she was quite shocked that it had actually happened, I am reasonably sure in my own mind that she was not at all surprised.

I went to stay at my friend Chris's flat in Docklands, East London, for a night of two, before moving on to stay with my brother Paul, Lyn and the children – Jamie and Emma aged ten and eight respectively, in Bracknell, Berkshire, not that far from where Mum was living in Ascot. I don't think Lyn was too happy with the arrangement and, after a couple of weeks, I managed to rent a one bedroom, ground floor flat in a small block of flats in Carshalton Road, in Sutton, Surrey.

I met with Jill a couple of times after I left her to discuss what we were going to do about getting a divorce and selling our home. I agreed Jill could say that my unreasonable behaviour in the last five years had led to the breakdown of our marriage so that we could push for a quickie divorce. This we did and, in the late autumn, six months after we first applied, we were granted a 'quickie' divorce. We had by this time put our house up for sale and, after a couple of months, it sold and we split the proceeds. Unlike some people I know, who have cheated their ex-wives out of their due entitlement when their marriage has ended in divorce, I was determined to do the right thing by Jill. Having redeemed the mortgage and paid the estate agent their fees, solicitor's fees, etc, we both walked away with fifty per cent of the remainder, £12,000 each, so I had enough money to put the rental deposit down on the flat.

I was not entirely happy but I was glad that I had made the break from Jill and determined to build a new life for myself. One unpleasant piece of news was that Jill had decided to have Susie put to sleep. Her mother had told her that if she were to stay with her after the house was sold Susie would have to go.

I suppose, under the circumstances, I could understand why Jill did it but I was angry with her for some time afterwards. Susie was old and needed a lot of care, so maybe it was kinder to have her put down.

I had become aware of a young woman who worked in the leasing department that occupied the whole of the ground floor office at the Saito Bank. She sometimes came down to the post room to collect or deliver mail, but we didn't make much conversation until she started to cover the switchboard and reception area on the directors' floor. I would regularly pop up to see my boss's secretary at lunchtime but it was primarily to have a few words with the young lady in question, Jacqui.

Towards the end of January 1991 during one of my visits to the directors' floor, Jacqui asked me if I would like to go to her birthday party at her family home in Bowers Gifford, in Essex. "Yes, I would love to," I told her. She gave me the details of exactly where and when and I went off happily.

Later, one of her work colleagues asked me if I had been invited to Jacqui's party and if I knew exactly how old she was.

"I'm not sure," I replied. "About twenty-six?"

"Oh, no," came back the answer. "She told me that it was going to be her nineteenth. She is only eighteen." What! No! Then I couldn't go as I was approaching my thirty-fifth birthday that March. Jacqui surely wouldn't want an old fogey like me at her birthday party, she would want friends of her own age. So I went to see her and told her that I was sorry but I felt that I was too old to come along to her party and would have to decline. She said that my age didn't matter to her and that she wanted me to come, so that's exactly what I did and a bloody good time I had as well. So good, in fact, that I was more than a little bit tipsy as I headed home late that night after the party.

With the help of Chris, I found a newly-built one bedroom flat for sale in at Green Pond Close, in Walthamstow E17. The old football stadium that had been on the site had been torn down and redeveloped into a small estate of low rise buildings containing one and two bedroom flats.

Once settled in I was reasonably happy, but had to quickly learn how to cook as I didn't want to live on takeaways. I also had to learn how to do the laundry and iron my shirts for work, so I didn't look scruffy. During the week everything was fine as I would get home from work relatively late, have a quick light supper then go to bed. It was the weekends that were a problem as I was lucky, or unlucky considering on your point of view, that I never worked at the weekend so consequently I found Saturdays and Sundays long and dull. I had my own car, a Renault 5 GT Turbo three-door hatchback finished in black metallic paint, a proper boy racer's car of the day, ha-ha. I would go over to see Jacqui and we would go out somewhere for a few hours, usually to a pub somewhere close by.

Her father, Roy, was dubious of my intentions for a long time. In fact, for many, many months he referred to me to Jax as 'your mate'. He would say to her, 'Your mate is on the phone' or 'Your mate has just pulled up in his car,' not calling me Brian until he decided that he wanted to. I guess he saw this thirty-something divorced man lurking around his nineteen-year-old daughter as something of a predator. Well, how wrong he was; from the moment I first saw Jacqui I knew that I was going to marry her.

We had been seeing each other for a while, and things were moving along well even to the point that we were making early morning phone calls to each other before we left for work, albeit that we were going to be seeing each other at the office in a couple of hours. Jacqui was always keen for our relationship to be kept as quiet as possible while at work, even to the point whenever there was a function at the bank she would stay with her friends and not come over and say hello, and never allowed me to take her for a pub lunch etc. Why? I don't know and, in all the years that we have been together, she has never told me the reason. Outside of work we were getting along really well; we were seeing each other most nights of the week, and I have to say that I was really smitten.

After a while, and with the summer fast approaching, we planned to go to Newquay in Cornwall for a week's holiday. Great, but how to do it? Jax was sure that her dad would not be happy about her going away with a man she had only known for six months, so a plan to keep him happy had to be concocted. And in stepped Jax's best friend from school, Danni.

At that time, Danni worked at NatWest Bank's offices on the south side of the River Thames close to Blackfriars Bridge. Together they come up with a plan; firstly, having decided where Jax and I were going to stay, they asked the hotel to fax confirmation of a one week stay on the agreed date, in a double room, to be sent to Danni at the bank. Then cutting off the top of the fax paper that showed the time and date and, most importantly, the hotel's fax number, Danni then doctored the contents to show that two single rooms had been booked, sent the new fax to Jax at Saito Bank and, hey presto, it looked like a genuine booking for such had been made, thus keeping Roy happy if he should argue the point about us not having separate rooms. Very devious of them both but, as they say in the Dordogne, *fait accompli*.

At the start of our holiday I drove to collect Jax from her dad's home in Bowers Gifford and we set off in my Renault 5 GT Turbo for the 300 mile plus journey that would take us down to Cornwall. With a comfort break and a fill-up of coffee for us and petrol for the car it took us about six hours to cover the journey.

While there we had a great time visiting many of the local attractions and just generally enjoying being away together. The weather was quite good as I remember, so all in all it was a pleasant week for us both, the first of many such holidays that Jax and I were to spend together over the coming years.

Jax was becoming ever more frustrated living with her dad. He expected her to help around the house with the domestic chores; washing, ironing, cleaning, shopping, etc, but Jax was loathe to do any of this, and caused a problem between them. In the end, I think to preserve some kind of peace between them, they just looked out for themselves, it wasn't going to last though, and something had to give.

Work was going well for us both now that my English boss at Saito had gone elsewhere and, as Chris had transferred to Saito Europe, I was now driving the new CEO of the bank. I was still there with Nigel who continued to drive the chairman. Chris and I would meet up at a small bakery in Robert Street, St John's Wood, every morning at around 7.00 am for a cup of tea, bacon roll, and a chat before we set off to collect our respective bosses who lived in the NW1 area and take them into the office, something we continued to do for quite some time.

Time was going by, and summer turned to autumn which in turn had started to give way to winter. I was invited to Christmas dinner at Roy's house mainly, I felt, to keep the numbers up along with Roy's younger brother, another Brian, and his wife Jenny. Jax's older brother David who was at that time was stationed in Poole with the Royal Marines stayed away, preferring to do his own thing. I have to say that I enjoyed that Christmas, mainly I think because I had spent a couple on my own since my split with Jill and to be in a family group again was comforting.

Jax and I were now getting serious about each other. We bought each other about a dozen quality Christmas presents that must have seemed a bit over the top to the others as we both had a pile of presents stacked up.

I was allowed to stay for a couple of nights over the Christmas holidays, in the front bedroom, of course, no sharing a room together under Roy's roof. Soon it was over, and things went back to normal, me going back to my one bedroom flat in Walthamstow, Jax staying in Bowers Gifford.

New Year came and went, and I returned to work. In

February, it snowed heavily. In fact, the late winter of 1992 was one of the worst that Essex had seen for many years.

Jax was becoming increasingly unhappy living with her dad, and I could tell that she would be better off away from the family home. So I made a bold decision and said that, if she felt it was right thing, she was welcome to move in with me. She made the decision to do so quite quickly and, pretty soon, we found ourselves living as a couple.

God knows what her dad thought about it, but it never concerned me, so I neither asked nor thought about it. Actually, I think it suited the pair of them because, even though they were father and daughter, they never really knew or got on with each other at this point of time, but that's a story for another time, perhaps.

Jax found it quite easy to adapt and settled in quickly, helped no doubt by the fact that it was just as easy to travel into work from Walthamstow as it had been from Pitsea.

Towards the end of the year, Jax started to plan her 21st birthday party and asked Roy if she could have it at the family home in Bowers Gifford. Roy agreed and Jax got stuck in to what she does best; organising and planning. She arranged everything by herself, it was no good asking or relying on me to do any of it as that's not my thing at all.

She arranged for invitation cards to be printed, made quite a number of compilation music CDs of the songs that she had grown up with and liked. I thought this was strange as Roy's taste in music was definitely not hers. Something that she had to tolerate over the years was his playing the recordings of most of the jazz greats played endlessly on his reel to reel tape machine, or having to listen to BBC Radio 2 on a Sunday evening. She worked out the food and drink requirements, and the thing that I think that she was most proud of doing, organising decorations for the house, not just the usual shop bought, banners and balloons, oh no, Jax sourced out a supplier to make an arch out of royal blue, and white, latex balloons. I have to say that it did look stunning when it was placed at one end of the large sitting room in Roy's house for all to admire.

On the evening of the party the guests arrived with presents and good wishes. It was a picture to see Jax's beaming smile as she graciously accepted the gifts. There was a mix of family, Jax's friends and friends of Roy who had known Jax from when she was a baby. Everyone was enjoying themselves until, all of a sudden, there was a commotion in the kitchen.

Roy had tripped over something and, stretching his arm out to steady himself, had put his right arm through the glass of the back door. It was quite a nasty cut and blood was pouring out of the wound. A melee of people gathered round in an attempt to help out, but it was a case of too many different people, although well-intentioned, trying to deal with the situation.

Eventually matters calmed down, and Roy was taken to Basildon Hospital A&E by one of the guests, Pete, a friend that Roy had known since they were at primary school together. Roy had damaged a tendon which meant that he would have restricted use of a couple of fingers on his right hand for the rest of his life. As you can imagine, this event put a bit of a damper on things and, although the party didn't end there, people did start to drift away.

Well, it was quite late by this time so maybe if the accident hadn't happened when it did the party would have started to wind down to its natural end anyway. After almost everybody had left and there still being music playing, Jax's friend from work, Sam, who was quite tipsy by now suddenly grabbed hold of me and made me dance with her. It was not altogether an unpleasant experience but one that I would not be keen to endure again. I have never been much of a dancer, in fact, I find it quite embarrassing. I know my limitations in life and try to stay within my comfort zone of which this was not one.

Roy returned home after midnight, after the party had finished, sporting his right arm in a sling. He let us know what the hospital had said and how he should do this and not do that in an effort to aid his recovery. Whether he did heed the advice that he was given only he knew. Eventually, there was just the three of us left, saying goodnight and leaving the clearing up until the morning I was again directed to the spare room at the front of the house. I can just hear, even now, Roy thinking, *No fraternising in my house.* Quite rightly, I suppose.

Before Christmas 1992, I had suggested to Jax that as part of her celebrations for turning twenty-one, we take a holiday in Orlando, Florida in the spring. For me, having been a couple of times before, I had found this to be a great time of year to go. The climate was not as harsh as it is in the summer months, with the temperature in the mid-seventies and without as many rainy days that can happen due to the high humidity and temperatures in the summer.

Jax thought that was a great idea and then left it up to me to do all the planning, ha-ha, so I booked a fourteen night package holiday with a rental car thrown in, staying at the International Inn on International Drive, Orlando. Now, it's called the Rosen Inn and is one of the most popular budget hotels in the area. Back then, International Drive was where all the popular, affordable hotels were located and was dominated by British tourists for most of the year. The whole area had cheap and nasty gift shops in abundance selling all kinds of knick-knacks such as Mickey Mouse T-shirts, snow globes, keyrings, pens and pencils. The Beltz outlet area at the northern end of the road had stores owned by the big designer brands, Reebok, Nike, Timberland etc who sold their manufactured seconds off cheaply, and I do mean cheaply, sometimes up to 70% of the regular retail price. Although the goods were classed as seconds they were virtually impossible to tell apart from the originals so these goods sold exceptionally well and we Brits snapped them up.

On our first day, I suggested to Jax that we pop out and get a sandwich at Denny's Restaurant that was located virtually next door to the hotel. She agreed and we walked the minute or two it took to reach the restaurant. It was a typical American basic food establishment, one that we have all seen in a million American TV programmes, nothing fancy just practical and clean with the archetypal waitress ready to pounce as soon as eye contact was made. Having perused the menu we decided on a ham sandwich each, ha that's a laugh.

We both got caught out here, as an American sandwich is not like an English one. It is about three times the thickness, toasted and served up with a large portion of French fries and salad to boot. Jax couldn't believe her eyes and we both laughed at what we had ordered.

Over the next couple of weeks we crammed it all in; Disney World, Universal Studios, Sea World and so on. Eating out at many different places all added to the great experience that we were having. We had a really good time and, before we knew it, we were packing up our suitcases, bringing to an end the first of many trips to Florida. In fact, Orlando and Florida were to play a huge part in our lives.

We really liked the Orlando area and decided that, when we got back home, we would book again for the following year, only this time we would want to rent one of the many privately owned villas located in and around Disneyworld, namely the boroughs of Kissimmee and Davenport which are both within a fifteen minute drive away from the major theme parks and downtown entertainment areas.

We booked a lovely three bedroom, two bathroom villa with a pool, via an internet company that matched up owners and renters. The villa was located near an area called Four Corners in Davenport, and the company was called Florida Choice – remember the name – and when going through the booking process we found it to be easy and straight forward.

We booked our holiday for a couple of weeks after the Easter holidays knowing that the number of tourists would be fewer as the kids would be back in school by then and that would make it not only slightly cheaper, but the theme parks would be less crowded.

This second holiday was much better than the first because when you are in a villa there is no need to vacate the room by a particular time, and return once the cleaners have been, and you can come and go as you please and relax in and around the swimming pool. In mid-April the weather suited both Jax and me as neither of us like the heat, sunbathing is definitely not our thing.

We hired a car, an absolute must in Orlando, as public transport is practically non-existent. The villa was located about an hour's drive from the main international airport MCO. On the few days of our two week holiday that we didn't fancy a theme park we explored the area during the late morning after I had made breakfast, later stopping somewhere for a coffee or having a late lunch before returning to the villa and enjoying the rest of the day in and around the pool, usually with a beer for me and a soft drink for Jax. Occasionally, we would fire up the BBQ and sit and have that as the day gave way to night.

As we were doing okay financially due to the long hours at work that I was doing, we decided to have nice holidays, as and when we could, to recharge the batteries as the saying goes. In the autumn of 1993 I booked a holiday to the Dominican Republic via the Teletext holiday service – Google it! The hotel would be allocated upon arrival on the island. There had been stories in the national press about an outbreak of dysentery in many hotels on the island and I knew that we had to be careful where we stayed but we needn't have worried because we had been booked into a German-run TUI all-inclusive resort hotel, which I have to say was very nice indeed.

We had a great holiday there, spoiled on the last couple of days by a party of Brits who were loud and brash with unruly kids who had obviously been taken out of school as this was term time, wore football shirts and made a right nuisance of themselves! Still, it was only for a couple of days. The flight home was not that good either as the airline was Monarch and, if any of you remember travelling with them around about this time, you can sympathise with me when I tell you about the size of the seats in economy; very small. I had to squeeze myself into the seat and practically stay put until we got back to London's Gatwick Airport (LGW).

While I am on the subject of Caribbean holidays, our next venture to this part of the world was to Jamaica, a place I had always wanted to visit mainly because of the song 'Montego Bay' recorded by Bobby Bloom, a hit in September 1970. It conjured up a picture of an island paradise, but the reality could not have been more different and what an utter disappointment it was.

We had a straightforward flight to Jamaica from LGW, and we actually landed at Montego Bay airport, a good start. I was excited and eager to see the place after nearly a quarter of a century waiting to do so. Having cleared customs and with luggage in tow we were directed to the coach that was to take us to the Holiday Inn Resort, Montego Bay. The first experience of Jamaica for anyone is to fend off the constant barrage from the local baggage boys, coach drivers et al who continuously ask, "Do you want any smoke man!" Well, no actually, but I am sure that many people do.

Having secured the luggage in the coach and with the holiday rep perched at the front by the driver we set off. Firstly, we drove through the palm tree fringed archway that proclaims 'Welcome to Montego Bay' then turned west away from the town the few miles to the hotel. And what a lovely hotel it turned out to be, located right on the beach with the Caribbean sea lapping up to the edge of the immaculately manicured gardens where on many a night after dinner in the open air restaurant Jacqui and I would watch the sun go down with a drink or two.

Across the road from the hotel, partially hidden from view by mature trees, was a small upmarket collection of jewellery, clothes and general shops which we took a look around one day out of curiosity. While looking at the jewellers front window display Jax spotted a diamond and emerald bracelet that she immediately took a shine to. She wanted to know more about it so we ventured inside and made enquiries. The shop assistant could not have been more helpful and, after showing it to Jax and allowing her to try it on, she gave her the number and carat value of all the precious stones, oh and the price $600.

Knowing that her dad knew a jeweller, Jax telephoned her dad and gave him the details to pass on to his friend to see if it was worth the money. Roy said to call him back in a few days and he would have the answer from his friend, so that's what we did. Not only did Roy's friend say it was a reasonable price, but it would have cost twice as much in the UK.

That made up her mind, and the next day we went back to the shop and bought it. Having had it valued a few years ago for insurance purposes it is now worth about £5000 and permanently lives in our home safe.

We looked at going on a couple of excursions from the hotel and chose three; the Red Stripe cruise, a half day trip to Montego Bay, and a day trip to Dunns River Falls. First was the Red Stripe cruise; a large catamaran was the vessel of the day and took a party of about eighty people to one of the tiny islands a few miles offshore for a BBQ lunch. It was, supposedly, where some of the Cadbury's Flake TV adverts had been filmed. I have to say that it was one of the most beautiful places I have ever seen, made even more special by the ocean currents coming from two different directions when the tide comes in to join forces in the lagoon, how cool is that!

The much-anticipated trip to Montego Bay was one of the biggest let downs of my life. The coach, well, minibus actually, collected us from the hotel at about 9.00 am and drove via a couple of other hotels on the way, collecting other tourists, before continuing the short drive to the centre of Montego Bay. We were dropped off by a small row of select, expensive shops and told to report back by 12.00 pm lunchtime.

On the drive through the town I was not at all impressed. My image of an idyllic little Caribbean town with brightly painted wooden houses was not how it was in reality. It was more of a shanty town, in fact, with overcrowded roads and hordes of locals going about their daily business. The river that runs through the city was practically dry and was so full of rubbish that it stank. We were so disappointed that we made our way back to the minibus and sat inside and waited until the others returned and couldn't wait to get out of the place. We hoped that Dunns River Falls would be better, and boy was it.

Again, we were collected at the hotel, this time by a larger coach-type minibus, and were driven about fifty miles along the north coast of the island taking in a few local villages along the way. We stopped for a Red Stripe and Jerk chicken/pork delicacy at a roadside café which just so happened to be owned by a member of the driver's family. Still, good luck to them. It was a welcome addition to the official trip, a trip I might add that was thoroughly enjoyed by all.

One last thing to mention, as we are all only too well aware, the island of Jamaica is financially poor compared to many other countries, but what is worth taking note of is how immaculately dressed the children are in their brightly-coloured uniforms of blue, red or green tops, white shirts or blouses, shorts and skirts of grey or black with polished black shoes. They can be seen along the roadside travelling on foot to and from school in the morning and late afternoon carrying their books in their arms. Nearly all of them get excited when a busload of tourists drive by. The children wave and smile the most engaging and delightful of smiles giving the outward appearance of happiness towards their fellow human beings.

Jax and I did go back for a second time and spent a quiet, relaxing ten days out of season at an American-run hotel which, not being quite such fun as the previous time, did have its moments mainly when we tried water skiing offshore. Not being very interested in it I gave it a go but was utterly useless at it even to the point that as soon as I stood up, wallop! Down I would go and so gave up fairly soon after starting. Jax, on the other hand, proved to be a revelation, not only did she get up on the skis first time but managed to stay up for quite a time. Beginner's luck I have always said, ha-ha.

Once back home from this holiday, Jax and I were beginning to realise that we had a future with each other and maybe we should buy a house together. We wanted to move further eastwards and, after doing our homework regarding the logistics of travelling into central London, me by car as I was still chauffeuring and Jax by public transport, we found a lovely, newly-built three bedroom semi-detached house on the airfield estate near to Elm Park in Hornchurch. The estate was so called because the area had one of the most important frontline RAF fighter bases during World War II from which Spitfire and Hurricane squadrons were scrambled to go and intercept the might of the Luftwaffe during the Battle of Britain

The house was one of a pair of semi-dethatched houses that were located in Maybank Avenue, Elm Park, backing on to Scotts Primary School. We lived there for about five years and all was well except for a gang of teenagers that would hang about outside, sit on the fence and generally make a racket starting at about 9.00 pm. After a while it wore us down and we decided to look elsewhere to live, something that we had planned to do anyway. I knew that the best way for us to secure our future was with property and as it didn't seem likely that Jax and I would get married and start a family anytime soon; we were both happy to stay as we were. Being in quite a good position financially we also considered buying our own villa in Florida.

We looked around for a suitable place to relocate to and found Chafford Hundred or, as Jax calls it, 'Toy Town'. It is a vast, modern private housing estate created on the old chalk quarry near to Grays in Essex. We bought a lovely, new, five bedroom house from Bovis Homes that included a large, double garage facing a pedestrian footpath that basically led nowhere and was very quiet, just what we were looking for. Even better, Bovis part-exchanged with our house in Maybank Avenue for just under the market value. Ease of access to London was important for Jax and me, and we were within ten minutes' walk of Chafford Hundred railway station which fed into London Fenchurch Street Station, so it was ideal for Jax. Being five minutes from the A13 trunk road into London it was also perfect for me.

To maximise our position, we decided to buy a villa in Orlando, as discussed, and consulted, amongst others, Florida Choice, remember them? We decided to talk to their salespeople who operated out of Chelmsford, not a million miles away and easy enough to get to from our new base.

Having worked out the size, budget and location of said villa we decided that we were going to rent it out to help pay the mortgage and running costs. As Florida Choice were in the business of doing this, it felt right to go ahead and take the plunge and ask them to put us in touch with the builders that they used in Florida.

Arrangements were made, and Jax and I found ourselves on the plane to Orlando to not only enjoy another fourteen days of fun in the sunshine state but also to start the process of owning our own dream home there. Firstly, we met with the salesman responsible for new builds on a relatively new development called Hampton Lakes located in Polk County, Davenport, Orlando, just off Highway 27 (H27) about four miles north of Interstate 4 and within fifteen minutes' drive of Disneyworld. At that time, H27 had few such developments scattered along east and west of the road and was predominantly Orange groves owned by the PepsiCo Corporation and used for its Tropicana brand of orange drinks

As we were renting a villa through Florida Choice on Hampton Lakes we had time to get to know the area before we met with the salesman to, hopefully, start the process of buying one of our own. After a few days we met the salesman in the show home near the front entrance to the development, a curved open entry structure that had been tastefully planted with palm trees combined with a variety of tropical plants that gave it an inviting facade.

Upon meeting the salesman, I immediately had a good feeling in my gut that here was a man who knew his stuff. He wasn't pushy and made both of us feel relaxed during an experience that was new to us. Purchasing a property in the USA is relatively straightforward, but there were many things to consider that do not necessarily apply to a house purchase in the UK. All of this was explained slowly and thoroughly to us by him.

Once we understood what was required, he set about telling us what position the company was in regarding new builds and what size of property and prices they offered. We had an idea of what we were looking for and, with the salesman's help, we decided on a three bedroom, two bathroom, double garaged, single story 1500sq ft. pool home with purchase price inclusive of all taxes for $166,000 plus $17,000 for the upgraded furniture package, located in one of the quieter areas of Hampton Lakes. It would be ready for occupancy in about three months' time, and we had to get cracking and arrange to meet with the internal furniture supplier recommended by the builder to ensure that on completion/handover day the property was ready to be occupied and have the appropriate thirty day county rental licence in place. In addition to setting up the utilities, a bank account in the US was needed and Florida's Sun Trust Bank was recommended to us as they were one of the best when it came to helping those like us who were as naive as can be when it came to operating such an account there for the first time.

As everything was falling into place, we felt excited about our new home, but we also had a holiday to enjoy. Many discussions took place between us about the whole process. Were we doing the right thing? Were we going to get enough bookings to cover our costs? You know the kind of thing.

Three months and a few days after our return from Florida we were on our way back to collect the keys to our new villa and, what was soon to become, our second home. We had already spent so much time in Orlando that now having our own base we fully intended to make great use of it.

When we walked into the property we were not disappointed. It was everything that we had thought and hoped that it would be. When we saw the sparkling water of the pool we couldn't wait to get changed into our swimming gear and get right in.

And so what had once been our dream, had now become a reality.

# Chapter Ten

As previously mentioned, Jax is exceptionally efficient when it comes to the organisation and administration of all things in life, and so the record keeping, booking, advertising and daily running of the villa from over 3,000 miles away didn't faze her in the slightest. We were guided initially by Florida Choice who took care of all those things, at a price mind, a price that after the first year of ownership we found a little bit excessive. As Jax had organised our own bookings on the weeks that FC hadn't we thought that we could do better renting it out ourselves with FC filling in the gaps for us, not as easy as it sounds.

You see, what we hadn't realised was the scale of development of the rental market that was taking place in the Orlando area not only in Davenport, but also in the neighbouring district of Kissimmee. In the one to two years since we had bought our villa there seemed to building work on new community and rental developments everywhere you looked. The potential for good rental occupancy was depleted by the number of villas, townhouses, etc that were now available for holidays.

We kept the same kind of level of occupancy in ours as we had from the beginning, but the indicators were there that it was going to get tougher to rent out, but for now, Jax and I were content to let it continue as it had and to enjoy many holidays there.

In the spring of 1996, I mentioned to Jax that I thought it might be nice to visit Florida with Roy; his lady friend, Wendy, whom he had known for some years having first met at a dance of some kind; Pete and his wife, Ann and Wendy's sister, Mavis. We would propose to them a week in Orlando to visit the theme parks and then drive over to Florida's west coast for a week in the St Petersburg area, rent a large villa with a pool in each location and rent a large minibus for the duration. They all jumped at the idea and so I began to put together an itinerary for the trip that we had agreed would take place the following spring, 1997. This would give us all time to save up the not inconsiderable cost.

The time soon passed and, before we knew it, we were heading to Gatwick Airport to catch a scheduled Virgin Atlantic flight to Orlando. Upon arrival we made our way through immigration, collected our luggage, then our rented vehicle, and drove to the first villa that I had booked some months earlier. Once at the villa, a large two-storey, five bedroom property, bedrooms were sorted, suitcases unpacked, before going out to look around the area and shop for essentials, bread, milk tea, etc. We then returned to the villa for a little rest before finding somewhere for dinner.

That first week was hectic. We visited amusement parks most days; Walt Disney World, Universal Studios and Sea World to name a few. Wendy, Mavis and Ann were amazed at the range and low prices of designer goods on offer at the large outlet stores at the northern end of International Drive and spent many dollars on clothes for their children and grandchildren.

Every evening we spent dining out at a different restaurant, okay not always five star, but we didn't do too badly. I think we went downmarket once or twice but still had an enjoyable time. The company helped a lot, as we all got on really well.

Soon the week was nearing its end, and we packed up ready for the two-hour drive to the next villa in the New Port Richey area forty miles north of St Petersburg. And that's when things turned a bit sour.

When we reached the villa and started to sort out the sleeping arrangements it was democratically decided that as three of the bedrooms were doubles these were allocated to each couple, Wendy and Mavis being one. Roy would have the huge and spacious converted garage that contained at least two beds. That didn't go down at all well with Roy as from his point of view he had been put in the garage space, something that irked him for years afterwards. I agreed to take him to the rental company's local office to see if they could relocate us but, alas, they had nothing available on their books, so it was a simple case of Hobson's choice, basically, take it or leave it. We took it.

Still, it didn't spoil things too much. We just picked up where we left off and Roy made the most of it. Actually, after a day or two, he was okay about it and enjoyed, like we all did, going on various trips like the offshore, evening dolphin and sunset cruise out of Clearwater or the glass bottom boat ride on Tarpon Springs although I think that discovering a Krispy Cream Donut shop with all the goodies that Roy liked helped a great deal.

The two weeks passed quickly, and it was time to pack up and return the villa keys, take the minibus back to the car rental drop off point at MCO, check in and board the Virgin Atlantic Boeing 747 Jumbo Jet and settle down for the nine-hour return flight to LGW.

After a little while back at home, the group remarked over dinner in a local pub near Roy's house one Saturday night how they had thoroughly enjoyed the whole experience and could we possibly do something similar in another year or two's time? Yes, of course, we could. I was actually quite chuffed with all the praise being heaped upon me and, quite naturally, was eager to rise to the challenge of organising another trip, but where to next time?

The answer lay in California, I was confident that the group would go for that, having been brought up on classic Hollywood movies and TV shows, plus they knew of the iconic sights that the state contained and were keen to go and see them.

So I set about organising the next holiday with Roy, Wendy, Pete and Ann. This time our party would include Roy's best mate from his National Service days, Ray, and his wife, Barbara. When I mentioned that I had started planning the trip to California, everybody agreed that this would be a holiday of a lifetime and by the end of the evening everybody was quite excited at the prospect of spending a couple of weeks touring such iconic places as Los Angeles, San Francisco, and Las Vegas.

Having been tasked by one and all to plan the trip, I eagerly started to search various websites for flights, hotels, and places of interest. If you're going to that part of the world there are a few must-see places to visit; Las Vegas and San Francisco being the two that the group wanted to go to the most. Vegas speaks for itself, the dazzling array of hotel front entertainment would, and does, give any theme park a run for its money. It would be best for you to look it up online as there is too much for me to explain in detail here. As the Grand Canyon is not too far away from Vegas that was also on the list.

Having spent many weeks putting together, what I thought it was, an excellent 'package', I informed the group at another Saturday night dinner the details of the itinerary that I had put together. To be honest, I think the detail went over their heads, but they were only too eager to visit the iconic places that they had seen in the movies or read about over the years. Over dinner and a few drinks it was agreed that they would leave it all up to me to arrange. Gee, thanks guys, they said to let them know how much they needed to pay and when it was due by.

I set to work finalising the arrangements and after a couple more weeks of tinkering I had the final details planned. What a great thing the internet is. All the bookings that I needed to make were made via my home computer. Once everything had been confirmed and priced I informed the others of dates, monies owed and reminded them to make sure that their passports were valid for the duration plus six months validity after our return. All was in order and agreed by all; the countdown had begun.

The year of 1998 wasn't all about the good things that life has to offer though, because this was the year that my dear, sweet, ever-loving, ever-understanding mother passed away.

As I mentioned earlier, Mum had moved out of Battersea to

a warden controlled ground floor flat in Ascot, where she spent quite a number of happy years. Unfortunately, she had a persistent ulcer on her lower right leg, which meant her having many, sometimes daily, visits from the district nurse to clean and dress the ulcer, as it was pretty stubborn and not healing at all.

As time went on, she became less and less mobile and because of that bloody ulcer she started to spend time in one of the local hospitals as they tried to find an answer to the problem. By now, Paul was spending the weekday nights at Mum's flat, sleeping on the settee as he was finding it quite a journey from his home in Castle Cary, Somerset, to his place of work at De Beers diamond merchants whose main office was in Sunningdale, Berkshire, where he was employed as a chauffeur.

After many stays in hospital, and with her ulcer not healing, it got to the point where the doctors advised Mum to have her lower right leg and foot removed. This was partly because the ulcer had spread quite a bit and if it continued to do so it could put her health and life at risk.

Mum had a one or two of stays in hospital over the next couple of months, due to her deteriorating condition. Paul and Chris – again I was not part of the decision process – agreed that it would be best all round if Mum could get into a local nursing/care home where she would be properly looked after as she couldn't really manage alone at home any longer.

A suitable home was found for her in the Ascot area, and she duly moved in. I only saw her at the home a couple of times, but she seemed to be happy and settled.

Saturday, 15<sup>th</sup> August, 1998, was a warm sunny day and one which started full of excitement as it was the first day of the new football season and I was driving up to the Midlands to see Coventry City v Chelsea at Highfield Road for the 3.00 pm kick off. On the way I picked up two fellow supporters who were, like me, season ticket holders at Chelsea, and we had planned to make a day of it.

Chelsea were losing 1-0 at half time and as we started to

discuss the events of the first half I heard my name being called on the stadium's PA system asking me to call home. At first, I wasn't sure that I had listened to the announcement correctly, but nonetheless I called Jacqui and she told me that Paul had phoned to say that Mum was very ill and that I should make my way to the nursing home as soon as I could.

That gave me a bit of a problem, as I didn't feel that I could just leave my fellow supporters in Coventry to make their own way home. So I stayed until the end of the game, drove them back to West London and then on to the nursing home in Ascot.

When I arrived at about 7.00 pm I saw my brother Chris talking to my nephew Jamie. I listened in and discovered that Mum was in a bad way, and things didn't look good for her. Having waited until their conversation had ended I then expected Chris to explain to me exactly what was wrong with Mum but, to my disbelief, he just turned on his heels and walked away not talking to, or acknowledging, me!

I found Paul, and he told me that Mum was in a coma and not in a good way at all. We went to her room together and I saw Mum was lying asleep in her bed. We sat with her for the rest of the evening, not knowing what to say or do. Occasionally, a nurse would come in to make sure that Mum was all right and one time a doctor came to speak to us about Mum. I don't remember much about the conversation that took place, I suspect he was factual about Mum's condition and what treatment she would receive the next day, but for now resting was the best thing for her.

Paul thought that it would be a good idea, under the circumstances, if I went home and got a few hours' sleep as I had been up early that morning and had driven quite a few miles already and was looking tired. I agreed with him, kissed Mum goodnight and set off for home, leaving Paul to stay with her.

As soon as I walked through the front door the phone rang. I instantly knew what that meant. Paul told me that Mum had passed away a few minutes before he rang and that I should come straight back to the nursing home. Saying hello and goodbye to Jacqui at the same time, I set off back to Ascot.

I went straight to Mum's room and found Paul sitting with her, visibly upset. He then told me a tale that makes one think about how we are as human beings. He said that a second before Mum actually died she tightened her grip on his hand and he swears he felt a warm tingling sensation flow up his arm and go around his body. I will leave it for you to make up your own minds about what that may have been.

After kissing Mum's forehead and saying my last goodbye to her I left Paul with her and made my way home again. I got back about breakfast time and told Jacqui the events of the previous few hours.

I am not going to dwell on what happened in the following weeks and months after Mum's passing, only to say that she was cremated, a lifelong wish of hers, and her ashes are buried alongside my father's coffin.

*RIP Mum, love and miss you more than ever xxx*

*****

A couple of months later Jacqui and I were preparing to go on holiday again.

When departure day arrived we met the others at the Virgin Atlantic desk at London Heathrow Airport and checked in, went off for breakfast and waited four our flight to be called. Once on board the Boeing 747 (Jumbo Jet), we stowed our hand luggage and sat back and looked forward to landing at Los Angeles International Airport (LAX) some eleven hours later.

Upon arrival I told the group not to rush off the plane but hang back until most of the other passengers had departed the aircraft, the reason being that immigration into the USA, even in those days, was quite thorough and time-consuming. There was no point in rushing to the queue only to be standing in line for God only knows how long before being called forward. When we did get to the front the wait was minimal and all were let through except for yours truly!

For some reason, they held me back at the desk while they double-checked my paperwork. A few worried faces peered at me from where the group was waiting. I was delayed, but all was in order and was let in.

After we had collected our luggage we made our way to the car rental desk. I had booked two vehicles, a seven-seater MPV and a large Buick Sedan. Having decided weeks ago that Roy and I would do the driving he chose the Buick, and I had the MPV. We entered the vast labyrinth that is the Los Angeles freeway road system that leads to all parts of the great state of California, looking for Highway 405 to take us south to join Interstate 5 to San Diego a little over two hours' drive away if the roads were clear.

An episode that made us all fall about laughing occurred when Roy discovered that his car had radio volume controls on the steering wheel, a discovery that he had a lot of fun with for a couple of days. Roy's front seat companion was Pete, now Pete and Roy loved their music and Pete would often lean across and turn up the volume on the radio to enjoy a particular song that was playing. Roy would then sneakily, and with a straight face, turn down the volume via the steering wheel control that he was shielding from Pete who, incidentally, had no knowledge of what Roy was doing.

Pete just couldn't work out what was going on and complained that something must be wrong with the radio as peculiarly it only happened on the songs that he liked. In fact, he became that concerned that he almost demanded that we return the car to the rental company in exchange for a different one. Eventually, Roy had to come clean and poor old Pete felt such a fool for falling for the trick.

Both are deceased and I can't imagine what the pair of them are up too now?

*RIP the pair of you wherever you may be.*

*****

San Diego being our first stop for a couple of nights meant that we would spend a Saturday night in the city and get a chance to see what it was all about. Having checked into our hotel and freshened up we were ready to take the short walk into the city centre. It just so happens that Saturday nights can get pretty busy in downtown SD, the part that we found ourselves in was indeed busy, busy, busy.

We found a restaurant and booked in for dinner, no mean feat as there were eight of us in total. Afterwards we started to walk in the general direction of our hotel along the bustling and crowded sidewalks, these having metal crash barriers in the gutter making it impossible to step into the road to get away from the crowd. Somewhere along the way Roy found a gap in these barriers and walked into the street alongside the fence. Almost immediately, a policeman came towards Roy frantically blowing his whistle and gesticulating furiously, demanding that he should get back on the sidewalk. Roy spoke to the officer protesting his innocence and, much to our surprise, the officer upon hearing Roy's accent suddenly became a lot less hostile. "Hey, I love you Australians!" he said.

"No, no, we're British," said Roy.

"Oh, I love you more than the Aussies," came the reply.

After a brief exchange of pleasantries, Roy asked where we could get a couple of cabs to take us back to our hotel. In response the officer promptly walked out into the traffic blowing his whistle for all he was worth and waved a couple of passing cabs over in our direction. With a thanks and a cheerio from us and a salute back from the officer he held up the traffic to allow the cabs out and we set off on our way. It just goes to prove what I have always said, being English – all right, British – is simply **being the best!**

The itinerary that I had drawn up meant that from San Diego we would drive to Las Vegas the next day, via San Bernardino to Barstow and, after a few hours on the road, we all fancied a stop for a beer or a coffee and a visit to the smallest room in the house. We stumbled across a bar called the Slash X Ranch (incidentally this is where the bar scenes from the film *Erin Brockovich* (2000) were shot). Upon entering I wasn't sure that we had made the right choice of venue to stop, outside was a collection of Harley Davison chopper bikes that said, 'Noooo don't enter!' but here we were and here we were going to stay a while. To say it was rough would be a bit of an understatement, in fact, Jax asked me why there was sawdust under and around the pool table? That, I told her, was to soak up the blood from the many bar fights that would regularly take place. No, no, don't look so worried, Jax, I was only joking, or was I?

Then it was on to Las Vegas, a journey that was to take in a couple of out of the way Old America towns over a couple of nights before we were then to stay at the famous MGM Grand hotel for two nights. Vegas is just an ordinary, fairly drab, place during the day time but, oh boy, by night does it come alive. As you walk down the strip after dark the skyline is aglow with a billion lights, and free entertainment abounds from the front of the hotels as they all try to entice the tourists into their particular establishment.

We didn't venture far during the daytime on the first day, but I had planned an early start for us the following morning to visit the Hoover Dam and Lake Mead and we all enjoyed a pleasant, relaxing day. However, the next day was anything but.

After an early breakfast we set off for the southern rim of one of the wonders on the planet, the Grand Canyon, a five hour drive away, or so I thought. The problem was that the road was extremely busy with lorries and the radar enforced speed limit of 55 mph meant that it took us nearly six hours to reach our destination.

Arriving at about 4.00 pm we had to quickly make up our minds as to whether or not we were going to take a helicopter trip over the Canyon. Roy, Wendy, Jacqui and I elected to do so while the others decided to keep their feet firmly planted on terra firma.

What an experience it turned out to be though, I don't know

about the others but I absolutely loved it. Up until then it was one of the best touristy things that I had ever done. After a quick visit to the rim of the Canyon to experience what really is quite an impressive sight, and one that I would recommend that you try and see in your lifetime, we set off back to Las Vegas hoping to reach our hotel by about 10.00 pm that it wouldn't take as long as the journey out to the Canyon. I think that after stopping for dinner we made it back to the MGM by about midnight, not good really as we were due to check out in the morning and head towards our final destination, San Francisco. I had planned a route that would take us about four days of leisurely driving.

So having loaded up the vehicles we set off on our journey towards SF, planning to go via Red Rock Canyon, through Death Valley National Park, Lone Pine, Independence, Bishop, Lake Tahoe, and Sacramento. We made sure that we had plenty of bottles of water as we were passing through Death Valley just in case we should break down. The advice is to take plenty of water, just in case. After a while, I noticed that we were a bit low on fuel, no matter I thought we are bound to stop for a coffee soon and we can fill-up then.

Meandering through and admiring the beautiful colour and rock formation of Red Rock Canyon I was conscious of the need for fuel but not unduly worried as the vehicle's fuel gauge showed that we still had about a quarter of a tank, I was sure that was enough to get us to a petrol station.

As we drove on and on towards Death Valley I was getting concerned that we hadn't passed any towns or even seen any signs for fuel at all. Roy, who was driving the other vehicle, suddenly indicated to pull over to the side of the road. Pulling up behind him I then got out of the car to see what was going on.

Roy announced, "I don't know about you, but I am just about out of petrol."

"Me too," I told him. Great, what a pair of numbskulls we were, we had plenty of water but no fuel!

We decided to do the only thing that we could do, and that was carry on in the hope of finding somewhere pretty damn quick or we were going to be in big trouble, stuck out on a desert back road with not one, but both vehicles, having run out of fuel. After little more than ten minutes later, I thought I saw something shimmering through the heat haze up in the distance, a sign of some sort. As we got closer, the sign began to take on a more familiar shape, that of a fuel pricing board high up on a post. Yes, unbelievably we were heading to a fuel stop not that far ahead.

As we got closer I could see that it wasn't only a petrol station, it was, in fact, the frontage for a golfing and holiday resort. As we pulled in off the road, we were met by an enormous expanse of perfectly manicured lush green lawns, water fountains and the elaborate and ornate entrance to the resort's hotel and casino.

Any old petrol station would have done us; they didn't need to have gone to all this trouble, ha-ha. Having filled both vehicles to the brim with petrol, we decided that this was where we would have our coffee break before driving through Death Valley on our way to San Francisco.

Although there is nothing in particular that stands out in Death Valley, the sheer enormity and beauty of the place has to be seen first-hand to grasp what the place is all about; the brightness, the crisp blue of the sky, the darkness, even during the day, of the far off mountains give it an almost a magical feel. It is an experience that I will never forget.

We stayed the night in Lake Tahoe and drove on to San Francisco the following day. Seeing the iconic Golden Gate Bridge sent a shiver up my spine I can tell you. Other stand out moments were riding the famous cable cars up and down the hills of SF, visiting the Hersey Museum, Coit Tower and eating Lobster Thermidor at Fisherman's Wharf. We also spent an informative and relaxing day at the Benziger Family Winery in Sonoma.

On our last night, we went to the famous Chinatown for our

farewell dinner before returning to our hotel and packing up ready for the short drive the following morning to San Francisco Airport for the long flight home.

Having had such a great time we got together and planned our next adventure once again. It was to be to Canada in a couple of years' time on what Ray ultimately referred to as the 'Brits on Tour' trip. He actually wrote that in the dirt that had gathered on the rear windscreen of one of the SUV vehicles that we hired for our trip and one and all "Do not wipe it off!"

We flew into Calgary the day before the annual Stampede was due to start on 5<sup>th</sup> July. It was to last for about a week, we, however, would be out of the city and on our way to our final destination, Vancouver, via Banff, Jasper, Kamloops, Whistler, Vancouver Island and many small 'one horse town' overnight stops, one of which was the Tyax Lodge and Heli-Skiing Resort.

I was not very popular on the day we travelled from Kamloops to Tyax as I made a slight error in calculating how long it would take to drive there, approximately five hours with a 150 mile drive, mostly on a mountainous, twisty dirt track, it being a main route for the logging lorries, of which there were plenty to keep us occupied, that is me and Roy who were doing the driving. It wasn't altogether bad as we broke the day up with plenty of coffee and comfort breaks in little off the beaten track places that everyone seemed to enjoy.

The resort itself was more than we had expected. It could have been the set of a Hollywood movie with its grand, expansive reception area and local wood panelling around the walls adorned with the heads of various stuffed animals, stags mainly. However, there was also a huge, erect bear, arms and paws reaching out to give someone a hug, ah shucks just like a big old teddy bear, NOT! The centrepiece was a grand stone fireplace, which made for a welcoming sight, not that it was working at the time but it was still impressive.

We stayed at the resort for a couple of days relaxing as we had been on the go pretty much full on for the previous week.

This was the ideal retreat to recharge the batteries. We four men rented quad bikes and explored the surrounding forest for a couple of hours while the ladies relaxed with a coffee and, no doubt, had a good old chinwag. Then in no time at all, it was time to retrace our steps back down the logging road where we would eventually head further west to catch the ferry that would take us over to Vancouver Island for another two-night stay.

This part of the trip was to be one of the most memorable times of my life. I had planned a choice of two excursions; the first a city bus tour with a visit to The Butchart Gardens, which Roy and Wendy elected to do. The other option was to go out into the seawaters off Victoria with the Canadian Meteorological and Oceanographic Society in a large RIB boat on a killer whale watching trip, which the rest of us elected to do.

Firstly, we all had to put on bright yellow buoyancy suits for safety. Once were we seated in the RIB, about twenty of us altogether, we were taken a few miles offshore to search for orcas. Almost immediately, after stopping at a point that the guides had been to previously, one of them spotted large dorsal fins a little way off from where the boat was stationary in the water. The engines had been stopped so no noise would disturb the animals, and they started to approach the area of the boat. The guides told us that the orcas were chasing Pacific salmon along known and historical swims that were centuries old and that we were in for an extraordinary day.

They were not wrong. The sheer numbers alone were breath-taking. The guide estimated there were approximately seventy orcas split up into groups of between five to six in individual pods. The size of the males was staggering, majestic as they rose out of the water thirty feet away from the boat and then dived underneath to emerge on the other side. Bearing in mind that some of these big boys are about twenty feet long and can weigh in at about four tons they didn't leave much room for manoeuvre. With many smaller females and juveniles in the pods following close behind it made for the most spectacular and thought-provoking of sights, truly a day that I will never forget.

We took the ferry back to the mainland the following day and drove off to find our hotel in Vancouver. On the way we passed close to the International Airport where I spotted a sign for early morning, tourist seaplane flights to some of the smaller islands in the area, to deliver/collect the morning post and to bring in commuters to Vancouver for their workday.

*Now, that would be worth doing*, I thought. So once we reached the hotel and had checked into our rooms I went to see the concierge to make enquiries. Sure enough, these flights took place every morning, lasted about ninety minutes and were available for all to experience. Later that day, I asked all those in the party who might like to go on one of these trips. Roy and Ray said yes straight away but Pete was a bit hesitant and said that he would let me know later. When I spoke to him about it, he explained that his funds were running low and that he would have to pass. "No way," I told him. "You can't come all this way and pass up on a trip like this." I said that I would pay for everybody on my credit card and that he could settle up with me at a later date.

Having called ahead and been given a time to be at the jetty the next morning, we arrived and checked in early. Upon meeting the pilot he said that one passenger could sit beside him and the rest could occupy the two rows of seats behind. I bagged the front seat next to him, saying to the others, "My idea, I booked it, and I paid for it, so that seat is mine." Once aboard the pilot manoeuvred the little seaplane out into the middle of the channel and got the all clear to take off. With a slow acceleration of the engine the plane roared into life and started to propel us across the calm waters until the point of take off. Way hey, hold on, here we go.

Climbing up to about 1500ft the pilot set us on course for his first destination, a small island about thirty minutes flying time away where he told me that he would pick up and deliver a couple of sacks of mail and one lady passenger who lived on the island and commuted every day to her office in Vancouver.

On the way we flew over lots of little islands just big enough to accommodate a traditional sized house made of wood where families lived. Boats were moored alongside small jetties ready to take passengers over to Vancouver so that kids could go to school and parents go to work for the day. During the flight the pilot told me that this work made a nice change from his day job, as he usually flew heavy passenger aircraft such as the Boeing 747 or the McDonnell Douglas DC-10 on Transpacific or Transatlantic Routes for Air Canada. *Nice, if you can get it,* I thought, ha-ha.

Once we had got back to the jetty the pilot was off to photograph a section of the river a few miles away where a logging company was sending down a vast number of trees for him to fly over and capture on film so the numbers could be calculated at a later date. Having met up with the ladies at the hotel we went for lunch before packing for our eleven hour flight home to London the following day. Wow! Where had the time gone.

A last little story about our Canadian holiday will have you believing in Karma. You remember the story of the policeman who burnt his wrist on my RE5? Well, guess what? While at the Calgary Stampede the local police motorcyclists did a little display for the onlookers at the opening parade, and afterwards some stayed behind to chat with the spectators. Taking my opportunity I asked one of them if I could sit on his bike. He agreed and I eagerly positioned myself on the machine, guess what? That's right, I burnt my leg on the exhaust pipe! That will teach me to wear shorts.

So all packed up and ready to go we made the short journey to Vancouver International Airport for the long flight back home to LGW where we all said our goodbyes and made our separate ways home.

# Chapter Eleven

The next few years brought Jacqui and I both great joy and sadness and certainly changed our lives forever.

After being made redundant, firstly in 1998 by Saito Bank and again by my next employer the insurance broker Aon back in the summer of 2004, I decided that I had been in the chauffeuring game long enough and would use this opportunity to try something different. Courier work seemed to be where the future lay, so I used part of my redundancy money to buy a second-hand Mercedes Sprinter van at the British Car Auctions site at Blackbushe Airport. Paul came with me (he lived a few minutes' drive away) and helped me with the procedure required to obtain a vehicle and to get it to home.

I set myself up as a self-employed courier under the name BG Courier Services, BGCS, as it was later to become. Having registered with HMRC and obtained the relevant insurances I was ready to go. At first, I worked for a courier company based near Southend-on-Sea, and what an eye opener that was! Working all the hours God sent was tough, especially if I was waiting around for a long time in between jobs. Distance work was what I really liked but those kinds of situations usually came at a price. The controller would offer a job to say, Liverpool, mid-afternoon, now that was a good paying job worth about £200, but it would usually mean a pick up very early in the morning from a local company that had goods to be delivered by say 8 o'clock on the same day.

Great, but for a couple of things. Firstly, going to the north west of England meant that whatever route I took it was going to be busy with traffic all the way up to Liverpool. Once the goods were delivered by, let's say, 7.30 pm, it was a four or five hour drive back home, usually getting in by midnight, then up again by 6.00 am to be ready for the next day's work, sound good? Well, think again! More often than not the next day would be quiet, and the work would be thin on the ground. You see that's a ploy that these companies use as, quite often, they look after the driver one day then don't bother the next. Thus, your overall takings might only just cover expenses. After a while I got fed up with being treated like that and decided to look around for something better.

I would walk into a local transport company and offer my services to them. Mostly I was offered the next opening that became available but I soon realised that this was an easy way for them to get someone like me off their back and out the door quickly. However, my luck was to change when a prominent local company were interested from the outset. The transport manager must have liked what I had to offer when he checked out the van and documents. He then told me, "Be here at 6.00 am tomorrow and we will give you a day's work. Don't forget to bring a hi-vis jacket and wear strong boots." Just what I wanted to hear as I knew that they paid well, £185 per day was the going rate and usually it meant working Monday to Friday. The company ran a large fleet of articulated HGV vehicles doing bulk delivery and collections throughout the UK, Europe and Scandinavia, a bit like Eddie Stobart only on a slightly smaller scale. My job was to do the smaller deliveries and collections that didn't warrant the use of such a large vehicle.

The first day it was all new to me. Taking direction from the transport manager I was given my own call sign for recognition purposes and handed a small A5 sized group of printed delivery and collection sheets from which to sort out the best order and routes to take. Then having done so, with the help of my own knowledge and a TomTom satnav I would present myself to the loader and tell him in what order I wanted the van loaded. Once this was done I would be on my way. I usually worked the southern Home Counties anywhere between say Sandwich in Kent down to Weymouth in Dorset, not on the same day, of course, as that would be too great a distance to cover in one day.

I felt I had been very fortunate. I was now earning a decent wage after all the rubbish that I had put up with when doing the odd day here and there for lots of small courier companies and felt quite at home. I did have one day that didn't go so well though. One morning the TM greeted me with, "Brian, if only you had been here five minutes ago." He told me that he had a job in mind for me but somebody else who got in extra early that day was offered the prime job by somebody else in the office. It was to load up five empty Euro pallet sized cages that had contained sacks of packages that had been delivered to the company the night before for return to a DHL depot in Birmingham ready to be used the following night and to be returned once again the next morning. It was a Monday to Saturday routine and paid £200 per day ie £1,200 per week and that's all you had to do. *Well, thank you very much!* I thought. In fact, I wish I hadn't been told about it in the first place as I was gutted knowing that the other driver, whom I didn't much like anyway, had been given the work.

Oh well, that's how it goes, I suppose. I still had decent work and it was to last for at least another couple of years.

During the winter of 2006/2007 Jax started going to the local gym in an effort to get fitter. Her daily routine of walking approximately a third of a mile to Chafford Hundred train station in the morning was not sufficient for her to achieve the level of fitness she desired. Her weekly routine was now attending the gym about three times a week.

During January and February of 2007, she went down with what, on the face of it, seemed to be a series of colds, one after another, complaining of minor to severe headaches. She put these down to her strenuous workouts at the gym and cut back the number of visits that she was making, but still the headaches persisted to the extent that Jax felt it necessary to visit her GP. He carried out a brief examination and told Jax that he was making an appointment for her to see a specialist at Basildon Hospital as soon as possible. After a few days, she received a telephone call from the hospital asking her to attend a clinic.

This she did and during a consultation a doctor told her that she was going to be admitted as he was not happy with her condition and wanted to carry out further tests.

Jax called me at work and explained what was happening and asked if I could bring her some things in a bag that evening when I got home from work. It concerned me greatly that the hospital had deemed it necessary to admit her and told my boss that I was leaving early to go and see her.

When I arrived at the hospital ward she had been admitted to I found Roy already with Jax. He soon left to wait outside until I had spoken to her. She told me that the doctor had asked her all manner of questions as to what she had experienced over the past couple of weeks. He had made lots of notes and said that he would be back in the morning and he was now going to arrange for her to have, amongst other things, a CT scan on her head. She said that the left side of her body felt numb and she feared that she may have had a minor stroke. Her movement when she got out of bed to walk across the small, six-bedded room to use the lavatory was akin to an old lady. She looked like someone who had, indeed, partially lost the use of one side of her body. To say that I was shocked and concerned is an understatement. I was extremely worried about her.

When I left, I found Roy waiting for me outside the ward, and as we walked to the exit he asked if I knew what was going on. I told him that the doctor was arranging various tests for the next day as he wasn't sure what to make of Jacqui's condition but hoped to have a clearer picture by the end of the following day. As we continued walking Roy showed a side of him that I hadn't seen before, that of a concerned father.

I guess Roy, like myself, had had more than his share of visiting hospitals over the years. His wife, Eunice, had died not that many years earlier from stomach cancer in the very same hospital that his youngest child had been admitted to with an, as yet, unknown condition.

The following day at work I couldn't stop worrying about what the hospital tests would discover about Jax's condition.

When I saw her that evening she told me that the doctors were none the wiser as to what was causing her problems after carrying out many neurological and physical tests. However, they had noticed a minuscule dark patch on her brain. One of the doctors surmised that the colds she had been experiencing during the previous few weeks may have been a virus. He suggested that as she was going to the gym as often as she was the virus could not attack her immune system but had, in fact, attacked the brain instead. It seemed a bit fanciful to me, but who am I to suggest otherwise? During my visit a doctor came along to see Jax and inform her that he wanted to carry out a lumbar puncture.

*Lumbar puncture (LP), also known as a spinal tap, is a medical procedure in which a needle is inserted into the spinal canal, most commonly to collect cerebrospinal fluid (CSF) for diagnostic testing.*

I was asked to leave while the procedure was carried out and so waited nearby until it was over. Only it didn't all go to plan. The doctor couldn't, if his life had depended on it, insert the needle into Jax's spine to withdraw the fluid, so after about five attempts he had to concede defeat and summon his consultant to do it which she duly did at the first attempt.

Over the next couple of days, Jax made a remarkable recovery from walking like a little old lady to one who was happy and robust in her outlook even though the hospital, despite all the tests that had been carried out, were unable to come up with a definitive diagnosis of her condition. She was discharged and they advised her to keep a close check on herself and if she had the slightest of concerns about her health she should return to her GP immediately. I am happy to report that she suffered no more 'incidents' as we refer to it. We are still baffled to this day about the whole event and are none the wiser as to what happened to her.

It did lead on to a relationship changing event though. Out of the blue, Jax, who, up until the above incident occurred, was quite happy just going along as we were, announced that, perhaps, we should think about starting a family. I was over the moon as I was desperate for us to marry and start having children. After all, the clock was beginning to count down for both of us. I was already fifty and Jax was – can't reveal a lady's age here can I? – no doubt aware that her biological clock was also ticking down.

Being a traditionalist in these sort of matters I wanted to do things properly so one evening while watching TV I walked over to where Jax was sitting, went down on one knee and said, "Jacqui, will you marry me?" to which she replied something along the lines of 'Oh, go on then'. Not what I was expecting. More of a 'yes' is what I was hoping for, ha-ha.

Still, it was the answer that I had wished for ever since I first asked her years earlier and had been soundly rebuffed with the comment, "I am too young just now." Next we told our closet family and friends, and one or two remarked 'about time too'. Well, we had been together for fourteen years. Others just wished us well. We sat down to discuss what kind of ceremony we wanted. Neither of us are religious and felt that, as we had been together for quite a long time, a traditional church wedding was really not for us. Likewise a mundane civil ceremony in the local Town Hall was also out of the question.

Then we both had a light bulb moment. Why not get married in the one place that felt like a second home to us (well, we did have one there anyway) Orlando, Florida. Why not marry there, lots of British couples do and we wanted to too.

But first things first, the transport company that I was working for decided to reschedule the way they operated and were, in future, to redeploy their own drivers to do the work that I and others had been doing for them. This came about because of the influx of the Eastern European freight companies that were allowed to operate in the EEC from such countries as Romania, Bulgaria, Hungary etc having joined the great European Union experiment.

This meant that operators from those countries could now openly compete with others located anywhere in Europe for the freight that needed to be transported there. As these 'new boys' came from economies that were much smaller than those of the established first world countries inside the EU they could, and did, offer their services at a fraction of the cost. Tt's a hard fact that operating costs for these new joiners was much smaller as the pay, fuel, road tax and insurance costs were much lower than elsewhere in the EU. As the effect of this is documented elsewhere I won't bore you with the details but just to say that my job/work disappeared overnight.

With an upcoming marriage to pay for, I had to move pretty quickly in finding another job if were we to fulfil our ambition of marrying in Florida. So, reluctantly, I decided to call an end to the courier work, don my collar and tie and get back to doing what I did best and look for a job as a chauffeur.

Jacqui had been busy organising our upcoming wedding in Orlando and had sent emails out to the local county office who dealt with the legalities of marrying in the state of Florida. Another was sent to Celebration Golf Club in Celebration, Davenport, Orlando, enquiring about their wedding packages. A photographer also received an email along with an entertainment company, a hairdresser and a wedding car/limousine company all enquiring about their services.

One Saturday morning we visited a company who sold Virgin Atlantic tickets at a discounted price whom we had dealt with for many years. When our contact there discovered that we were planning to marry in Florida he invited to his visit his office so that he could find us the best possible deal they could offer as a token of their appreciation of the many, many trips to the USA that we had booked through them over the years.

Having got our travel plans in place we asked our family and our close friends if they would be able to travel to Orlando for our wedding. All of them said yes, and we had the beginnings of the plans that needed to be put into place.

While all this was going on I sent out my CV and references to a few select specialist chauffeur employment agencies, putting myself forward as a candidate for any suitable positions that might become available. All said it was great to hear from me and they would undoubtedly try their best to find me a job. *Yeah*, I thought, *at 17.5% commission of the salary offered I bet you will.*

I received a phone call out of the blue from an old friend that I had known years earlier who ran as small employment agency asking if I was still chauffeuring and was I looking for work? Well, yes, I was, so I asked him what he had in mind? He told me about a particular, special job that he had been asked to fill and felt that I was the best candidate for what turned out to be a magnificent job. He gave me details about the position and when he got to the part about it being the personal chauffeur to a Saudi Arabian billionaire prince, I shouted down the phone, "Jim, I'll take it!"

When Jax arrived home from work I could barely contain my excitement and repeated the conversation about the job. Indeed, I was called back by Jim with a date for an interview to be held at the central London residence of the said principal, not with the man himself but with his personal finance guru, a hard-nosed man of English/Arab descent.

On the day concerned I presented myself at the residence and was greeted at the front door by a small Asian man dressed in a smart black suit, white shirt with black tie, and the shiniest, black shoes that I had ever seen. He looked and smelt 'military' and, as it turns out, the principal had ex-Ghurkha soldiers as his security guards. I was led to a waiting area where I was greeted by one of the two butlers that worked in the house. Having introduced himself he told me what working for such a high worth (reputed to be about £8bn) individual would entail and it all sounded rather wonderful.

I was then introduced to the finance man and taken to a rather grand library where the interview took place. I was told what my duties would be and that I was the only interviewee as the principal had been impressed by my CV and credentials and if we could broker a financial deal the job was mine.

Now, I had done my homework to the extent that the

finance man was impressed with my knowledge of the boss, as I later called the principal, but we hit an impasse when it came to the salary and benefits. I knew exactly what the job was worth and I told the FM precisely what I wanted. He scoffed at my terms and said that the job only paid X amount. "No," I said. "I won't do it on the cheap. If you want the best, as the principal obviously does, then I expect to be paid what I am worth."

"Okay," he said eventually. He then suggested that maybe the next move should be a meeting between the principal and myself to see if we liked each other and said that he would be in touch. I called Jim as soon as I left the house to let him know how I had got on, but the FM had beaten me to it. He told Jim that he had been impressed with me, and was arranging a second interview.

A couple of days later the FM called me directly and told me when my interview with the principal would take place.

"Do you have a current passport?" he asked.

"Yes," I replied.

"Good, you'll need it as you are going to be interviewed by the boss at his villa in Cannes, in the south of France. Come prepared to stay for a week."

*What! Are you serious?* I thought. Well, yes, he was, and he gave me my travel itinerary over the phone. I excitedly called Jax at her workplace and relayed the conversation to her. "This is the big time," I told her. It was what I had always dreamt of, and now it looked like it was going to be a reality.

The wedding plans were taking shape, and we were both excited about what the future held for us. These were good days. Jax's health was excellent, her job was going well, and I was on the cusp of an exciting future on the job front. Yes, we were doing just fine.

The day came around when I was due to go to Cannes for my interview. Having packed a holdall with enough clothes to last me for the week, plus my suit in a carrier, I set of for Heathrow where I would take the early evening British Airways flight to Nice on the Cote de Azur. From there, I would be met by a limousine driver in the terminal building and driven to the villa in Cannes. As it turned out it was quite a nice limo, an obsidian-coloured Mercedes Benz S600 V12 driven by a well-built, and I guessed right again, ex-military man, who drove at an almost constant speed of 150 KPH, approximately 95 MPH.

As we approached Cannes, all sorts of visions came into my mind as to what the man and his villa might be like. However, nothing that I had imagined would match the reality. Cannes is a coastal town situated in a vast bay and we seemed to pass through the posh end before leaving the city behind and travelling up into the surrounding hills. As we drove higher up into the mountains, even though it was late on a summer's night, it became apparent that the higher up we went, the more extensive and expensive the villas became.

I was quite taken aback when we finally reached the villa sometime just before midnight. I was met by the sight of a large pair of ornate black iron gates, which must have been twelve feet high and ten feet wide, stretching out into the blackness of the night across a tarmacked driveway flanked by an immaculately cropped hedge. The gates were manned on either side by two men armed with automatic rifles. *Jeez* I thought, *what is going on here?* The driver having shown the armed guards his credentials the electronic controlled gates opened and we were allowed on to the complex. I looked back at the two armed guards taking up their positions. *This is the big league now, Brian,* I thought. The driver drove us up to the front door of the villa and told me that he would take care of my luggage. He then got out of the car, opened the door for me to get out before the he and car disappeared towards a large outer building.

As I watched him go, the front door opened and I was greeted by an altogether more relaxed FM who beckoned me into the villa. He led us along a long, wide corridor adorned with gold-framed paintings painted by, as I later found out, some of the world's most renowned old masters with a few modern ones thrown in for good measure. We entered a large conservatory that had, at its heart, a large table covered with plates of food, all manner of Champagne, wine, spirit and beer bottles, surrounded by about a dozen people.

I was immediately greeted by a large and stocky man whom I presumed was the principal but was, in fact, the boss's right-hand man cum bodyguard (I have changed his name) called Omar who nearly broke my hand when he shook it. Now, I like a firm handshake, but this was ridiculous. I later found out that Omar had been a colonel in the Saudi Special Forces.

He nearly roared the roof off with laughter when I called him sir. He then excused my mistake and introduced me to the boss who was sitting across the table from us. I saw an elegant, well-dressed man in a casual open-necked shirt and light-coloured trousers. He got up with a big smile on his face and an outstretched hand saying, in a well-educated English accent, "Hello, Brian, I am Sheik…"

I replied with, "Hello, sir. I am pleased to meet you."

I don't know if this has ever happened to you, but both he and I had that gut feeling that said: 'Yes, you are the one' and from that split second when we shook hands I knew the job was mine.

After some small talk he suggested that I be shown to my room and that we should meet and discuss things in the morning. So I was led by the other butler from the London house who I hadn't met, to a guest room and left to unpack, shower and get a good night's sleep before meeting the boss one to one in the morning.

As it was summer time the sun was already peering through the curtains when I awoke at about 7.00 am. I have always been an early riser so, once up, I made my way through the villa trying to find out where I could get a cup of tea, if at all possible. I heard voices coming from what I assumed to be some kind of staff quarters and, sure enough, I had found the kitchen that the staff used. When I entered, there was a look of shock on the man's and woman's faces who were enjoying a coffee and croissant for breakfast.

"Pardon Monsieur," they said, as they both jumped up in tandem offering their apologies to me in French.

"Non, non," I said followed by, "Parlez vous Anglais?" in my best South London accent.

"A little," replied the man. I explained who I was. "Ah, oui," he said. They both relaxed and a coffee and croissants were offered up to me for breakfast. They told me in their best English that it was usual for the boss and his guests to be late risers. Considering that they didn't go to bed until about 2.00 am I am not surprised.

They suggested that I look around the villa but warned me to stay away from the first floor, as that was where the master and guest bedrooms were situated. Good tip, I didn't want to walk into somebody's bedroom unannounced.

I set off back towards my own guest room that was located at the back of the villa on the ground floor. I must tell you that my room was akin to one in a five star hotel, exquisitely furnished with an enormous double bed, seating area and the biggest bathroom that I have ever seen complete with walk-in shower, WC and bidet. It had large French windows that opened up on to the most beautiful garden with immaculately manicured lawns and a mix of fruit trees in their own sectioned off orchard.

Leaving the room and wandering into the gardens I turned past the corner of the building so I had a view of the entire complex. What I saw was like the set from a James Bond movie. What I hadn't realised the previous night when I arrived was that the villa was built into the rock of the hill that it sat within. Stretched out before me was an enormous, kidney-shaped swimming pool that glistened invitingly in the morning sun. When I turned around I was met with the most stunning view of the harbour and bay of Cannes below.

By now the staff were starting to go about their duties. It was evident that the boss and his guests had held a party around the pool as the whole pool area was being cleaned by three or four cleaners. They were clearing away empty bottles that had once contained the finest of Champagnes, vintage wines and a good few spirits, together with beer bottles and the remnants of last night's BBQ.

I continued on to the outer buildings that lay beyond the pool area via a winding garden footpath through a myriad of sweet-smelling shrubs and bushes all lining the edges of the pathway and with palm trees as their backdrop. These outer buildings were, in fact, garages where I found a few of the cars that I would be expected to drive. So here goes the list; a Mercedes Benz S500 AMG, Bentley Continental, Bentley GT, Range Rover, Porsche Cayenne, custom built Porsche 959, Lamborghini Gallardo Spyder. Wow, that's enough hardware to take anybody's breath away, but wait there is one more supercar to add to the list.

A supercar that is still coveted to this day, a Ferrari supercar, a red Ferrari supercar, a red Enzo Ferrari supercar. Oh, and a little silver Toyota Yaris. And I was expected to be able to drive them all. Well, I could and, each in turn, did.

As I was pushing my dropped jaw back into place a slightly younger man than me appeared and started shouting at me in a heavy French accent.

"Calm down, old son," I said.

He responded in reasonable English, "Who are you?"

"I am your new boss from England," I replied. With a puzzled look upon his face he calmly introduced himself as Patrick. *That's better*, I thought, *being a bit more civil won't do you any harm.*

I gave him the briefest of details as to why I was there, and had to be a bit cute as I hadn't officially got the job yet, but all was fine with us both.

As I walked back to the central part of the complex I passed two armed guards who shot me a suspicious glare as our eyes met.

"Bonjour, parlez vous Anglais?" I asked.

"Yes," one of them said and so we had a little Q&A session mostly from me, I admit. It turned out that the boss had a dozen or so ex-French Special Forces and ex-French Legionnaires guarding the property on a permanent 24/7 365 day rota.

There had been quite a few burglaries in the area and a few kidnappings of high-value persons or members of their families in recent years and the boss didn't want to leave anything to chance.

"Fair enough, but what are the weapons for," I asked?

He shrugged and said, "It's okay", and they carried on their way.

Upon entering the main part of the villa I was met by the butler, a young Arab man who spoke perfect English, was built like a brick outhouse and had an engaging smile. He ushered me away from the main area and explained that staff NEVER entered by the front door unless accompanying the boss. Slap on the wrist accepted.

Next up was Omar and the FM who said, "Let's get a coffee and have a chat." Omar started the conversation with all the usual pleasantries, then told me about the boss and what he liked and disliked about staff working for him, how I had great responsibility for his safety when driving him anywhere and not to chit chat, keep the things heard in the car to myself, blah, blah, blah. *Yeah, I know the score, I've been there and done that*, I thought as he rambled on.

The FM then gave his two penneth; another load of blah, blah, blah, yawn, yawn, yawn, I've heard it all before, but I know that you won't let Omar pull rank on you. The politics had begun, and I hadn't been there twelve hours yet. Anyway, Omar told me that the boss was going to the International Carlton Hotel, in Boulevard de la Croisette, and asked me if I knew where it was? "Yes, of course I do," I lied. So he asked me to bring the Bentley Continental to the front door just before 12.00 noon.

I looked up where the hotel was situated using the car's satnav, muting it so I wouldn't get caught out. At the appropriate time, the boss and Omar got in the car and we set off for the hotel. On the journey, they started talking in Arabic, but quite soon the boss apologised to me and they changed to English. Nice touch.

When we got close Omar gave me 1000 euros and explained that this was a float that I should use in case the boss wanted anything small while we were out. He also said the going rate for the number one spot outside any hotel or restaurant was 200 euros and this is what I should give to the head doorman to ensure that we had the best place. For the uninitiated this meant bunging cash to the doorman so the car could be right by the main door so that the boss didn't have to wait while I went to get the car, and he also wouldn't have to walk far.

Sure enough, that is precisely what happened. When the door staff saw the car approaching they immediately removed the cones that were reserving the space for us and, once parked the boss got out. Now, contrary to popular belief, the chauffeur doesn't open the principal's car door, only for a female who is a passenger seated behind the driver if present. The door is opened by the doorman, and in this case he got a 50 euro bung.

About an hour later the boss and Omar reappeared, got in the car and off we went. After a couple of pleasantries to me, the boss made one or two calls on the phone. It was a short journey back to the villa, about fifteen minutes and, once there, Omar informed me that I would not be needed for the rest of the day as the boss had just invited people over for dinner. The next day, however, the boss had lined up something special for me.

Mid-afternoon and my day was done? Can't be bad. When I next saw Omar I asked him if it would be okay for me to take the little Toyota and explore the area.

"Sure, no problem," he said. "But don't go to Monaco." His last words were said with a smile. So I drove down through Cannes, along the seafront to the marina, then worked my way to Mandelieu and on towards the coastal town of St Raphael via Frejus. After stopping for a coffee in a local café, I started my journey back to Cannes, driving through scenery up in the hills that I am sure that most of us have seen in films or on *Top Gear* over the years, spectacular it is too. Once back I put the car away and went to the staff kitchen for dinner. Patrick passed on a message to me from Omar to be ready at 10.00 am sharp in the morning as the boss wanted me to take him to the Hotel de Paris in Monaco.

As I sat down for dinner I contemplated which car he would want to go in and thought it prudent to make sure that the non-sports cars in the fleet were prepared with water, soft drinks etc and, above all, that they were clean and tidy. I needn't have worried as Patrick had already taken care of it as this was part of his duties. Having seen the boss's guests arrive I decided to go to my room and get an early night.

The next morning I was up early. I had breakfast and got ready, showered, shaved and dressed in my finest collar and tie. I then waited by the front door for the boss to appear and give me instruction on what the day ahead held for us. A little after 10.00 am the boss, accompanied by Oma – this was to become the norm – said good morning and asked me if I could go to the garage and get the Enzo? *Can I what? Had I heard him right? 'Get the Enzo' is that really what he had said?* Yes, it was!

As I was making my way to the garage with a feeling of dread, Omar called after me, "Don't worry," he said. "I will give you a quick rundown on how the car drives."

And so, with his guidance, I strapped myself into the eight-point racing harness and straightened my suit jacket. I felt a bit stupid wearing a suit as I was about to drive what was, at that time, the most desired sports car of its day. I drove the Enzo Ferrari to the front door of the villa, which by now had attracted an audience to see the boss off, or as I thought to come to see me make a fool of myself.

Omar opened the right passenger door for the boss, left hand drive you see, who slipped into the car and said, "Hotel de Paris please, Brian."

"Yes, sir," I said as we slowly pulled away from the villa and made our way along the long driveway to the big black gates at the front of the property. It felt like every bodyguard and security man had turned out to have a good laugh at my expense when I inevitably stalled the car somewhere along the route. But I was determined not to and we got to the gates okay, pulled out and headed north towards Le Cannet and then on to the A8 eastbound that would take us to Monaco.

Not much had been said between us as the boss had been reading some papers which was a relief as I was struggling in my mind to make sure that I remembered the way to the motorway. Once we reached the A8 I was fine, still nervous but fine. After a few minutes the boss lowered his papers and asked if everything was all right.

"Yeah, great, I assured him."

"Then why are we going so slowly?" came his reply.

I told him that we were doing about 110 KPH to which he replied, "That's far too slow. Put your foot down." What! Give me a break I was nervous enough about driving this million dollar icon as it was. "Go on, you should be in the outside lane doing at least 150 KPH." Having explained to him that I didn't want to lose my licence due to speeding he, roared with laughter and told me that I should take it up to 160 KPH and not to worry because the local Gendarme loved having these exotic cars on their patch of motorway. Yes, they will blue light you in their little Peugeot hatchbacks but once alongside they will give you the thumbs up and encourage you to blast away from them.

*Yeah, right,* I thought, *this is a test of some sort, isn't it? But here goes.* I increased the speed up to 160 KPH. The cars in front soon got out of the way when they saw what was coming up behind them. Well, blow me down, I would not have believed it if somebody else had told me the story, but sure enough, that is precisely what happened. I must admit that I was dumbstruck, but the police actually did what he said and then waved me on to go even faster, unbelievable.

Pretty soon we were making our way down the D6007 towards Monaco. This is where it became a chore to drive the Enzo, not because the roads were quite narrow and the Enzo felt like I was driving a bus as it's so wide, but with a low permitted speed, all and sundry were beginning to gawp and stare at us. I guess it's because the Enzo is not a car that you see every day, not even in Monaco, people were actually posing alongside the car when we stopped in traffic or at the traffic lights to have their photo taken. In a way I thought that it would be a relief to get to the hotel and park up but, oh no, it was even worse, once we were stationary all and sundry wanted to take a look. I was saved by the doorman as he ushered the crowds back and beckoned me out of the car so that he could park it in the hotel's secure underground car park. As per instruction, when he came back 200 euros found their way from my hands to his, very discreetly of course. I then followed him to a part of the hotel overlooking the front entrance where he and his fellow doormen holed up for a coffee until it was time for him to get the car. He handed it over to me and pocketed another 50 euro note from the boss for services rendered. The journey back to Cannes was uneventful and, once back at the villa, I was told the same as the precious afternoon; that I would not be needed until the next day.

However, the next day there was a total change of plan. Omar told me that the boss had to go to Maryland in the USA for an urgent business and so my week-long interview/assessment would have to be curtailed. I was to bring the Porsche Cayenne to the front door at 1.00 pm ready for the boss to travel to the airport in, Patrick would drive the Range Rover ahead with the luggage and meet us on the tarmac at Cannes-Mandelieu Airport where the boss would board his private Boeing 737 jet for the journey to the USA.

On arrival we were escorted out on to the tarmac where the plane was indeed waiting with engines turning over. The pilot or co-pilot, I'm not sure which, greeted the boss at the bottom of the stairs that led to the front of the plane and, almost immediately, the boss climbed the stairs and disappeared inside the jet. Omar had stayed back and walked over to me and said, "Brian, the boss is impressed by the manner in which you have presented yourself, your discreet manner, your excellent driving skills and your obvious overall knowledge of how a chauffeur goes about his duties. He is offering you the job here and now and on the pay and conditions that you have asked for, and with the understanding that you are to drive him and him alone, so I need a decision from you, yes or no?"

Well, naturally, it took me a millisecond to say yes. Omar was delighted with the answer and told me he would tell the boss the good news. I could stay in the villa for the next few days until my original departure day came around and, with a shake of hands, he too boarded the plane. Patrick helped the loaders to secure the luggage in the hold and we were told to drive back to the terminal building. As we did so the plane started to taxi to the far end of the runway.

As the plane was taking off I picked up the car phone and called Jax on her office number to tell her the news, simply saying, "We've cracked it!" I told her that I was staying on until the original departure date and that the future certainly would be rosy from now on.

On my return to London, I waited a few days for confirmation of the job offer to arrive, which it duly did. It confirmed the terms that I had asked for and contained a proposed start date, which I agreed upon. I signed the top copy, returned the contract in the next post and excitedly waited for my official start date to come around.

On my first day I was shown around by the butler, and advised of the dos and don'ts before being taken to the garage underneath the house that housed a much smaller collection of vehicles than the one in Cannes. The cars here consisted of a Rolls-Royce Phantom, Mercedes Benz Maybach, two Range Rovers, Ford Galaxy and another Toyota Yaris.

My insight to the world of a billionaire certainly caused me to inwardly gasp a few times. The boss would quite often have me drive him to a lunch engagement in Mayfair in his Rolls-Royce Phantom, or Mercedes Benz Maybach. Again I had a float, only this time it was £1,000 and the doorman's bung was now £200.

Usually, as he exited the car, the boss would lean over and

give me a £50 note so that I could buy myself lunch. Had I got lucky, or what? Yes, I had and couldn't believe how my fortune had changed. I was beginning to feel that Jacqui and I were going places.

# Chapter Twelve

Having been introduced to the staff in the London house by the butler and familiarised myself with the layout of the property, I was given a mobile phone and advised to keep it switched on at all times day and night. I was not officially on call 24/7 but Omar thought that, in an emergency, it would be a good idea if I could be contacted. Gradually, I began to develop a daily routine of making sure that the cars were clean and presentable and stocked up with water and soft drinks and a selection of the boss's favourite sweets and cigarettes. People asked me if I objected to him smoking in the car but, quite frankly, for what I was being paid who cared? In any case, he always sat in the rear nearside seat and, no matter the weather, he had the window open when he lit up, so I didn't really suffer from it at all.

The boss would go to a different restaurant in Mayfair or to one of the big hotels on Park Lane, (The Dorchester, Grosvenor House to name but a couple) most nights of the week. He would occasionally meet up with friends but, being a bachelor, he usually went by himself. Sometimes he would conduct business meetings over dinner but, being quite a shy man, he seemed to prefer his own company. The same parking criteria applied at all of these establishments, bung the doorman and get the number one spot.

I was dumbstruck by his wealth, as I will explain. Having worked for the boss for a couple of months he asked me to drive him to a certain jewellers in Bond Street, the family jeweller. Here I was to later see some of the family's jewels; fabulous pieces made from precious stones arranged in all manner of items, necklaces, bangles, tiaras and cuff links that would only be surpassed by our Monarch's collection of Crown Jewels in the Tower of London.

On this particular day he was going to buy a new watch, not

your usual Rolex, TAG Heuer etc, no, he was going to see a Patek Philippe that had been specially commissioned for him and handmade to his own design, costing a cool £500,000.

On the way back to the car we stopped at a Watches of Switzerland shop where he beckoned me over to look at the watches on display. Having scoured the window display he pointed one out.

"That's a nice watch, Brian, do you like it?" Thinking that he was buying a cheap one for himself – £30,000 cheap – I played along and agreed that it would be a nice everyday watch for him.

"No, no," he said. "It's for you."

What me! No, I told him that I couldn't accept such a gift from him. "My mum and dad would turn over in their grave if they thought that I would accept such a gift so soon going to work for you," I explained.

With that he turned and headed back to the car in silence, travelled back to the house in silence, and even when I said goodnight to him I was met with silence. After work and once back home, I told Jax the story and she thought that he had taken offence and that I would probably be sacked in the morning. *Bloody hell!* I thought. *She is most likely right!* It's all right having principals and standards but not if I was going to get the sack in the morning.

Sure enough, the next day my fears appeared to be found. As soon as I appeared at the house one of the staff told me that Omar wanted to see me in the library, a place staff never set foot in as it was where the boss conducted most of his business. Sat behind his desk was the boss, next to it was Omar and then there was me feeling like a schoolboy called up to see the headmaster. Omar asked me for my version of the events in Bond Street the previous morning and I explained what, in my view, had taken place, clenching the car keys in my hands behind my back ready to give to him. Omar turned to the boss and said something in Arabic. The boss nodded in agreement and this is what Omar then said.

"The boss was shocked when you told him why you couldn't accept a gift of the kind he was offering. Coming from such a wealthy family, all through his life, all kinds of people had done nothing but take advantage of him at any opportunity and in any way that they could. When you refused his offer he was deeply touched that, for the first time in his life, someone wasn't interested in him just for his money. I am instructed by the boss to give you a substantial pay rise, together with a promise that you will never be replaced, and that you have a job here for life. Oh yes, and he won't allow you to resign either."

I was shocked, to say the least. I never expected that. Feeling quite proud of myself, I said thank you and left the room, saying under my breath, "Wow, that's what happens when you do the right thing." Following me out, Omar also told me that the boss was paying for a dinner for my friends and me in celebration of my forthcoming marriage, a kind of stag night, at a local restaurant to be arranged by Omar. This took place a few days before Jax and I were due to head out to Florida and a bloody good night was had by all.

Jacqui was putting our wedding plans together in a very professional manner. She had booked the venue, catering, photographer and so on and sent out invitations to family and friends, namely, Roy and Wendy; David, her brother, his nine year old daughter Katie and his latest girlfriend Karen; Pete and Ann; Jacqui's cousin Suzanne and her husband Ivan. On my side there was Paul; his second wife Emma (Paul and Lyn were divorced by this time); my best friend Steve and wife Kathy; and friends, Lee and Mandie.

So come the time, we all travelled to Orlando with Virgin Atlantic on their direct morning flight to MCO, except for Paul and Emma who had made their own arrangements and would meet up with us at the wedding location. On arrival we collected our rental cars and made our way to the accommodation that Jax had booked for everybody. We, of course, stayed in our own villa.

The next couple of days were spent preparing for the big

day. Firstly, Jax and I visited the wedding venue, then we checked sundries like the car arrangements, Jax's hair appointment etc, to make sure all was in order. It was, of course, because Jax had been meticulous in her arrangements.

On the eve of the wedding we had arranged for a get together at an Italian restaurant in the small town of Celebration, a 1950s themed creation by the Walt Disney Company. When I say 'themed' it is an experiment in living by a community of like-minded souls who seek out a more gentler way of living. It has all the modern conveniences of a regular town; hospital, gym, police station, that you would expect to find and an area with a limited number of shops and, of course, the venue for our wedding, the Celebration Golf Club.

As our dinner guests began to arrive I was getting a little concerned that Paul and Emma were leaving it rather late as we were starting to take our places. Steve, amongst others, asked where I thought they might be.

"I don't know," I replied. "But I'm sure they will be here soon. Paul won't let us down, after all, he is my best man."

We all sat down and dinner started to be served. I was concerned that something had happened to them. Maybe Paul had got lost? Extremely unlikely! Or maybe their hire car had broken down. Or they may even have had an accident.... Course after course arrived with them not having appeared and, the longer the evening went on, the less likely I felt it was that they would come. The following day when I met up with Paul he told me that he and Emma had wanted to do their own thing.

That night, Mandie stayed in our villa so that she could help Jacqui get ready on her big day while I stayed with Steve, Kath, and Lee, as tradition demanded that the groom cannot see the bride until at the altar. Come the morning of the wedding we each got ready and when presentable Lee drove us to the Celebration Golf Club. Upon arrival we were greeted by the club's event organiser, a pleasant young woman called Robyn, who offered us a drink from the bar. Fairly soon our guests started to arrive and, with drinks in hand, began to chat amongst themselves.

I greeted David and was asked by him where he could get changed. David, you see, was under orders from Jacqui that he would attend her wedding dressed in his Royal Marine blue dress uniform. Robyn directed us to the men's changing room used by the golfers. While chatting with Dave as he was getting changed it became obvious to the other occupants that here was a military man as revealed by his uniform. It soon became clear that he was a Royal Marine and so the men changing in the room shook his hand or clapped and said, "Thanks for what you did in Iraq and Afghanistan." David was extremely embarrassed by all the fuss and couldn't wait to get outside and away from the adulation. Not so easy as, when we walked from the changing room to the venue, lots of golfers stopped and clapped at David.

Everybody was assembled and ready to go out into the garden where the wedding would take place. The ceremony was to be held on a beautiful, raised, white, open-sided octagonal gazebo. A few minutes ahead of the bride-to-be's arrival the wedding party, under the direction of the man officiating, were told to take their seats. I was told where to stand in the gazebo and duly took my place and waited for my bride to arrive. I think Paul was on lookout duty and nodded to us that the limousine carrying Jacqui and her father had arrived. Looking straight ahead, and not wanting to spoil the moment, I sensed Roy leading Jacqui up to my side. As he came alongside he uttered these words, which I will never forget, "Just you watch yourself, all right."

When I looked at Jacqui standing beside me I saw the most beautiful woman in the world who was ready to be my wife. She looked absolutely fabulous, no princess ever looked as pretty as my Jacqui. I will always remember saying "Wow," to myself as my breath was taken away by her looking so gorgeous.

The official started to say the wedding vows which were a mix of the old, traditional, and the new. We had decided to include a small narrative of a Native American blessing which, unfortunately, I cannot remember but was liked by both of us when we were choosing the words to be spoken. Having placed rings on each other's fingers and declared under oath all the usual commitments, the official declared us to be husband and wife.

The guests offered their congratulations and much kissing and handshaking took place. Photos and video were taken – a professional photographer took the stills and Lee was commanded to make the video, thanks for that Lee.

The photographer walked us to various locations around Celebration and took photos of us crossing bridges, seated together by a stream and walking hand in hand along tree-lined footpaths. When we arrived at the old town square I spotted a white four-wheeled open carriage that had a pair of the whitest-grey horses you would ever see standing resplendent in their shiny black tack waiting for their first clients of the day to be taken around Celebration. Having chatted-up the driver and dropping him a $20 bill, Jax and I climbed inside the carriage and had a few wedding photographs taken. When the photos arrived back home in England a couple of weeks later the photographer had cleverly photoshopped a 'Just Married' sign to the back of the carriage.

Back at the venue, our guests were having a merry time. Nibbles and drinks had been set out in the garden for them to enjoy while being entertained by Mystic NRG, a Florida-based reggae steel band.

Later, we went inside to have an early evening dinner and while this was being prepared we had the odd glass of something. Robyn asked Jacqui to inspect the wedding table to make sure that all was laid out per her instruction. Jacqui concurred that all was to her satisfaction, place names cards had been laid out correctly, small gifts for the bridesmaids were within reach and so on.

When it was time to take our places Robyn invited us to take our places for dinner. All was going well until Mandie was served her dinner and she told the waitress it wasn't what she had chosen.

"You are Emma Gaskin, aren't you?" asked the waitress.

"No, I'm not actually. My name is Mandie Briggs." It turned out that Emma had switched place name cards as she wanted to sit next to Paul. Not what we had intended and, thus, it caused a problem, a minor one granted. Happily, it was the only problem we had the whole day.

After dinner, speeches were made, the cake was cut, and gifts opened. The adjoining room was opened up to us so that the original room could be cleared and Mystic NRG could set their instruments up for the party. A great time was had by all that night. Mystic NRG had had a minor hit called 'Hold ya Head' and performed this song and said that whoever danced best would get a prize. The winner was Ann, Pete's wife, although what the prize was I don't know. All too soon, it was time to end the most wonderful day of my life thus far. Jax had always wanted to travel in a white stretched limousine, and so the transport back to our villa was the biggest, longest Hummer you could imagine, complete with a setting that wouldn't go amiss in a disco; roof lights, dark glass around the crushed velvet seating for eighteen people and an interior roof with a night time effect that beamed with a million tiny stars.

Back at the villa, our guests started to make their way back to their own accommodation, some by taxi and others, those who were capable, drove themselves. Eventually, we were left alone together and all too quickly the day was over.

The next week or so we met socially with our guests until it was time for them to depart for home or go on elsewhere, as was the case with Paul and Emma. Jax and I were disappointed that they left the day after our wedding and didn't spend any time with us. After all, they had come 3,000 miles to attend our wedding and were my only family there. A day spent with them would have rounded things off nicely for me personally.

On our return home little did we know what lay in store for us and rest of the world as the financial system around the globe went into near meltdown in the financial crisis of 2008. It was primarily caused by deregulation in the financial industry that permitted banks to engage in hedge fund trading with derivatives. Banks then demanded more mortgages to support the profitable sale of these derivatives that created the financial crisis and led to another recession.

We, like many, saw the value of our villa plummet overnight. We decided that the only sensible thing to do was to sell up as quickly as we could and, fortunately for us, we didn't lose any of our initial capital as we sold at just above the original asking price.

What a blow this was. We believed our financial future was secure. The value of the villa had rocketed at one point to $330,000, the house in Chafford Hundred was going up faster than a space rocket and, with my new position as head chauffeur to a billionaire, all looked very rosy indeed.

In April we held a wedding party for friends and family who were unable to attend our day with us in Florida. This was held at Berwick Manor Hotel and Restaurant, in Rainham and was very much a traditional wedding party knees up. Thanks, once again, to all those who attended. Jax and I had a great time that night.

This was a disappointing and tragic time for us, more so for me than Jax. She had managed to keep her job as a personal assistant at the Swiss bank UBS, not through any luck of the draw as others were made redundant, no, it was because she was really good at her job and was too good an asset to lose. One thing about Jax is that, as far as work is concerned, she is diligent, loyal, trustworthy, knowledgeable and reliable.

For me, things were going to get worse. On the work front all was going really well. My relationship with the boss was good and I felt very settled. I knew that I was accepted and, in some cases, looked up to and admired by the staff. Everything was good, and then it happened. Little did I know as I made my way home one night, but my life was to take a tragic turn for the worse.

During the night, probably about 4.00 am my phone rang. Wearily, I looked at who was calling and saw that it was the house number of the boss. On answering, I was told by one of the Gurkha security guards to, "Come quickly back to the house, Mr Brian, the boss is dead!" I told the little fella that if he was playing some kind of sick joke he would be for it in the morning. "No, no, please come now," he begged and from the tone of his voice I knew that he wasn't joking at all. Quickly explaining to Jax that I had to go and why, I said that I would update her as and when I could.

When I arrived at the house there were a couple of police cars parked outside and, indeed, two police officers stationed outside the front door. Having told them who I was and being let into the house I was immediately told by a shocked Omar that the boss was, indeed, dead. At about 3.30 am one of the patrolling guards just happened to be passing past the boss's bedroom door and heard a crashing noise coming from inside. He then went to wake Omar and the pair of them returned to the boss's bedroom. Having knocked on the bedroom door a couple of times Omar decided to enter. Upon doing so, he saw that the bed had been slept in but was empty. The bathroom light was on and visible under the door. Omar opened the door to see the boss lying on the floor. He knew immediately, probably by his military training, that the boss was dead.

The security guard was dispatched to stand outside the bedroom with orders not to let anyone in, and he meant anyone. Omar called the family doctor and the police who arrived quickly. By now, of course, all the staff were awake and knew what was going on. The doctor confirmed that the boss was dead and had started, even at this early hour, to make arrangements for the body to be removed.

Being who the man was, the coroner gave permission for the body to be removed to the Westminster Morgue in Horseferry Road, SW1, where an autopsy would be carried out as quickly as possible. It is customary for a Muslim to be buried as soon as possible.

The body was removed later that morning by a black 'private ambulance', seen off by almost the entire staff, most of whom were in tears or in shock at what they were witnessing. The butler turned to me and said, "That's us out the door mate, but at least we'll all get a decent pay off." Great, that's all I wanted to hear. The staff didn't know what to do that day, but Omar told them in a meeting that we were to carry on as usual until such time as a strategy had been worked out for us, so that's precisely what we all tried to do.

The next day I was to learn that the boss was to be taken to his homeland of Saudi Arabia and buried almost upon arrival there. The autopsy had taken place and the coroner had released the body for burial within twenty-four hours of death. He was only thirty-nine when he died of a heart attack. I don't know what caused it, I guess working all the hours that God sent and smoking a couple of packets of cigarettes a day didn't help!

Later that day Omar, together with a few close friends of the boss, were driven by myself and the butler to the private VIP area at Heathrow where they were to accompany the boss's coffin that had already been loaded on to a luxuriously fitted out Boeing 747 for the six hour flight to Jeddah, the capital city of Saudi Arabia.

As the butler and I stood watching the plane take off and disappear into the night sky, little did we realise that things were going to get worse. The senior butler took charge of running the house over the next couple of days and had told the other butler what provision had been made for the thirty or so staff that the boss employed both in London and at the villa in Cannes. All were to be let go and would be paid off accordingly taking into account their position and length of service. As most of the domestic staff were Pilipino in origin whatever payout they got would tide them over until they found another job or decided to go home.

The butler told me I would be taken care of as the boss had really liked me, especially after the watch incident, and that I would be okay financially. Apparently, £3,000,000 had been set aside for the staff with some naturally, like Omar and the senior Arab butler, earmarked to have big six-figure pay-outs coming their way and the rest distributed accordingly. Great, except for one thing.

By the end of the week, a couple of days after the boss's body had been repatriated back to Jeddah, I was presented with a formal thank you letter for my service to the boss over the past eight months. However, the letter continued to say that they were very sorry but my employment had been terminated at once and further communication would follow in due course. I took that to mean the money would be paid to me later, once the legalities had been dealt with. *Fair enough*, I thought. I quickly said my goodbyes and made my way to Victoria train station to go back home. Funny that, hours earlier I had been driving a Bentley Continental 6.0l Flying Spur 48 and now I was on Shank's pony to the train station.

The next day, I received a telephone call from the butler who, through the anger in his voice, told me that Omar had run off with the money and was nowhere to be seen. He explained that was it, no payout for any of us, the money had gone. I knew the boss was dead and gone, and I was genuinely sorry for that, but s**t.

Having spoken to the boss's lawyer and got nowhere, I had to accept what had happened and get on with finding another job pretty quickly.

I bummed around trying out one so-called executive car service company after another over the next couple of years until I was forced to give up work altogether, but more of that later as I am getting a bit ahead of myself here.

One night, in the early autumn of that year, 2008, Jacqui said to me the words that I had been longing to hear her say but never thought that I would. "I would really like us to try for a family."

After all the bad stuff that had happened to me, and us, over the years, yes, of course, I would. It would be wonderful if we could have a little family. I have to admit that I was both elated and frightened at the same time when, around Christmas time, Jacqui told me that she was three months pregnant. It was excellent news that we passed on to family and friends as soon as we possibly could.

In addition to the appropriate GP/midwife appointments, Jacqui decided that we would attend evening NCT childbirth sessions, once a week, at the health clinic in Stanford-le-Hope, Essex. During these sessions we made friends with couples who were in a similar position to us.

As the weeks rolled by, and Jacqui got bigger and bigger, from time to time, I had little moments where, due to my past experiences, I would begin to imagine the worst happening all over again. Completely irrational, I know as I knew that the problem didn't lie with me. Jacqui was healthy with no history of any problems associated with childbirth in her family.

We were given a due date of late June 2009 and the weeks seemed to fly by. With a couple of months to go, Jax told me that she would like to find a doula to be present at the birth as her mother was not alive to help her during childbirth.

"A what?" I asked.

"A doula," she explained, "is an independent person, trained in such matters, who is by the expectant mother's side to help and encourage her through the labour until the baby is delivered." I agreed, as it sounded like a good idea.

Jacqui found a lovely lady, who lived nearby, named Sandra Cowley. When we met her I could tell that Jacqui and Sandra got on well together and that she was going to be the one. Jacqui kept in regular contact with Sandra as the time grew ever closer to the due date.

On Friday, 26<sup>th</sup> June, 2008, Jacqui told me that her contractions were close enough for us to go to the maternity unit at Basildon Hospital. Once there, Jacqui was examined and told that it was not quite time just yet so we should get something to eat and keep an eye on what was happening. We went to the hospital public restaurant and each had fish and chips. Well, it was Friday after all. Halfway through the meal Jacqui said,

"Oops time to go!"

We went back to the maternity unit and, sure enough, they agreed it was all systems go. I rang Sandra and asked her to make her way to Basildon Hospital as it was all happening. Jacqui was taken to the delivery suite and linked up to a monitor. The attending midwife administered, and dealt with, other things while I made a swift exit.

Sandra arrived, and we all settled back for nature to take over. And take over it did! After a lot of massaging and encouragement from Sandra, Jacqui had consumed copious amounts of gas and air up to the point where she was encouraged by the midwife and Sandra to push for all she was worth.

Holding Jacqui's hand, the most wonderful moment came for all of mankind, the moment a child is born, and it was happening right in front of my eyes. I was so relieved when the baby was born okay. Upon hearing the baby cry for the first time all the heartache, sadness and sorrow of the previous twenty-nine years were gone in an instant. I sank to my knees and burst into tears as absolute relief and joy flooded through me.

At 6.50 am on Saturday, 27th June 2009, George Stanley Gaskin came into this world weighing 7lb 4oz; our son was born. George was checked over by a nurse almost immediately the umbilical cord was cut, laying him down on a set of scales I could hear her say, "Yup, all there, two eyes, two ears, ten fingers and toes." Then George was brought back to Mum and Dad, and when I held him for the first time I cried and cried, not through sadness but with joy. The horror of the past was put to one side for a moment, but soon, Mark, Charlotte and Andrew were very much in my thoughts.

I popped outside for a moment while Jacqui and George were made presentable, and my thoughts turned to the ones who would never have the joy of knowing their grandchild George; Eunice, Jacqui's mum who had died from stomach cancer when Jax was only fifteen and, of course, my mum and dad, Elsie and

Stanley, who had also died many years beforehand. I said, "Mum and Dad, we did it at last," shed a few more tears, and went back to mother and baby.

Jacqui and George were eventually taken to the maternity ward where they were to stay for forty-eight hours before being allowed home the following Monday morning. We all went home to Chafford Hundred where our little family was to spend the next few years.

My emotions were not as under control as I thought they might be after George was born. Every time he cried I felt incredibly sad, why? I think it's because it brought back to me the fact that I never heard Mark, Charlotte or Andrew cry. I know it sounds crazy, and I could never work out why I felt that way, but I did and still felt that way for many years after. I guess it must have been hard for Jax to see this and, on one occasion when I was a bit tearful, she said to me, harshly, in my mind at least, "Get over it!" I thought that was a bit cruel as I will never forget the traumatic times that I went through all those years before. I didn't take it to heart too much as I know that if she had experienced half of what I had she would never have said it. I hope and pray that she never does.

Jax was on six months maternity leave from work to get acquainted with, and look after George. During this time she took many videos and photos of them together for me to see when I came home from work, and lovely they are too.

Before it was time for her to go back to work, Jax enrolled George into the local nursery, where he would attend every day Monday to Friday, aged six months, right up until his first day at Harris Academy Primary, ten minutes' walk from our house. He blossomed at nursery and became very attentive to the other children to the point that, if they hurt themselves or got upset for some reason, he would immediately run over to cuddle and comfort them.

George also enthusiastically joined in all the events, play and stories they enjoyed. At tea and lunch times he would help to clear the tables, and he was a real help to the staff there. I know they were genuinely sad to see him go when he eventually left.

When George went on to primary school, he was so excited and happy on his first day, proudly posing for photos in his new, grown-up school uniform with school bag to match. He broke my heart with the joy and happiness he portrayed going in to meet his first teacher, Miss Davidson, and all his new classmates that he was to make friends with. From the first day at the end of class he would give Miss Davidson a hug, without fail, until the day he left.

The reason for his leaving was due to another sad event in our lives.

# Chapter Thirteen

Over the years, Roy had had his fair share of bad luck with health issues. I understand that, for many years as a young child, he had worn leg irons. Later on in life he had fallen and badly hurt his left ankle. Jax thinks that he may have dislocated it and never had it looked at but just got on with it. You may think that was a stubborn thing to do, and I for one agree, but you have to bear in mind that when Jax's mum was ill with cancer Roy felt that the medical profession had let her down severely due to the treatment that she had received.

In a way, I suppose Roy felt that, unless it was necessary, he would not want to be part of the system that had let them down, instead dealing with it in his way. He had an accident at work while working as a bus driver when he got his neck caught in the automatic doors on one of the newer driver only buses. How that happened I never really got to the bottom of. When he crashed through the glass door during Jax's 21st birthday party, he severed nerves in his right arm, resulting in the partial loss of movement in his right hand. All while he was running the sorting/Post Office at Ingatestone in Essex.

This meant that he was up at 4.00 am to drive the fifteen miles or so from home in Bowers Gifford to open up for the postmen and women at 5.00 am to allow them to take delivery and sort the day's mail ready for their rounds. He would then run the counter service until closing up at 5.00 pm, then either going straight out for dinner with Wendy or spending the evening with her at home, finally getting into his own bed usually after 11 o'clock at night.

In all the years that I knew Roy he never once complained about anything related to work even though it was a punishing regime and one that a much younger man would have found it difficult to keep up with. I think part of the reason for his willingness to work so hard is that both he and his younger brother were born into a poor family, like so many born during or just after World War II. I believe that this fear of poverty drove him on but, whatever the reason, I admired him for it.

His health was an issue, and here was a man doing excessive hours with a body that would have tried the best of us. The fact that he was unable to walk properly, suffered from a persistent neck injury and had a hand that was not functioning correctly didn't seem to worry Roy, but did concern the rest of us. This was not helped by a fall on to a railway track at a station in Norway while on holiday with Wendy. He was all right but Wendy insisted that he went to see his GP on their return to the UK.

Once home, he did indeed go and see his GP. Sadly though, they had known each other for so long that the consultation was more about the weather or how well/badly West Ham United was doing that season. A medical examination certainly was not the order of the day on these visits, if they had been maybe Roy would be with us today in 2019.

He was diagnosed with bowel cancer in the summer of 2011 which saw him deteriorate rapidly, because sadly the cancer had gone too far for any treatment to be effective. He had been told that he had, at most, two years of life left, quite upsetting for those closest to him. Initially, his health wasn't too bad but, as the months passed, he got worse and worse. He was forced to sell the Post Office as he was no longer strong enough to continue with the long hours that he had been working.

For his age he was always on the go, but now he was reduced to taking a multitude of tablets to keep going and couldn't go out as much as he had been used to in previous years. David had a stair lift fitted in the house as Roy found it difficult to walk up the stairs to the bathroom and his bedroom.

One evening, Wendy called Jax and asked if I could come to the house and help Roy to his feet as he had collapsed in the doorway of the downstairs WC. I was soon on my way, leaving Jax to look after George and put him to bed as he was only four at the time. When I got to the house Wendy was quite upset and quickly showed me where Roy was. He was lying in an awkward position which made it impossible for me to help him to his feet and the only way to get him up was to dial 999 and get an ambulance crew to help.

Poor Roy had to wait for over two hours for an ambulance to arrive. When one did eventually turn up the two male crew members struggled for a while but did, finally, manage to get Roy on his feet. They were reluctant to take Roy to hospital although, quite clearly, he had to go to be checked over, at the very least. When Wendy explained that Roy lived alone and he, therefore, didn't have anybody to care for him all the time, they decided to take Roy to Basildon Hospital A&E department for assessment. What a nightmare that turned out to be.

I drove behind the ambulance and stayed with Roy at the hospital all that night. Having been assessed by a doctor, and with the information that I gave as to why we were there, the doctor found Roy a room where he could be further examined.

I am aware that the NHS is underfunded and services in A&E departments are stretched so I will be as kind as I possibly can here.

Having arrived at the allotted room in A&E, the porter left, and a nurse came into the room to check that the patient was whom they were expecting. As she was leaving she said that it would not be too long before a doctor would come and see Roy. Two hours came and went and nobody appeared so I went looking for someone who could help. As I did so, a middle-aged man was walking in front of me holding a can of strong lager in one hand and a bandage on his arm with the other, followed by his loudmouth wife who was moaning that they had been in A&E for about fifteen minutes before he arrived in this department to have his arm seen too. No doubt the injury had been self-inflicted as he was worse the wear for the amount of alcohol that he had consumed, she was no better.

Having spoken to somebody on yet another reception desk I was rudely told, "Yes, Mr Brenchley will be seen to, don't worry." On my return, I could see that Roy was in considerable pain as he had been lying in the same position for some time. After another hour of being left I went back to the same nurse on reception and, in a much firmer tone of voice, demanded that Roy, after waiting for three hours to be seen, needed seeing to NOW. Never mind about the scumbag drunks coming in to be patched up due to either getting into a fight or just collapsing and banging their head or getting a cut or blooded knuckles. This man was a cancer sufferer and needed urgent attention.

Within five minutes a doctor arrived at Roy's room. Well, I say doctor, she looked about fifteen. She was of oriental descent and had a strong non-English accent as she asked what the problem was. Having asked her if she had read the notes she began to do just that. After quickly reading them she obviously hadn't digested any of the information, as she began to examine Roy who, by now, was in agony with his legs as he hadn't moved for hours. I explained to her why Roy was there, because his legs had given way at home some hours earlier and he was now incapable of walking.

Now, here it comes…wait for it…you know what the dozy imbecile said next? Yes, you've got it. "Can you stand up for me, Mr Brenchley, and walk to the door so I can see how steady you are on your legs?"

"What the f**k! Are you deaf or just plain stupid?" I said to her angrily, but before she had a chance to answer I told her to get out a send a proper doctor to attend to Roy. Two minutes later, another doctor came in with her in tow behind. He took a look at Roy's notes and told her to go and get a porter as he was admitting Roy immediately. He didn't apologise for the way Roy had been dealt with, but I could tell by his body language that he was annoyed that Roy had been treated in the manner that he had been.

Very soon afterwards two porters arrived to take Roy to a ward. I followed with the few things that Wendy had put in a bag for him. When we got to the ward it was in darkness except for a few night lights as it was, by now, about 2.00 in the morning. As they wheeled the bed into position by the large window overlooking an inner courtyard I caught Roy's reflection. He was staring out of the window with the same look that a frightened rabbit has when it gets caught in a car's headlights. At that instant I don't think I had ever felt so sorry for anybody in my life before. I was absolutely gutted for him.

When I arrived home I told Jax all about the previous night and what ward her dad was in so that she could visit him in the morning. She called David and filled him in on events and also called Wendy to relay the night's events to her.

Wendy had been a stalwart for Roy. She did everything for him while he had been laid up at home; she took care of his washing and ironing, cooked and cleaned for him and sat and held his hand when he needed it.

The following day when we went to see Roy, he had been moved to a side room and was by himself. *Not a good move*, I thought, as Roy was the kind of man who thrived on company. Anyway, he was settled and being looked after and that was the main thing. Various doctors came and went over the next few days, but didn't really tell us that much.

David had visited a couple of times and had second guessed what was about to happen next. The hospital wanted to discharge Roy as, in their opinion, they had done enough to stabilise Roy and now they wanted him out so they could have the bed for somebody else.

David had recently undertaken a course in law and had obtained his degree and was about to put this to good use. A meeting had been arranged between Jacqui, David and myself with the discharge manager to discuss the next move. David, dressed in a smart suit, with his black briefcase, looked the part of a man who knew his stuff and was going to fight for his father's rights and well-being no matter what. Also at this meeting were two social workers from Basildon District Council.

Having given her reasons for the need for Roy to vacate the hospital bed that they thought he had no right to remain in, the discharge manager handed over to the social workers. I must emphasise that they were far from social, forgive me for believing that they have the patient's well-being as their first consideration. Oh no, these couple of clowns started off by saying that they wanted to know Roy's financial position, house value, bank accounts, stocks and shares and investments as they said Roy had to go into a care home and would be footing the bill for the privilege.

Right on cue, David produced a sheaf of official looking paperwork from his briefcase and started to tell the social workers precisely what was going to happen next. He quoted case after case of high court judgements that had been declared in similar cases. Their superior demeanour dropped in an instant, their chins hitting their boots as he told them what they had to do. No, they were not entitled to know Roy's financial position, instead, as a terminally ill patient he was entitled to a place in a nursing home and they, the council, were liable to pay for it. Oh, and by the way, they had twenty-four hours to find him a place or he would be taking them and the council to court. He said he would be returning at the same this time the next day, and they had better have a satisfactory answer for us. Well done, Dave.

Low and behold twenty-four hours later the discharge manager had, indeed, found Roy a place in a local care home, Godden Lodge, in Thundersley, Essex. It was located about ten minutes' drive from where Wendy lived so it was convenient for the times that she visited him, which was frequent.

For both Jacqui and I it meant that we could only manage to visit him a couple of times during the week, but almost every weekend we would get to see him. George always liked going to see his granddad as it meant that he could sit in a big armchair all by himself. He would come with me to the kitchen where he knew that he would get a couple of biscuits while I made us all a cup of tea. I'm sorry to say that Roy's stay was short-lived. He grew desperately ill after a few weeks and, unfortunately, Roy sadly passed away on 23$^{rd}$ November, 2013.

I do miss old Roy. He could be the most cantankerous, argumentative, stubborn old so and so, but he had a heart of gold and was, at times, too generous to those he loved. I cannot possibly mention here all the stories that I could tell about Roy, but what I will say is that over the twenty years or so that I knew him I had my fair share of really good times with him, mostly when we got together on a Saturday night and went out for a meal at one of the local pubs that he knew.

One last thing, George loved riding up and down on Roy's stair lift whenever we went to see him at his home in Bowers Gifford, and I think that memory will live with George forever.

I want to back up a couple of months at this point and tell you a little story about how I came to meet one of the nicest people that it's been my fortune to call a friend and a good one at that.

In late September 2013, while working as a so-called executive car service chauffeur, I was given a job by control late on Thursday evening to collect a passenger from his home in Walthamstow at 5.15 the following morning and take him to his place of work, Planet Rock, in Winsley Street, just off Oxford Street in London W1, where he presented the morning show from 6.00–10.00 am every morning.

When he got into my car, he introduced himself as Paul Anthony, and I could immediately tell by his generous smile and overall demeanour that here was a nice bloke – you get to know the signs after nearly thirty years of chauffeuring. He asked my name and gave me his mobile telephone number in case I had a problem getting to him again so early in the morning. Taking this as a sign that he might prefer a regular driver, and being entirely mercenary on my part, I made sure that his office spoke to my controller and that I was requested for the job every day from then on.

Within weeks of Roy dying, early December as I recollect, I was in the bathroom at home one evening about to have a shave when Jax remarked, "The mole on your left upper back has gone a funny shape and colour?" Unfortunately, I knew exactly what that meant but didn't admit so to Jax. "You had better get that checked out as soon as possible."

The next day I made an appointment to see the GP and, upon examining me, he called the hospital and made an appointment for me. In a few days' time, Jax and I found ourselves at a small clinic at Basildon Hospital. We were called in to see a young, female, Asian doctor who, upon examining my back, said that they would remove the mole there and then and send it to the lab for analysis.

We went back to the waiting area and took our seats until I was again called. I went on my own to a small medical room where a nurse administered local anaesthetic to the area where the mole was located, extracted it, told me to get dressed and on my way out make an appointment to see the doctor again. The receptionist made an appointment for 10th February, 2014 – the day before Jax's birthday. It looked like I was in for a merry Christmas then. Just think of it, knowing what it was likely to be, Christmas 2013 was not going to be a very jolly one for me, was it?

Christmas and New Year came and went, and when Jax and I returned for the follow-up appointment the doctor confirmed that the biopsy had shown the mole was cancerous. That's right, I had skin cancer.

The results of the biopsy confirmed the suspicions and fears that I had had from the moment Jax first told me about what she had seen, just before Christmas. The doctor had already made an appointment for me to attend the cancer clinic at Broomfield Hospital, in Chelmsford, Essex, in a few days' time. *Crikey*, I thought, *that's quick!*

By now I was getting on really well with Paul Anthony and decided to tell him that I would be retiring at the end of the week and, therefore, unable to drive him any longer and explained the reason behind my decision. He was very understanding and thoroughly nice to me and said, genuinely, that he wanted me to keep in touch with him. He gave me his personal mobile telephone number and said, "Call any time."

He also said that he was sorry to hear the news and wished me and the family the best for the future.

On the last day of driving Paul to work I was saddened that it had come to this and that I was probably not going to see him again. Well, I got that wrong! One day, when I was due to go to London Bridge Hospital, I called and asked Paul if I could pop into the Planet Rock studios. "Of course," he told me and so, on the day of my appointment, I first went to see him, he took me to the studio where he was broadcasting his live show and let me sit in so I could see first-hand what was going on. It is bewildering what Paul has to do to present the show in the professional manner that he does, and so expertly too. Paul has become a good friend over the years and, from time to time, I and have a coffee with him either in the studio or in the local coffee shop.

On one visit (November 2018), we went to the local coffee shop and had our usual chinwag. I was pushed for time, as was he, so we didn't get as much time as usual, and Paul said one of the nicest things to me. He told me that he cherished our friendship because I was just me, something that he valued very much. I can understand what he meant by that as I have seen it all too often. When someone is in the position that Paul is in, I can imagine a lot of people want to know you for what you are, not who you are, and I think that he recognised the latter in me. I also feel the same way, thanks for being a true friend, Paul.

On the day of the appointment I made my way to the hospital on my own. Jax and I had both agreed that it wasn't necessary for her to come with me as it was only the first consultation and nothing was going to happen other than him/her telling me what was going to happen next.

Having checked in I waited in the large waiting room, empty but for me and another patient, a middle-aged woman who, like me, was on her own. Within a few minutes my name was called, and I followed a nurse to the consulting room of the doctor I was about to see. The doctor introduced himself and began by asking me a few questions about what had led me to be seen by him that day. *Don't you already know all about it*, I thought, but I told him anyway.

Now I don't know of any way to explain what happened, other than to say how it transpired. Once I had finished speaking, the doctor responded to my explanation but, being from the Indian sub-continent, his spoken English was not very clear to me. In fact, I found it difficult to understand what he was telling me. After the consultation the nurse took me to reception and made another appointment for me in a couple of weeks.

Later that day, when Jax arrived home, I tried to remember as best I could what had happened at the hospital but I had to be honest and tell her that I hadn't been able to understand the doctor's accent and was amiss to know precisely what I had been told. "Still," I said to her, "when I go back next time, it's bound to be somebody else, as it usually is, and I might be able to understand them better."

When I returned, almost the same thing happened. The person I saw this time was a young, female, Asian doctor who, oh dear, I couldn't understand either. When I got home and spoke to Jax I felt troubled by this as I needed to understand completely what was happening.

I asked Jax to enquire about my condition being treated privately through the medical cover that the company where she worked provided and, if I was covered, I was going to look up the best skin cancer doctor that I could find. I have to say that if I could have understood what the doctors had told me at Broomfield, then I would have continued my treatment on the NHS.

Jax made an enquiry with the health insurance company that she had through work, and they agreed that I could be treated, as it wasn't a pre-existing condition, but laid down some limitation on where I could be treated. We chose the London Bridge Hospital and, being part of the HCA International Group, it was acceptable to the insurers. The hospital is located on the south side of the River Thames, almost next door to

London Bridge.

We had no idea who to make contact with, and not knowing where to start I penned a letter to the 'head of the cancer unit' at the hospital, a shot in the dark I know but we didn't know what else to do. Remarkably, within a couple of days I got a reply and was asked to attend the hospital to meet the 'head'.

I met Jax outside St Olaf House, the hospital's consulting and administration rooms, on Tooley Street, near to HMS *Belfast*, on the south side of London Bridge in central London.

Once inside we were met by a man behind a lectern holding an iPad, enquiring as to who we were and to whom we had come to see. He checked his iPad, and directed us to registration, from where we were directed to wait outside the door of the 'head'. I have to apologise as I cannot remember his name.

After about ten minutes we were called in to see him. We sat down and he produced the letter that I had written to him. He said something along these lines, "I am flattered that you should ask to see me, but the person that you need to see in the first instance is Mrs Jenny Geh. I have made an appointment for you to see her immediately after seeing me." He then called a nurse who promptly came to get us. I thanked him for his help and we made our way back to the seating area and waited to be called. I was feeling positive about things and calmly waited with Jax until we were called.

Mrs Geh called us into her consulting room and asked me to explain why I had come to see her and I started to relay the story to her in the sequence that the events had occurred. When I had finished speaking, she asked about the biopsy. "Did Basildon Hospital still have the sample?" I told her that I didn't know the answer to that and she said she would make enquiries. She made an appointment, there and then, for me to see her in two weeks' time and thanked me for coming.

At this point, I should like you to read the following about Mrs Geh, taken from her web page:

*Mrs Jenny L C Geh is Consultant Plastic Surgeon at Guy's, King's and St Thomas' NHS Foundation Trusts.*

*She was the Chair of the Plastics Pan-Thames Specialty Training Committee (2011-2012). She is a graduate of the University of Nottingham Medical School, full member of the British Association of Plastic and Reconstructive Aesthetic Surgeons (BAAPS), The British Association of Aesthetic Plastic Surgeons (BSAPS), The Royal College of Surgeons of Edinburgh (RCSEd), fully registered with the General Medical Council (GMC), and was an advisory member of the UK Melanoma Study Group (MSG), now taken up as part of Melanoma Focus.*

*Her present NHS post is with Guy's and St Thomas' NHS Trust, King's College Hospital. Previously had outreach clinics at the Orpington and Princess Royal Hospitals at Farnborough, but now at Queen Mary's hospital, Sidcup for Guy's and St Thomas' NHS Trusts. Mrs Jenny L C Geh is a Consultant Plastic Surgeon with a particular interest in melanoma, sentinel lymph node biopsy, non-melanoma skin cancers, reconstructive surgery for all skin lesions, including eyelid, ear and nose reconstruction. She has experience in using Integra® artificial skin for cancer reconstruction. She treats all aspects of plastic surgery including trauma and hand surgery. She was the first person in the UK and Europe to treat patients with skin cancer in the pelvis with the Da Vinci robot. She is actively involved in research on melanoma and skin cancer treatments. She was a specialist participant in the Parliamentary Melanoma Taskforce and Skin Specialist Interest Group at BAPRAS.*

*Chair of Education and Research for BAPRAS (2011-2012)*
*BAPRAS Council (co-apted member 2011-12)*
*Specialist Advisory Committee (SAC) for Plastic Surgery training, UK (co-apted member 2011-12)*
*Chair of Pan-Thames Plastic Surgery Training Committee London (2011-date)*
*Plastics Lead for Clinical Governance Guy's and St Thomas'*

I think I was in the very best hands, don't you?

When Jax and I went back to see her approximately two weeks later, she informed us that she had, indeed, recovered the mole along with the biopsy report.

I am going to describe events from now on using nonmedical terms where possible, but some terminology will inevitably be necessary, I hope you will bear with me.

She told me that I was fortunate that I had had the mole removed when I did as it showed features of melanoma. Its vertical growth was 2.9mm, which she told me was almost down to the beginning of the body's fat layer and if it penetrated this it would have been quite dangerous.

To begin with, Mrs Geh arranged for me to have a full body PET & CT brain scan at the Harley Street Clinic on 19th March, 2014.

Then on 28th March, 2014, in the early evening, I had a sentinel node scan at the Wellington Hospital, in London.

*A sentinel node scan is a test to identify the first lymph node that drains your tumour. This is called the sentinel node. A small amount of radioactivity is used to obtain pictures of this node to guide your surgeon when you have your surgery.*

*The amount of radiation you receive is as small as possible and is similar to other X-ray procedures. The radioactivity leaves the body very quickly, and it will not make you feel sick or sleepy.*

As I am extremely claustrophobic, I was dreading having the above scans, but realising the importance of them, I had them done albeit with, quite literally, gritted teeth.

Mrs Geh reviewed the results of the scans and decided to operate in the area where the mole had been located. The procedure, a negative wide local excision with sentinel node biopsy, with a V-Y flap, was performed at the London Bridge Hospital on 29th March, 2014. My diagnosis had been revised from Stage 2b to Stage 2a, which seemed to me that my condition had worsened, and I was advised by Mrs Geh to have a follow-up consultation with her in three months' time. She also advised me to see a leading oncologist, Dr Mark Harries, who is a colleague of hers at the London Bridge Hospital.

*Dr Mark Harries MA, PhD, FRCP is a Consultant Medical Oncologist who is based at Guy's & St Thomas' Hospitals NHS Foundation Trust and is an honorary senior lecturer at Kings College London School of Medicine.*
*Dr Harries graduated from Cambridge University and underwent clinical training at The Royal London Hospital. He trained in Medical Oncology at the Royal Marsden Hospital and completed a PhD and post-doctoral work in the Department of Immunology at University College London.*
*Dr Harries is a member of the Association of Cancer Physicians, Royal College of Physicians, American Society of Clinical Oncology, European Society of Medical Oncology and the British Medical Association.*

*Dr Harries specialises in the treatment of Breast Cancer and Melanoma.*

Again, I think I was in the best possible hands, don't you?

# Chapter Fourteen

On 9<sup>th</sup> May, 2014 I had my first appointment with Dr Harries at London Bridge Hospital. He explained that I had a generally favourable prognosis following the diagnosis of melanoma but, in view of the proliferation rate and thickness of the melanoma, he would recommend a strategy of proactive imaging every three to six months over the next three years. Three years eh, that doesn't sound that bad does it?

My first scans at the London Upright MRI centre in Newman Street, London W1 on 23<sup>rd</sup> June, 2014 reported that no significant abnormality was shown from the MRI brain scan. However, a slight lung/chest infection was noted but of little consequence, happy days then.

Everything seemed to be fine during the summer and we got on with life happy in the knowledge that it seemed I had dodged a bullet. My next scans took place on 16<sup>th</sup> December, 2014 at the London Upright MRI centre and, again, the results were remarkably good, showing no abnormality.

I was seen by Mrs Jenny Geh in Clinic at London Bridge Hospital on 6<sup>th</sup> March, 2015. She gave me a physical examination and I was given a clean bill of health. She wanted to see me again in six months' time but, in the meantime, I would see Dr Harries and have further scans at three month and six month intervals.

I'm not too sure of the date on this one but I believe it was in July 2015. Mrs Geh decided to remove, from my left armpit, twenty-two lymph nodes; the vessels that play a vital role in the body's ability to fight off infection. They function as filters that trap viruses, bacteria and causes of illness before other parts of the body become infected.

This was the next procedure in the treatment of my condition. I had now been diagnosed as being stage 3b, which meant that my condition had again worsened, how this had happened I am not quite sure. Anyway, one lymph node of the twenty-two was reported as being positive. Did this mean that I did, in fact, have worsening skin cancer?

I remember that when I was discharged from St Thomas' Hospital, a day after the surgery, my friend Chris offered to collect me and drive me home. I must have looked a strange sight as resplendent in shorts and T-shirt I also wore knee length, white compression stockings. When Chris saw me he couldn't stop laughing.

On 16<sup>th</sup> June, I had further scans and in clinic on the 19<sup>th</sup> Dr Harries told us that the scan had shown something lurking in my left upper chest. It could be something as innocent as seroma fluid, but he would send me for an ultrasound test to discover more and, in the meantime, alert Mrs Geh to the possibility of further surgery.

Now to my mind it was a tumour, no more, no less, and it scared the life out of me because it was the first real sign that, possibly, all was not going as well for me as I had thought. Indeed, the ultrasound showed a mass and although Dr Harris was neutral about what it might be, he arranged for Mrs Geh to operate on me to find out exactly what it was. Within a couple of weeks I found myself, once again, in St Thomas' Hospital awaiting surgery.

Mrs Geh came to see me before the operation and reassured me that, whatever it was that she found, she would take the appropriate action required. Having been administered a general anaesthetic, I went into deep unconsciousness and Mrs Geh began the procedure.

When I came round in the recovery room Mrs Geh was called and within five minutes she was at my bedside telling how well the operation had gone and what she had found which was…nothing. Absolutely nothing!

She explained that when she opened me up she couldn't see anything. Having called another doctor to confirm this she put me back together again and did such an excellent job that I never had any discomfort from the surgery. Mrs Geh has such a lovely bedside manner and made me feel very much at ease and said that she would come and see me later that day and definitely before I was discharged.

On 31<sup>st</sup> July, 2015, Jacqui and I went to see Dr Harries at the London Bridge Hospital. At this consultation he asked if I would like to be considered for a clinical trial of a new drug being developed by the American drug company Bayer Squibb. It was open to qualifying patients at the Royal Marsden Hospital, in London SW3, under the guidance of his colleague Dr James Larkin. This adjuvant therapy was trialling Ipilimumab v Nivolumab, and he hoped that when he spoke to Dr Larkin I might be eligible to go on the trial. We said goodbye and Dr Harries promised to be in touch as soon as he knew if I might get on the trial.

Dr Harries arranged for me to see Dr Larkin on 13<sup>th</sup> August, Jacqui and I went to the Royal Marsden Hospital and had a consultation with both Dr James Larkin and professor Gore for them to assess my suitability of going on the Bauer Squib trial. During this consultation I was made aware that there might be a couple of obstacles in my way, however, I was going to be given the opportunity to go on the trial if these obstacles could be overcome.

I was given some documents to read and complete and, with Jacqui's help, I managed to fill them in there and then. I was then told by Dr Larkin that they would be in touch If I was to be admitted on the trial when, if successful, my care would be supervised at the Royal Marsden.

After recent events both Jacqui and I left the Royal Marsden feeling quite upbeat. Where it had looked like there was only darkness ahead, the possibility of being admitted on the trial gave me renewed optimism that my condition could be treated successfully. Within a day or two, I received a telephone call from a clinical nurse (Karen) associated with the trial who said that there was a potential stumbling block to my inclusion on the trial as my bilirubin (a yellowish substance in your blood, it forms after red blood cells breakdown and travels through your liver, gallbladder and digestive tract before being excreted, the condition of high bilirubin levels is called *hyperbilirubinaemia* and is usually a sign of an underlying condition) count was too high above the parameters set for qualification. She explained that this would need further investigation but the qualifying date for inclusion on the trial was only a few days away.

This news came as quite a blow to me. I felt that if I could go on the trial I would somehow be alleviated of any forthcoming problems associated with melanoma. After a day or so Karen called me back to say that my medical records had shown that, historically, my bilirubin count was consistently higher than the normal readings so this didn't disqualify me from the trial.

This news filled me with optimism that my application to join the trial would be successful and, indeed, in early August 2015 I joined the trial. I was to go to clinic at the Royal Marsden every couple of weeks for treatment. Firstly, I would have a blood test, then a consultation with an oncologist and, if all appeared to be well, I would go to a treatment room to have the drugs infused via a cannula.

As the trial was 'double-blind' it meant the Royal Marsden didn't know which drugs, or even if a placebo was being given to me. The hospital would monitor my condition at every forthcoming appointment every three weeks. I got into a regular routine of travelling by train to London Fenchurch Street Station from Pitsea then taking the District Line on the London Underground to South Kensington Station and walking the last half mile to the Royal Marsden. All was well until the first week in December 2015 when I felt quite unwell. I cannot describe all the symptoms I was suffering other than feeling lethargic and tired. On 10th December, I decided to make my way to the Royal Marsden to see what could be done to help me overcome my current condition. I took an overnight bag with me as a precaution to being admitted as I felt might be necessary and so it proved to be. I was admitted because I had:

1.  Panhypopituitarism hypophysitis
2.  Autoimmune hepatitis.


I was given a room on an isolation ward where I was to spend the next three days.

During this time, I felt very depressed and from time to time got quite emotional. I remember one evening feeling sick and upset. I was so down and depressed lying in my bed that when the young nurse who brought my medication stayed with me, holding my hand and comforting me, for as long as it took to compose myself.

While in the recovery ward I had a blood test carried out and it was discovered that my pituitary gland was not working and this resulted in the following symptoms; nausea and vomiting, weakness, feeling cold, sexual dysfunction, increased amount of urine, and an unintended weight loss.

On the morning of 14<sup>th</sup> December, 2015, I was due to be discharged, and a doctor came to see me and explained that, from now on, I would need to take supplements of steroid and Levothyroxine and, in time, testosterone. This was to replace those hormones that, because of the loss of my pituitary gland, my body could not naturally produce any longer along with others that were necessary for my glands to function correctly. He also commented that my recovery from the loss of the functioning pituitary gland could take up to two years.

A consultant endocrinologist Dr Morgenstein, who felt that I had *Ipilimumab induced hypophysitis*, told me he would speak to Dr Harries about how they could best treat my condition.

On 18<sup>th</sup> December, I was reviewed in clinic by professor Gore who officially signed me off the trial, wished me good luck and scarpered as quickly as he could leaving me with the clinical nurse Karen. Thank you and good night then.

As it was late on in the afternoon, about 5.00 pm I guess, on the Friday before Christmas 2015, the hospital reflected how I was feeling at that point; lonely, empty and cold.

As I made my way along one of the long corridors that led

to the exit, with all the side rooms in darkness I could just about make out a patient being pushed in a wheelchair coming towards me by, what appeared to be, another patient. As they got closer the full horror of what it means to be a cancer patient opened up right in front of my eyes.

The patient and her guide were both dressed in pyjamas and dressing gowns and it was very apparent that they were husband and wife, in their early to mid-forties and both obviously suffering from cancer as they showed the classic outward signs, she wearing a headscarf and he was bald.

I was shocked to behold such a sight that when we passed by each other all I could do was raise a half smile to them because I was getting quite emotional to think that, while most people were out shopping for Christmas presents and preparing for the big day, this poor couple and their family had only one thing to look forward too, DEATH!

I felt so sorry for this couple from the pit of my stomach as I made my way towards South Kensington tube station to make my way home. I had never felt so low in all my life, was this going to be my fate as well? I don't remember too much about that Christmas, all I know is that I spent it at home while that couple were going to spend probably their last together in the Royal Marsden Hospital.

I didn't know them but I pray that their final days and time together were spent in the love that they had for each other and may they rest in peace.

*****

In summary, in September 2015 I commenced CHECKMATE 238 adjuvant study, Ipilimumab v Nivolumab at the Royal Marsden Hospital. After just a few treatments I developed pan *hypo-pituitarism* and *autoimmune hepatitis* requiring steroids, therefore my treatment was discontinued on 18th December, 2015.

Basically, after about six infusions of the trial drug it had made me very ill. Not only was my pituitary gland now non-functioning but my liver was also affected.

A new left chest wall metastatic deposit was excised on 15th January, 2016 by Mrs Geh, which showed a large deposit of metastatic melanoma with tumour cells extending to peripheral margins. A repeat PET/CT scan showed a small subpectoral uptake and a low grade uptake to my liver. Basically my skin cancer/malignant melanoma was spreading.

On 5th February, 2016, I had a consultation with Dr Stephen Morris at Guys Hospital who upon reviewing my latest MRI CT scan confirmed that I had a 1.5cm subpectoral/lateral axillary lymph node in my left chest wall, he had spoken to Jenny Geh who felt that further surgery might be possible to remove the lymph node, or better still he would consider radiotherapy to the left chest wall to try and remove the tumour that had shown to be problematic.

On 11th February – ironically Jacqui's birthday – I had a consultation with Mrs Geh who informed me that she would have to operate again on my left chest wall for further investigation. Thankfully, Mrs Geh found no further active disease. When she reported back to Dr Harries that no further disease was noted, he was now not keen so on treating me with Nivolumab as he planned. Radiotherapy seemed to be the sensible way of treating the lymph node in my chest wall and Dr Morris was consulted about this.

In early April 2016 I started having daily radiotherapy at the Cromwell Hospital, in Kensington, London SW5. This meant that from Monday to Friday I would drive myself from home in Bowers Gifford, and this was to last for six weeks.

On my first visit, I was led to the room where the radiotherapy was to take place and boy was I in for a shock. The machine on which I was to have the procedure carried out was my worst nightmare. I was to be 'fitted' to the machine which, for all intense and purposes, looks like a PET scanner only slightly narrower, by means of lining me up with the use of a laser measurement on two tattooed marks on my body, one on my stomach and one on my side. They are permanent, by the way, so when on holiday they are visible for all to see.

Having been lined up by the staff, I had to lay in the most uncomfortable condition imaginable. My left arm was placed above my head in an unnatural position and my body slightly twisted to my right. It was made all the more difficult by the axillary clearance operation to remove twenty-two lymph nodes that I had had previously. Mrs Geh had told me that 1.5 lb of muscle had been removed and my left chest wall had tightened as a result. The pain was very evident as the procedure was about to begin.

As I was being manoeuvred further into the machine I was told that it would take about fifteen minutes to complete and to lie perfectly still and not move a muscle because if I did they would have to start all over again. Being claustrophobic, the panic started to set in and I only managed it through a great deal of self-control and fear of having to have it done again, as once did happen. I gritted my teeth and resigned myself to having the procedure.

Anyone who has been in a similar position will know that fifteen minutes is like Albert Einstein's analogy that, "When a man sits with a pretty girl for an hour, it seems like a minute. But let him sit on a hot stove for a minute and it seems longer than any hour." How right he was, because that's exactly what it felt like. I couldn't wait to get out of that machine, but to make matters worse I was to have to endure this another twenty-nine times.

On 3<sup>rd</sup> May, I reported to the duty nurse that I was feeling unwell. Upon examining me she suspected that I was suffering from severe dehydration and, as a precaution, I was immediately admitted into the Cromwell Hospital for treatment.

Later that day Dr Morris came to see me and told me that I was to cease having radiotherapy from then onwards as my overall condition had deteriorated to such an extent that it would be dangerous to my well-being to carry on. He said that he would make an appointment for me to see Dr Harries in the near future to discuss on going treatment and that he would arrange for me to have further scans in the meantime.

On 27<sup>th</sup> May, 2016, Jacqui and I attended Dr Harries clinic at London Bridge Hospital. He had invited Dr Morris to sit in with him while he gave us a brief version of the following results from the latest PET scan undertaken a few days earlier.


***Findings:***

*PET NTAP/lower limbs report.*

*Unfortunately, disease progression has occurred since the February data.*

*Liver nodal and bony metastatic diseases are now demonstrated.*

***Findings as follows:***

*Intense small volume signs of activity are now observed in the liver consistent with liver metastases progression compared with the previous scan.*

*New clustered FDG avid lymph nodes are present at the periportal level/superior retroperitoneum, individual nodes up to circa 2.6cm in size with a further low volume caudal retroperitoneal nodal tissue.*

*FDG avid new right anterior diaphragmatic adenopathy is now present measuring circa 2cm, a new site of intense small volume PET activity is present in the s3 bone segment consistent with a sacral bony deposit.*

*A new site of small volume PET activity is also present in the right femoral diaphysis just inferior to the mid-shaft, a circa 1cm site of high attenuation change being present within the marrow here on underlying CT soft tissue and bone windows settings, consistent with a small marrow based metastasis given the overall findings, not defined on the previous scan. Cortical destruction not defined here.*

*I note interval left-sided axillary region radiotherapy. The small site of nodal activity which was shown on the previous scan in the left axilla level 2/3 is again demonstrated, showing some reduction in activity. However, a small volume further FDG avid node is now present medial to this in left axillary level 2/3. Generalised left axillary cutaneous PET activity is also observed in keeping with radiotherapy related change.*

*Lungs well aerated, some atelectasis noted.*

*No renal or GI obstruction.*

**IMPRESSION**
**PET Conclusions**

*Unfortunately, scattered metastatic disease progression since the previous scan. Liver metastatic disease progression has occurred, new FDG avid nodes are present above and below the diaphragm involving the retroperitoneum and the anterior diaphragmatic groups, with low volume FDG avid bony metastases now being present, some PET activity in the left axillary level 2/3 may reflect a further small volume nodal disease at this level. I note the interval radiotherapy.*

He told us gently, and in a way that we could both understand, that my condition was now extremely serious. What had been quite a good outlook in February 2016 had turned into a very real, life-ending condition. He explained that the cancer had spread to my fibula, chest, liver and coccyx. He was cautious not to mention how quickly it could spread to other areas of the body or even when my life might end, but he did reiterate how serious my condition had become. It was at this point that Dr Morris left.

Both Jacqui and I were terribly upset at this news. Although we realised how dangerous melanoma is, and knew that the odds were massively stacked against me, we had both been optimistic that, through the surgery performed by Mrs Geh and the guidance of Dr Harries, I was going to be alright.

Dr Harries told us that he was going to treat me under the NHS at Guys Hospital with the drug Nivolumab, a drug then being licensed in the treatment of melanoma.

For a couple of days during the last week of May 2016, I experienced what were the worst two days of my life. Since my last consultation with Dr Harries the previous Friday I had become aware of my own mortality, it was a very fragile one indeed. Jacqui had taken George to school and then travelled to work as usual. We wanted to keep as normal a routine as possible for George's sake.

So Monday morning I was on my own, in a darkened living room, and all my fears and demons came to me at once. I have never felt so down in all my life. I was convinced that it was just a matter of time before I died. I didn't want to die, who does? Yes, I was scared of dying, but what hit me the hardest was that after waiting for twenty-five years to become a father, cruelly that was now going to be taken away from me. Was I really only going to be alive for the first seven years of George's life?

How awful for George to see his dad dying the most awful of deaths. He had been too young to understand the real horror of seeing his granddad Roy die of cancer, but what effect would seeing me die have on him? No, that thought was just too much for me to deal with. For two days I was tearful and depressed. I wasn't eating anything and couldn't even be bothered get a glass of water. I had lost about 20kg in weight very quickly. I was full of self-pity, lying on the settee too tired and fatigued to bother about anything. I was on the verge of giving up.

But on the third day, after suffering the darkest of days, I know it's a cliché but I said to myself, "What are you doing? This self-pity and wallowing in your own depression and crying like a baby is doing you no good at all. Pull yourself together and be a proper husband to Jacqui and father to George for the time that we have left together." And you know what? A dark cloud gradually lifted from me and I felt in a much better place.

On 2<sup>nd</sup> June, Jacqui had been to see the leading consultant psychologist at Guys Hospital for guidance as she had a number of things that she was worried about. She spoke of her fears for me and wondered if I would suffer 'a long, painful death' or would it be a quick one? Jacqui had taken a realistic approach in as much as she was ploughing through the internet, going on Facebook and reading blogs to find out as much as she could about the latest advances in treatments, whereas I had put all my faith and confidence in the doctors treating me. She was also concerned that I had lost my appetite, felt nauseous and had started vomiting bile regularly.

During Jacqui's foraging on the internet she found a story about America's 39th President Jimmy Carter. On 3rd August, 2015, the ex-president underwent elective surgery to remove 'a small mass' on his liver, and his prognosis for a full recovery was initially said to be 'excellent'. However, on 12th August, Jimmy Carter announced he had been diagnosed with cancer that had metastasized, without specifying where the cancer had originated. On 20th August, he disclosed that melanoma had been found in his brain and liver, and that he had begun treatment with the immunotherapy drug pembrolizumab and was about to start radiation therapy.

The former president has an extensive family history of cancer, including both of his parents and all three of his siblings. On 6th December, 2015, Carter issued a statement that his medical scans no longer showed any cancer.

On Tuesday, 7th June we had another consultation with Dr Harries at London Bridge Hospital and Jacqui asked Dr Harries if Tumour Infiltrating Lymphocytes (TILS) or TVEC could be given to me. Dr Harries said it could be considered, Jacqui also asked if Pembrolizumab was an option as she had read of success stories with that treatment. Dr Harries responded that oncologists tend to think of Ipilimumab or Nivolumab as they both go together, but Pembrolizumab could be considered.

Dr Harries commented that Jacqui had obviously done her homework as they spoke about things that went completely over my head. It was like two professionals talking about the ins and outs of my condition with complete knowledge of the subject. I was so impressed that I referred to Jacqui as Dr Gaskin during the rare light-hearted moments we shared from time to time.

The medical insurance company would not approve Pembrolizumab to be administered at London Bridge Hospital but would pay for it elsewhere. That would have meant transferring to a completely new team who were not known to me, which was something I didn't want at the time.

Dr Harries opted for Pembrolizumab as treatment is given on a three weekly basis, compared to Nivolumab which is given every two weeks. At that stage, Dr Harries considered that a trip to Guys Hospital every three weeks would be better for me in my current state. I would see Dr Harries the previous Thursday for a consultation.

So on that Monday afternoon I made my way to the cancer unit at Guys Hospital for what I hoped and prayed would be the start of as good an outcome for me that President Carter had experienced with this new drug. At the clinic I was shown to a that contained six open treatment areas consisting of a large comfortable chair for the patient to relax in, a monitoring unit and an area for the drip holder to be placed. A nurse came over and explained the procedure to me. Firstly, a cannula would be placed in my arm – in time I had a port fitted to the upper right part of my chest for ease of use – so that the drug could be infused via a drip. Next the treatment would be given and last about thirty minutes, the cannula would be removed and I would be sent on my way to return three weeks later when the whole procedure would be repeated, easy peezy.

On Thursday, 1st September, Jacqui and I attended Dr Harries clinic at Guys. As we had already waited for some time I asked Jacqui if she would mind going to get us a cup of coffee. Seconds after she left for the coffee shop my name was called and I made my way the short distance to Dr Harries room. Dr Harries was waiting for me at the open doorway to his room announcing to me with great joy, "Fantastic news, Brian. Your latest scan has shown a 90% reduction/partial elimination of your tumours." He asked where Jacqui was and I replied, "Unfortunately, Jacqui is getting us a coffee."

He replied, "Oh, that's a shame, if I had known she could have got me one."

What fantastic news. We were, of course, both delighted, but cautious as to whether the success would continue. We had a million questions to ask but they could wait for another day. Dr Harries examined me and was satisfied that no new lumps were present, just as the scan had shown, and told us how pleased he was that the first three infusions had gone this well. I guess it was as much a confirmation that his decision to use Pembrolizumab was the correct one from his point of view.

Happily, we left his consulting room and I made my way to have my bloods taken so that they could be analysed ready for my next treatment on the following Monday. Jacqui and I were leaving the hospital when, I suppose it was a wave of relief, I was overcome with emotion. I had to find a quiet corner to let it out. Yes, I cried, not with fear this time but with relief that things were going in the right direction after such a long time. We walked back towards London Bridge where we were to catch the bus to Fenchurch Street Station so Jax could go back to work and I would catch the train to Pitsea Station, collect the car and go to St Margaret's Primary school to wait for George and take him home.

On the way we stopped in a Starbucks coffee shop and got a drink each to take with us. When we came out and were making our way past the Shard, I suddenly stopped and told Jax that I was going to go back to Starbucks to buy a hot drink and sandwich to give to the elderly homeless man who always sat across the road from the shop. He never begged or harassed people as they hurried passed by hardly daring to stop near him for fear of, well, I don't know what.

When I gave him the drink and food a big toothless grin appeared on his face as his out stretched hands took the goodies from me. "God bless you," he said. "God bless you."

Digesting the news that I had just been given filled me with a better understanding of what we, as human beings, can sometimes go through. The man didn't know my circumstances and I didn't know his, but it just felt right to share the joyous moment with a fellow soul who was in need of some help.

Every third week I went for my treatment at Guys and every three months I had a PET/CT scan to monitor how my treatment was going. Oh how I hated every second of those scans. I realised, though, that the machine I hated and feared the most was actually one of my best friends because, without its help, I would not be in the place that I am today. From all the difficulties that I had endured since that fateful day when Jax told me about the change in my mole to being well on my way to making a full recovery. Then, on 21st September 2017, after receiving twenty-two infusions of Pembrolizumab and a little over one year after starting the course of treatment, Dr Harries declared me NED; no evidence of disease.

Jacqui and I took the news in our stride. Yes, I was happy but there would be no whooping, backslapping or partying. I am a realist and figured that all it would need is for a tiny molecule to be lurking undetected somewhere to kick it all off again. My frame of mind is one of, "If I get the all clear from my last scan then great. I am okay for another three months."

I had another five infusions with the last being on 18th December, 2017, ironically two years to the date of seeing the poor couple in the Royal Marsden just before Christmas. I was due to have another on 8th January, 2018 but on the way to Guys (I was now driving up as, in September 2016, I had been granted a Blue Badge because of my condition – as I was not expected to live that long a badge was granted to me quite quickly) I felt pretty unwell and when I eventually got in 'the chair' I told a nurse just how bad I was feeling. A doctor was called to examine me, bloods were taken and rushed to the lab and when the results came back later on in the afternoon I was deemed to be fine, although the doctor did conceded that I was showing signs of being unwell. The treatment was suspended on that day and an appointment was made for me to see Dr Harries on the Thursday of that week. When I saw Dr Harries he said that he had reviewed the episode that had taken place the previous Monday and decided, that as I was NED, to stop the treatment. He felt, after twenty-seven infusions, now was the right time to end. I still had many, many side effects from the failed trial that I had been on at the Royal Marsden and had a lot of side effects from the Pembrolizumab, which will remain with me for the rest of my life.

I felt that it was now the right time to thank Dr Harries for all that he had done. Modestly, he said that he was a small cog in a big machine that had got me to the position that I found myself in. I told him that may be true but he was the only one that I thank face to face. I realise that many hundreds of people, doctors and nurses that I had come into contact with since the beginning, research scientists and technicians from laboratories all over the world who helped to develop the drug deserved my thanks but I couldn't possibly do that. The only ones that I could thank were himself and Mrs Geh and I was going to thank her when I next saw her.

Dr Harries once told me that Pembrolizumab works for about 20% of those that it is given to, I do consider myself to be extremely fortunate that it has so far worked for me, it has given me a second chance at life and one that I am so very grateful for, How long I will live nobody can say, What I will say is that all those people that helped me, the ones that I will never know, you will be in my family's thoughts forever.

I find it difficult to walk as far as I once could and I am still tired from time to time. Some days are better than others but generally I am doing okay. We have been on holiday a few times since I was told that I am in remission but it's not all singing and dancing. Sometimes I am forgetful, have an intolerance towards people and can blow up or take offence at the slightest comment, but hey, at least I am here to be able to do so.

I am now looking no further than I need to, and intend to enjoy my life like never before.

# Epilogue

What started out as me writing a synopsis about my life for George to let him get an idea about who his dad is and where he came from grew into this book, a book firstly for George and then for all who care to read it.

I hope that you have enjoyed reading this book. I have enjoyed writing it, it has been a strange experience; from day one I have had a lot of laughs remembering the good and odd times and a lot of tears remembering the painful ones.

I need to mention a few people who have helped me along the way either sharing my experiences on a daily basis, or just being a bloody good friend when one was needed.

Firstly, for my beautiful, loving and dedicated wife Jacqui, Jax as I sometimes refer to her, without her undying love and dedication I don't think I would have been able to tell my story. She stood shoulder to shoulder with me in my fight against skin cancer every step of the way, gave me the privilege of being a father and, although our relationship has changed slightly, I need to tell her: I love you so deeply and I couldn't have done it without you by my side. It has been a privilege and an honour to be your husband and may we have many, many, more years together.

Next my brother Paul, when we were growing up as kids I looked up to him as he is my big brother. Sometimes, I would get angry with him like when we had our wrestling matches in the living room in Wickersley Road. He always got me in a headlock and I would have to give up, remember bruv? We were never in each other's pockets and really buddy-buddy, but when I needed help the most he was always the first one there. I thank you for that Paul, you have seen tragedy as well and I feel deeply sad for you, I have reserved a special place in my heart just for you.

Next is my mate Chris. I first met Chris back in 1988 when we worked together at the Japanese Bank Saito. We hit it off straight away and became good friends. We lost contact for a while but reunited in 2012 when he returned to the UK from a spell living overseas. If not every day, then certainly every other day, while going through my treatment Chris would call me up on the telephone with encouragement and words of wisdom. He would cheer me up when I felt down, talk sense to me when it was needed, be blunt when necessary but, above all, he was there for me. He and his lovely mother, Hilda, would light a candle and say a prayer for me every time they attended church. Thank you for being a true friend and may we remain so until our end of days.

And so on to Steve; good old Steve. We first met at Saito in 1988 and have remained close friends ever since. When I didn't think I would see out 2016 I bought a little Alfa Romeo open top sports car and asked Steve if he would like to accompany me on a French/Italian road trip. It turned out to be one of the best weeks of my life. Truly, from the moment we left home to the moment we got back, I have never laughed so much, sometimes to the point of having tears in my eyes and a pain in my stomach.

Firstly, we drove to Dover where we caught the ferry to Dunkirk before motoring down to Lyon, staying in a small hotel for the night. The next day we drove across the border into Italy and headed to Milan via Turin where we stayed for two nights while we visited the Alfa Romeo and Ferrari car museums in Maranello. Having enjoyed the day at them both we returned to our hotel to freshen up and change before going out for a few beers. We chatted to a lovely English couple in an open air bar before enjoying a meal in a typical Italian restaurant.

Over the next few days we drove to Monaco, through Nice, before making our way back up to Dunkirk via Grenoble and Reims, where we caught the return ferry.

Thanks, Steve, for being the best friend, just like Chris, that any man could ever have. Steady now, just a friend. Ha-ha!

To Madge, whom Jacqui and I have not known that long, but have come to respect and admire. You helped me through some dark days by telling me your cancer story. It was good to talk to someone who has experienced similar and has a greater understanding than most of what it's like to suffer from this terrible disease. I admire how bravely you have faced up to recent tragic events.

There are many stories that I could tell you but if I did this book would never end. I have lots of wonderful stories about the celebrities that I have met through work. There are many kind ones like movie directors Quentin Tarantino and Joel Schumacher, old time film stars such as Richard Todd and Jack Warner, rock stars Rod Stewart, Francis Rossi and the late Rick Parfitt from Status Quo, Ivana Marie Zelníčková, the 1972 Olympic Czechoslovak downhill skier and former wife of Donald Trump, now President Trump, various supermodels, footballers Thierry Henry, Emmanuel Petit and their one time manager Arsene Wenger. There have also been horrible ones, and mediocre ones, who I dare not mention. The list could go on and on.

The ordinary people I met who faced their own battles with illness, the work colleagues who infuriated me or made me laugh, those that have sadly departed far too soon or those that were there into their dotage. I remember you all and the impact that you made on my life.

Lastly, I want to single out you my son, George. When you were born you rekindled my life after so much tragedy, heartache and sorrow, and you remain my forever shining star. Yes, we do have our moments, good and bad, but every night I thank God that he sent you to me and may we be together for many, many, years to come.

And, lastly, taken from the internet, my thanks to 'Anonymous' for the following.

It made me smile as it reminded me of the things that we had, or didn't have, when I was a child.

If you love food and being a child of the sixties you may remember this:


*Pasta had not been invented, 'Kebab' was not even a word never mind a food, curry was an unknown entity, and Indian restaurants were only found in India.*

*The only vegetables were spuds, peas, carrots, turnip, cauliflower and cabbage. Mange tout and pak choi were made up words. Chilli was in South America and old ladies in Aberdeen wore scotch bonnets.*

*A take-away was a mathematical problem, a pizza was something to do with a leaning tower; oil was for lubricating your bike chain not for cooking. Olive oil was kept in the medicine cabinet.*

*Spice went in Christmas cakes (and so did peel, yuk). Herbs were used to make medicine, I think. All crisps were plain. All soft drinks were called pop. Coke was something that we put on the fire, we never drunk it and we certainly didn't sniff it. Ginger beer burnt your lips, when you stopped drinking. Rice was a milk pudding, and never, ever part of our dinner.*

*A Big Mac was what we wore when it was raining. A microwave was science fiction; tea was made in a teapot using tealeaves.*

*The tea cosy was the forerunner of all energy saving devices. Tea had only one flavour, it was tea flavoured.*

*Figs and dates appeared every Christmas, but no one ever ate them. Coconuts only appeared when the fair came to town. Mayonnaise was called salad cream and hors d'oeuvre was a spelling mistake.*

*Dinner consisted of what we were given, and not negotiable. Only Heinz made baked beans. Leftovers went in the dog. Sauce was either brown or red. Eating raw fish was called madness, not sushi. The only ready meals came from the fish and chip shop. Frozen food was called ice cream. Nothing ever went off in the fridge because we never had one.*

*None of us had ever heard of yoghurt. Brunch was not a meal.*

*Cheese only ever came in a hard lump. If we had eaten bacon, lettuce and tomato in the same sandwich we would have been certified insane. Eating outside was called a picnic not al fresco. Seaweed was not a recognised food. Eggs were not called 'free range' they just were, and the shells were white.*

*Pancakes were only eaten on Shrove Tuesday – it was compulsory. The phrase 'boil in the bag' would have been beyond our comprehension. The term 'oven chips' would not have made any sense at all. We bought milk and cream at the same time, in the same bottle, before you gave it a shake.*

*Prunes were purely medicinal. Pineapples only came in chunks in a tin. We didn't eat Croissants because we couldn't pronounce them, we couldn't spell them, and we didn't know what they were. For baguettes see croissants.*

*Garlic was used to ward off vampires in films, but never to be eaten. Water came out of the tap and if anybody thought about charging for it they would have been locked up.*

The Not So Famous
Battersea Boy